IMAGES
of America

Casper's Troopers Drum & Bugle Corps

On the Cover: The Casper Troopers Drum & Bugle Corps perform their world-famous circle formation at the World Open Championship at the Manning Bowl in Lynn, Massachusetts, on August 20, 1966. The Troopers debuted the circle formation in 1960. Over the years, it has also been called the wagon wheel or sunburst formation. (Photograph by Maurice Knox Jr., courtesy of Jim and Suzette McIntyre.)

IMAGES
of America

Casper's Troopers Drum & Bugle Corps

Michelle Bahe
Foreword by Tony Monterastelli
and Evan Stoddard

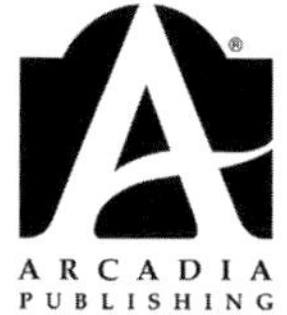

ISBN 978-1-4671-2908-4

Published by Arcadia Publishing
Charleston, South Carolina

Printed in the United States of America

Library of Congress Control Number: 2017964139

For all general information, please contact Arcadia Publishing:
Telephone 843-853-2070
Fax 843-853-0044
E-mail sales@arcadiapublishing.com
For customer service and orders:
Toll-Free 1-888-313-2665

Visit us on the Internet at www.arcadiapublishing.com

This book is dedicated to all Troopers past, present, and future. To all the Troopers' parents, families, and friends. To all the Troopers' staff and volunteers. And last, but by no means least, to all the Troopers Drum & Bugle Corps fans.

Contents

Foreword

The Troopers, in name and appearance, are what America was. The young men and women under the Trooper banner are what America is.

—Walter Brennan, 1970

Joining the Troopers changes a young person's life: traveling across the country in a bus, practicing and performing almost every day during the summer, constantly improving musically and athletically, and making lifelong friends. Few groups can offer the valuable lessons members learn after just one summer with the corps. Members of the Troopers join for a wide array of reasons. Some come for a challenge, others to just say that they marched in a world-class drum corps. Many come to the Troopers simply because they love the corps. While many arrive only caring about the scores and who is on staff this year, in the end, all they truly hold dear is the time they have spent with their Trooper brothers and sisters and the memories made while spending countless hours marching (and running) around on a field together, perfecting the 12-minute show.

During the hectic years of youth, we little realize the inspiration, the entertainment, and the honor and pride we bring to our families, our communities, and to the drum corps world, including our fellow members and the fans. In 60 years, wave after wave of dedicated young people have created a legend and a nationwide following. We march for those who marched before us. We march for the younger Troopers who will follow us. We march through our Trooper years and into adulthood, when we come to understand that the Trooper phenomenon is larger than us as individuals or age groups or eras. We find ourselves looking forward to each summer like fans, for the renewed thrill of music and performance and competition—but we also look with immense pride to the next group of young people following our path, the Trooper path, for 60 years and counting.

—Tony Monterastelli
Drum Major, 1985–1991

—Evan Stoddard, 2014–present

Acknowledgments

This book would not have been possible without the generous support of the Casper Troopers Drum & Bugle Corps organization, specifically Fred Morris, Michael Gough, Kristy Jackson, and Mathew Krum. They have been a great wealth of knowledge and were very helpful. The Troopers donated hundreds of images, many from scrapbooks put together by Grace Jones.

Another major source of photographs for the book came from Pat Chagnon. She marched with the Troopers in 1987 and is a professional photographer. Chagnon donated thousands of photographs that she has taken as well as ones she collected when she wrote *Troopers Drum & Bugle Corps: Celebrating 50 years of Honor, Loyalty & Dedication*. She has also been a great help in identifying and dating photographs.

I cannot thank the Troopers alumni and their families enough. Many—including Jim and Suzette McIntyre, June Hunter, the family of T.J. Simmons, Mike Monterastelli, Vickie Weber, Becky Steensland, Mike O'Hearn, and Linda Shultz—loaned or donated images that are in the book. The above mentioned and many, many others helped identify and date these photographs and shared wonderful stories of their time with the Troopers. Every effort has been made to identify everyone in photographs and to spell the names correctly. If your name is misspelled or missing, I apologize.

A giant thank-you to Tony Monterastelli and Evan Stoddard for writing the forward. They were able to write from the perspective of someone who marched with the Troopers, which added feelings that I could not capture.

I want to thank Vince Crolla and his staff at the Casper College Western History Center for providing additional images and helping me do further research on the Troopers. My coworkers Rick Young and Anne Holman spent many hours editing and proofreading for me. A couple of volunteers, including Carolyn Buff and Shannon Tippit, made sure it all made sense. I thank you all for your help.

All author royalties from the sale of this book benefit the Fort Caspar Museum Association and the Troopers Drum & Bugle Corps.

Introduction

These images are a journey through the 60 years of the Casper Troopers Drum & Bugle Corps for all those who performed and for those who watched. A lot of people in Casper have fond memories of watching the Troopers march down Center Street in parades or listening to them practice at one of the parks—or parking lots—around town. A smaller group of people have memories of playing with the Troopers not only in Casper but all around Wyoming and the United States.

This book is the result of an exhibit at Fort Caspar Museum in 2017 and 2018, Troopers: Celebrating 60 Years of the Troopers Drum & Bugle Corps. There were so many wonderful images, but only a few were used in the exhibit. This is a way to share more of them.

Whenever a significant anniversary draws near for the Troopers, there is discussion about which year it should be celebrated. While the Troopers were founded in late 1957, their first public performance was in 1958. Over time, it has been done both ways. The 20th anniversary was celebrated in 1977; all subsequent anniversaries have been celebrated from the 1958 date. For the exhibit at Fort Caspar Museum, the staff decided to have the exhibit span the summers of 2017 and 2018, thereby celebrating the 60th anniversary of both the founding of the Troopers and their first public performance.

This book is for everybody who embraces the "Long Blue Line."

One

1950s

Formation and the Early Years

The Casper Troopers Drum & Bugle Corps was the dream of one man, Jim Jones. As a teenager in the 1930s, he had been a drummer in the Sons of the American Legion Drum Corps in Casper, Wyoming. After serving in World War II and attending college, Jones returned to Casper and started his own contracting company. In the mid-1950s, he and other past members of the Sons of the American Legion Drum Corps formed an adult drum and bugle corps, the Commanders, and again he was a drummer.

In late 1957, Jones incorporated the Casper Junior Drum & Bugle Corps, and they quickly took the name Troopers. Over the winter of 1957–1958, the corps was formed. That first year, 1958, there were 54 corps members and nine color guard members. Jones's main purpose was to aid, encourage, and promote the welfare of the youth of Casper. He was quoted as saying, "I started the corps because I was in a junior corps myself here in Casper and we all enjoyed it a great deal. I felt the youth of today would enjoy it just as much as I did." He let any kids join who had an interest, whether they had any musical experience or not. The local American Legion and the Veterans of Foreign Wars (VFW) were early sponsors.

During those first couple of years, the Troopers stayed close to home, marching in parades throughout Wyoming and playing concerts year-round. The Troopers' first public appearance was in Riverton, Wyoming, at the Wyoming American Legion State Convention in July 1958. In addition, they competed at the Wyoming American Legion competitions. They performed for Vice Pres. Richard Nixon at a campaign stop in Casper in 1959.

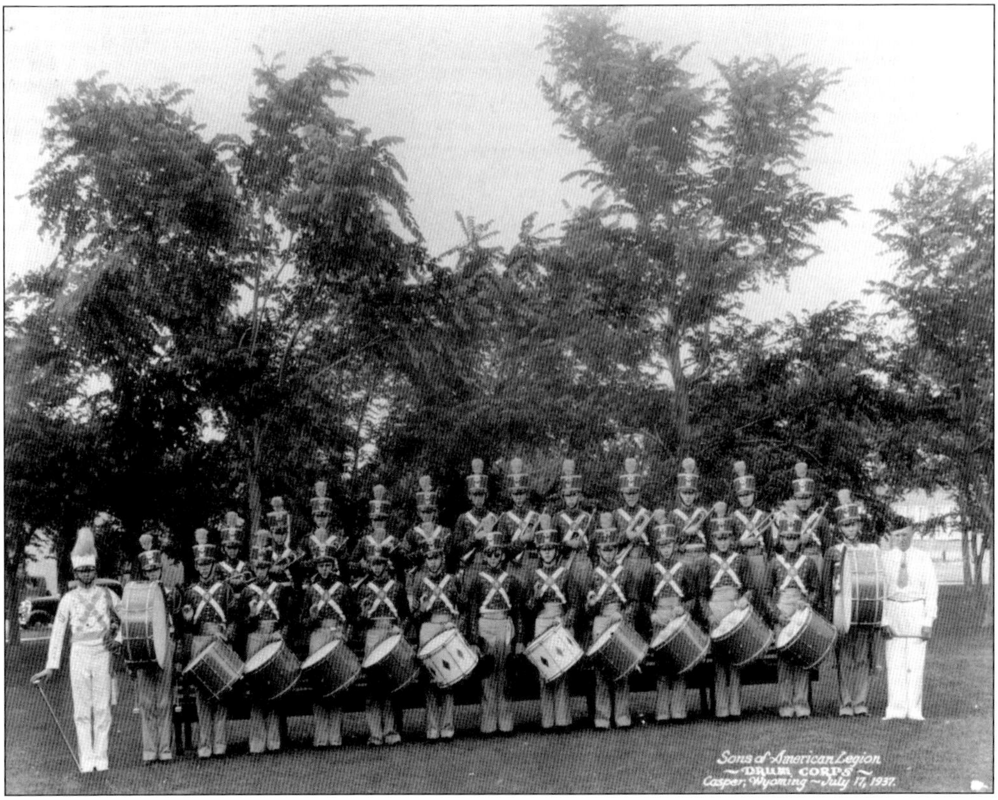

The Sons of American Legion Drum Corps pose for a group photograph in Casper on July 17, 1937. Troopers founder and director Jim Jones played snare drum with the corps. Jones is seventh from the left in the first row. (Photograph by Tom Carrigen, courtesy of the Chuck Morrison Collection, Casper College Western History Center.)

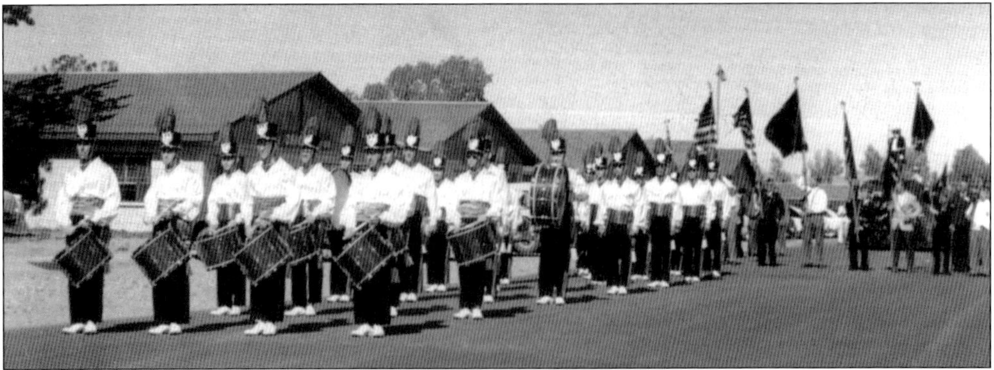

The Commanders, a senior drum corps, perform as part of a parade in Casper in the 1950s. The members of the Sons of American Legion Drum Corps from the 1930s formed the Commanders in the 1950s. Jim Jones is on the left in the first row. (Courtesy of the Chuck Morrison Collection, Casper College Western History Center.)

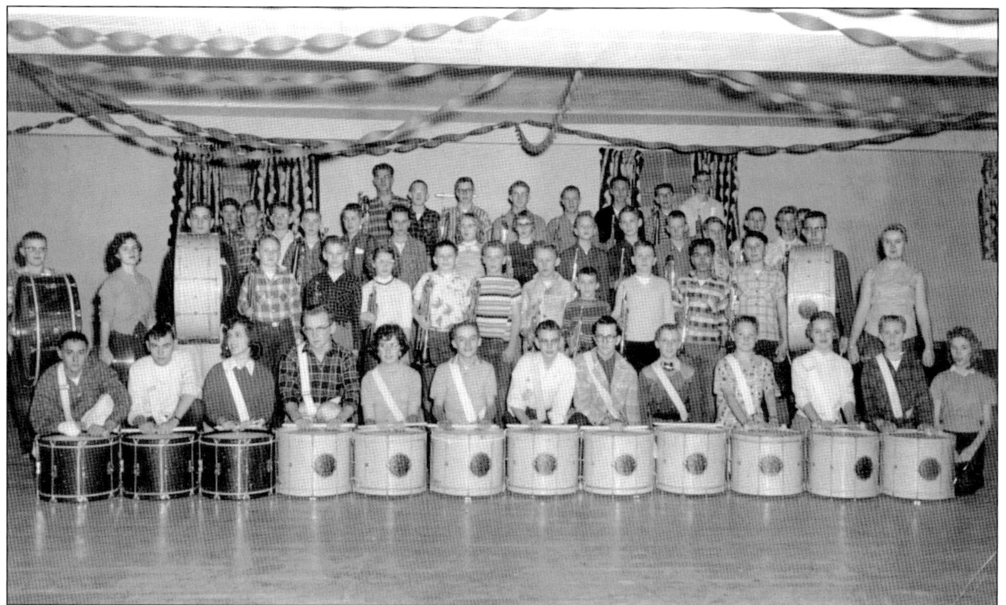

"Troopers at Rehearsal" was the title of this photograph when it ran in the *Casper Morning Star* on December 17, 1957. The caption reads: "Over 50 members of the Troopers, junior drum and bugle corps, are shown here at practice in the Legion house last night. . . . Support of the group is expected to come from several Casper organizations who will be represented in the color guard." (Courtesy of the Troopers Archives.)

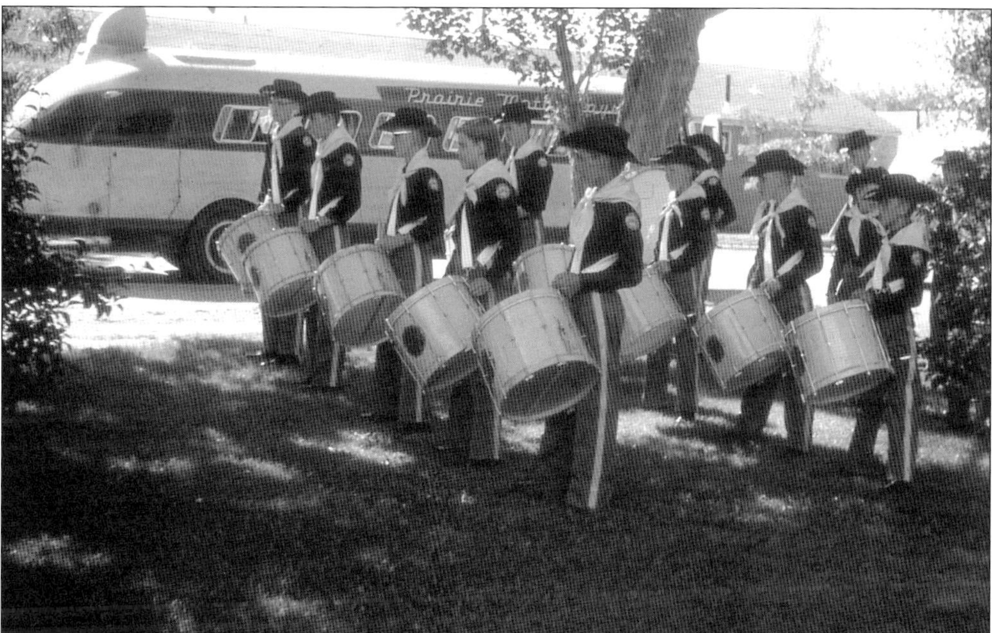

The Troopers snare drummers practice in a park before their first-ever public performance on June 27, 1958. They marched in the Wyoming American Legion Convention Parade in Riverton. According to an article in the *Casper Morning Star* on June 25, after the parade, "They will see the state drum and bugle corps contest and be entertained swimming and at the evening meal by the Riverton Legion." (Photograph by Guy Engle, courtesy of Lee Engle.)

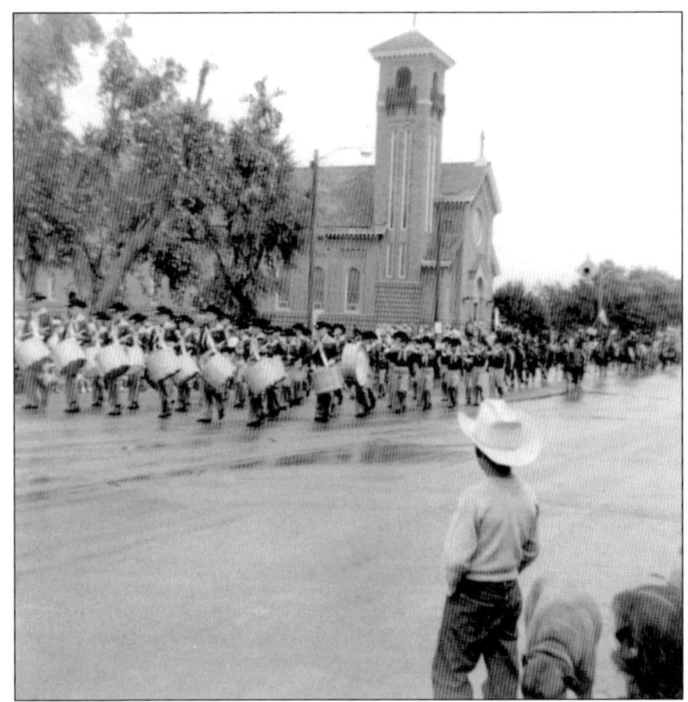

The Troopers' first performance in Casper was on July 30, 1958. They are seen here marching down South Center Street in the Central Wyoming Fair and Rodeo Parade. The *Casper Tribune-Herald* commented that day, "Parade viewers, too, were treated to their first good look at the 'Troopers,' a snappy junior drum and bugle corps which was recently organized here." (Courtesy of the Troopers Archives.)

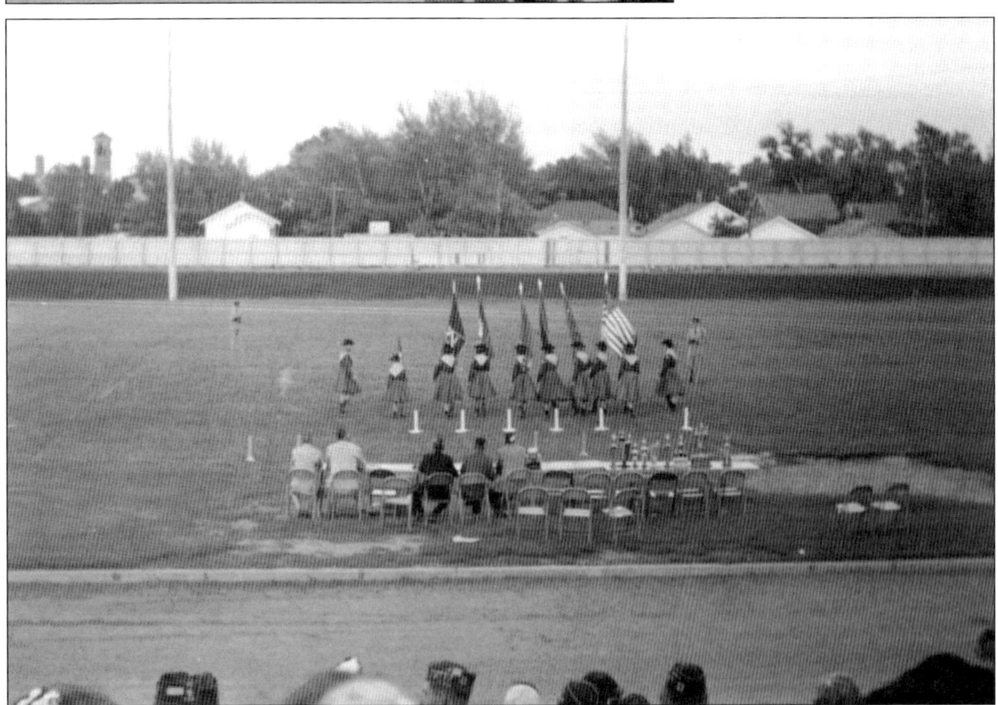

Trophies are lined up on a table behind the Troopers color guard as they perform at the American Legion competition at Natrona County High School in Casper on June 27, 1959. Martha Ackerman, at far left, was the guard captain in 1958 and 1959. The color guard competed as both a part of the drum and bugle corps and as a separate unit at American Legion and VFW shows. (Courtesy of the Troopers Archives.)

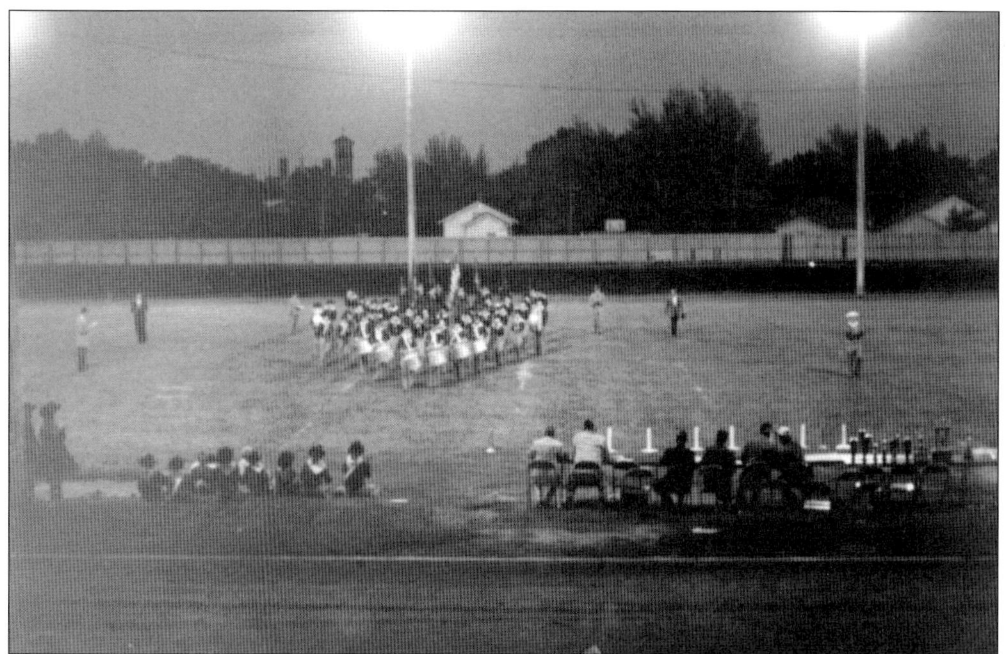

The Troopers perform during the American Legion competition on the football field at Natrona County High School in Casper on June 27, 1959. The Wyoming American Legion held its annual conference in Casper that year. The Troopers and six other corps participated in the festivities, which included a parade and the drum and bugle corps competition. The Troopers placed first in the junior division. Drum major William Snyder is standing off to the right. Snyder was drum major in 1958 and 1959. The musical selection the second year included "Ghost Riders in the Sky," "Battle Hymn of the Republic," "Cool Water," and "Wagon Wheels." (Both, courtesy of the Troopers Archives.)

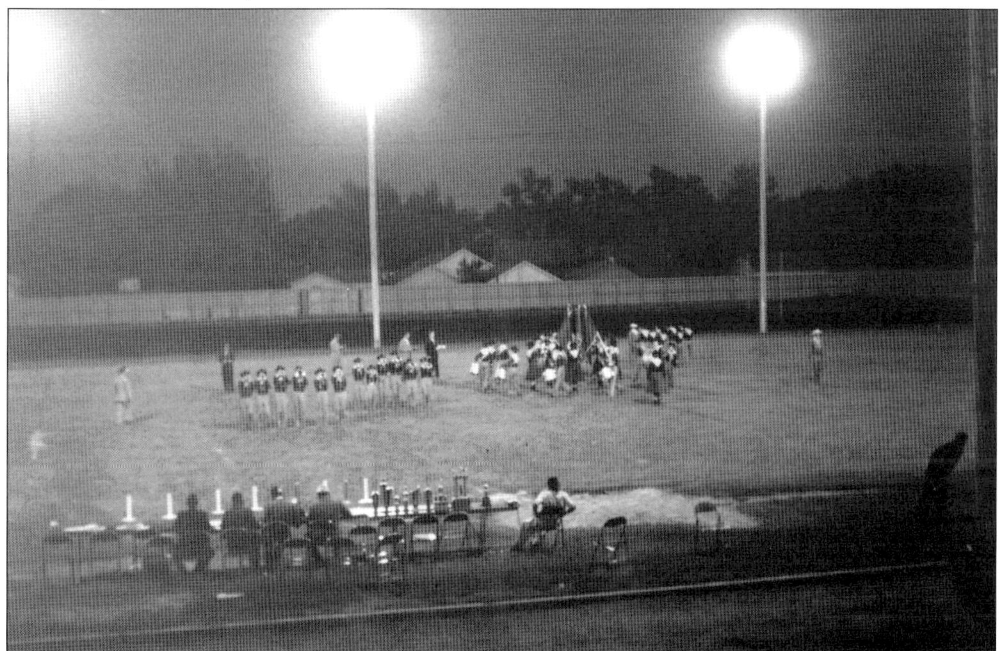

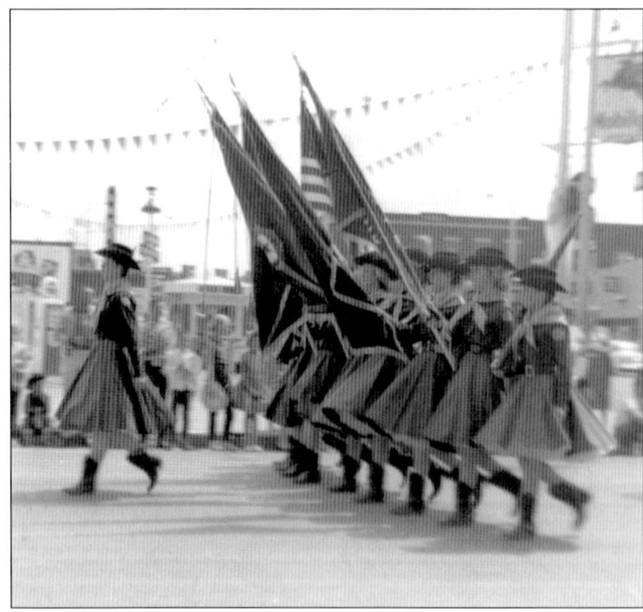

The Troopers color guard marches in unison during an out-of-town parade in 1959. Color guard commander Martha Ackerman leads the flag line. The Troopers and their parents helped raise funds to travel around Wyoming. That July, they raised $88.33 from a bake sale and $247 by hosting a car wash. (Courtesy of the Troopers Archives.)

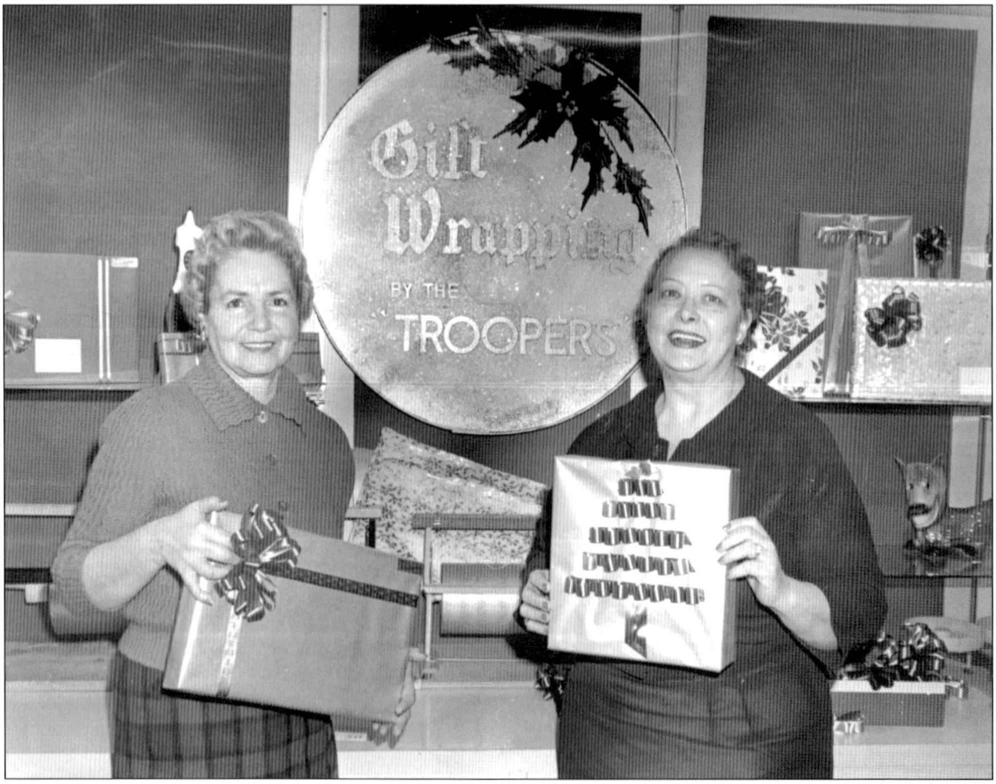

Kathleen Smith (left) and an unidentified woman hold examples of their handiwork at the gift-wrapping station in the Harry Yesness Store in Casper in the early 1960s. Beginning in 1959, local business owner Harry Yesness donated space in his men's store for the Troopers to have a gift-wrapping station at Christmastime. The tradition continues today with a wrapping station at Casper's Eastridge Mall. (Courtesy of the Troopers Archives.)

Two

1960s

Taking the Drum Corps World by Storm

The Troopers Drum & Bugle Corps was very popular in Casper in the early 1960s—so popular, in fact, that in 1961, Jim Jones started the Troopers Cadets as a feeder group for the corps. The Troopers' first national competition was at the American Legion National Championships in Denver, Colorado, in 1961. They finished a very respectable fourth place. They followed that up with a third-place win in Las Vegas, Nevada, the following year at the same event.

In order to compete in regional and national events, they had to travel great distances. Competitions were predominantly located on the East and West Coasts and in the Midwest, a long way from Wyoming. The Troopers pioneered long-distance travel for drum and bugle corps out of necessity. They had their own buses and trucks to move them and their equipment.

The Troopers performed at the Seattle World's Fair in 1962 and at the New York World's Fair in 1964. As the 1960s progressed, they proved to be very popular with drum corps fans across the country. In 1967, they were designated Wyoming's Musical Ambassadors by the Wyoming state legislature. In addition, they were the featured halftime entertainment at a Denver Broncos football game in both the 1968 and 1969 seasons.

The Troopers Color Guard also performed competitively; it won its first national championship in 1963, when it became the VFW Junior Color Guard national champion. Between 1963 and 1969, the color guard brought home first place 12 times at the VFW Color Guard National Championships, the American Legion National Color Guard Championships, and the Midwest Color Guard Championships.

The Troopers Drum & Bugle Corps won their first national championship in 1965, becoming the World Open national champions that year. Over the course of the next five years, they placed first six times, twice at the World Open National Championship, once at the VFW Junior Drum Corps Championship, once at the North American Championship, and twice at the Catholic Youth Organization (CYO) Championship.

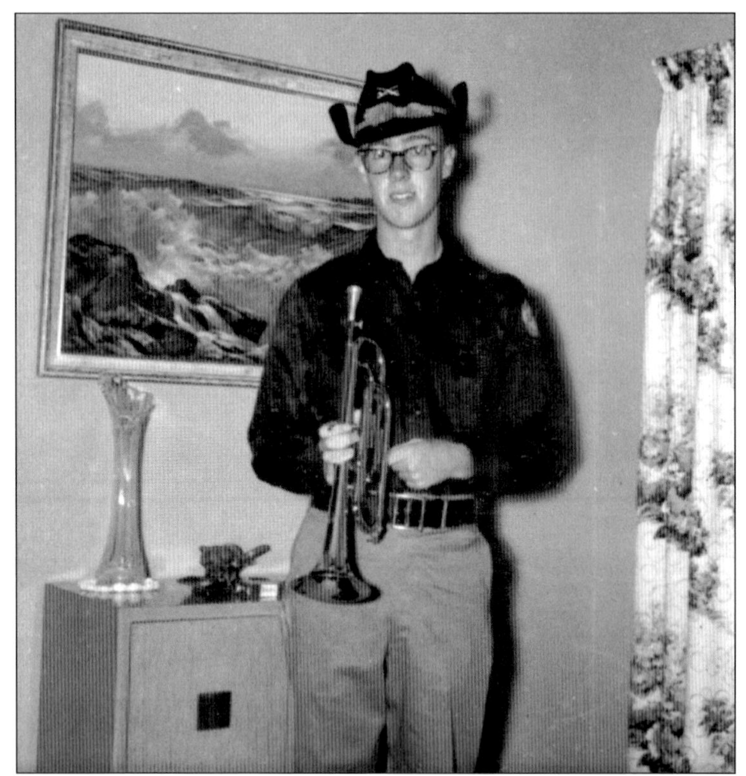

Trumpet player Ray Wilson was photographed in 1960 wearing the original Troopers uniform. The uniform consisted of light blue slacks with a gold stripe down the leg, a dark blue long-sleeved shirt with a Troopers patch on the left shoulder, and a black cowboy hat. The hat displayed a gold hat band with tassels and a gold pin of crossed sabers with the number 11. The 11 on the Troopers uniforms is for the 11th Ohio Volunteer Cavalry, who were stationed at Fort Caspar between 1862 and 1865. (Courtesy of the Troopers Archives.)

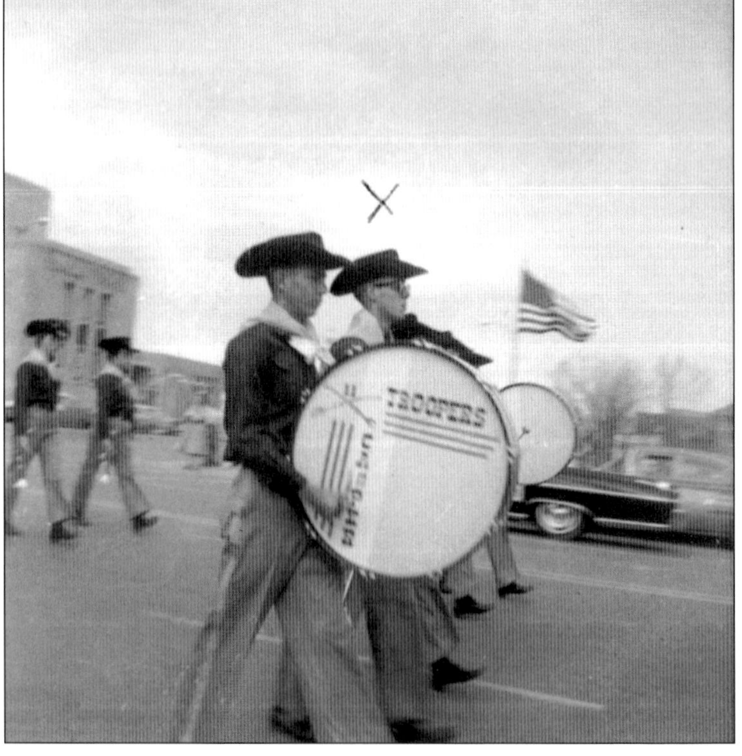

Ray Wilson (X over his head) marches down East A Street during a parade in Casper in 1961. According to the *Casper Tribune-Herald & Star* on May 11, 1958, "The uniforms are patterned after the U.S. Cavalry following the Civil War." (Courtesy of the Troopers Archives.)

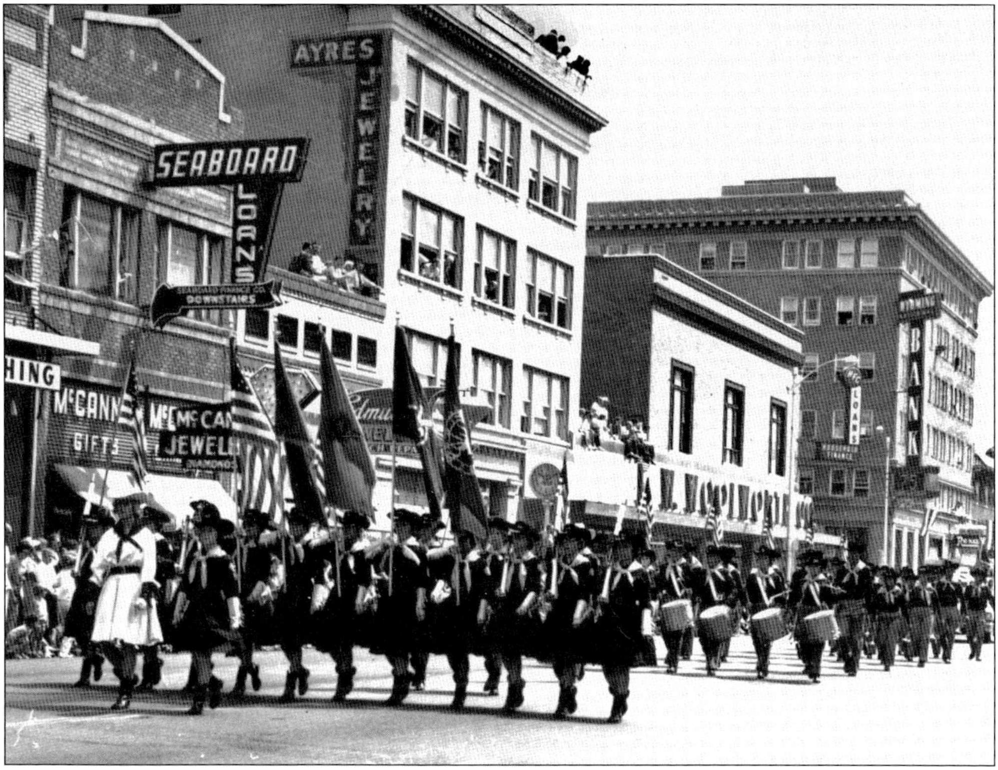

In this 1961 photograph, the Troopers march down Casper's West Second Street in the Central Wyoming Fair and Rodeo Parade. Color guard commander Kathy Davis is in the lead. The Troopers covered about 2,800 miles in 1961, traveling all around Wyoming and participating in competitions in Colorado and Kansas. (Courtesy of the Marion Alexander Collection, Casper College Western History Center.)

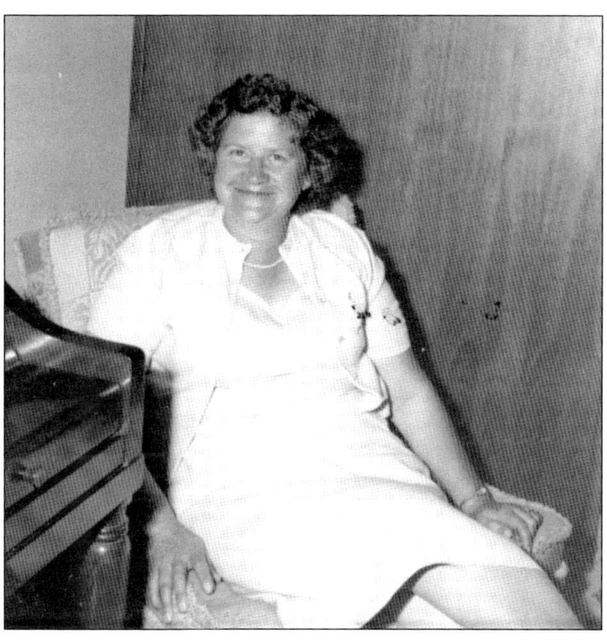

Volunteer Betty Campbell, shown at the 1961 Christmas party, served as a Troopers chaperone, cook, and more. Volunteers are essential to the Troopers' operation. They are the bus drivers, cooks, seamstresses, laundry crew, check-in personnel, and souvenir-stand sellers. They provide administrative assistance and general help, and also operate the Christmas gift-wrapping station and help run Troopers Bingo, a full-time fundraising bingo hall. (Courtesy of the Troopers Archives.)

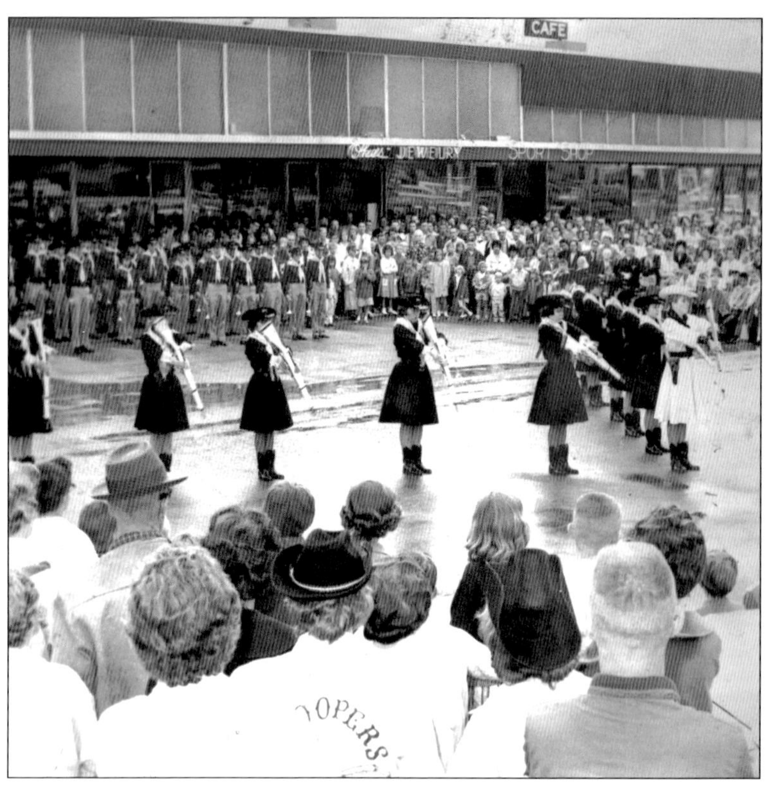

The Troopers color guard performs in the parking lot of Westridge Village on May 27, 1962, in front of the corps. An advertisement in that day's *Casper Tribune-Herald & Star* read: "Come See the Troopers Today—2 P.M. at Westridge Village. Bring the Family and Enjoy this Fine Performance at the Westridge Village Parking Lot. Help Send the Troopers to Portland!" (Courtesy of the Troopers Archives.)

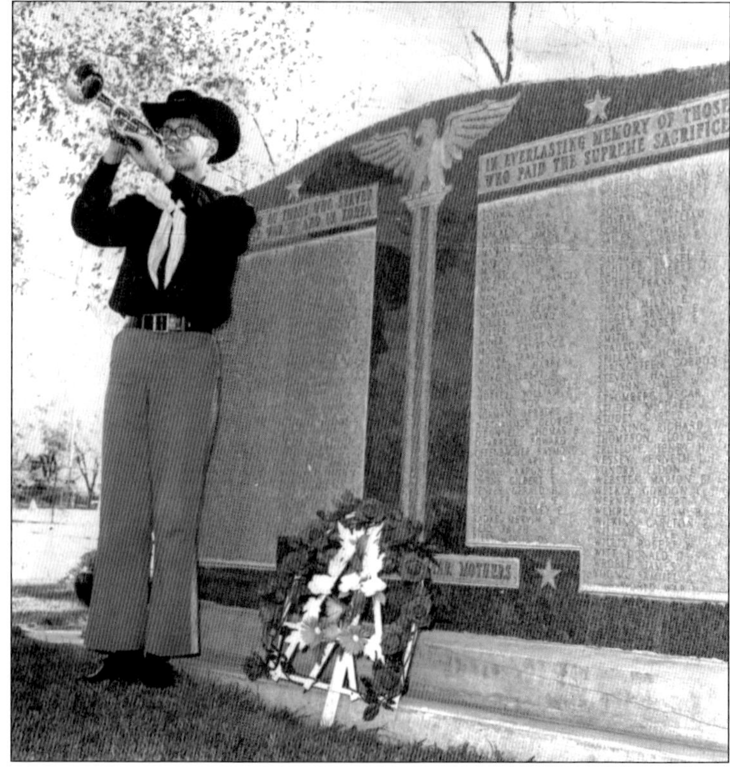

Troopers trumpet player Jim Wade plays "Taps" in front of the Gold Star Mothers War Memorial in Casper. The photograph ran in the *Casper Morning Star* on May 30, 1962, with the caption, "Traditional Taps. Trooper Jim Wade, in his 11th Cavalry Regiment uniform, sounds taps at the Gold Star Mothers War Memorial, Eighth and Center, where services will be conducted this morning." (Courtesy of the Troopers Archives.)

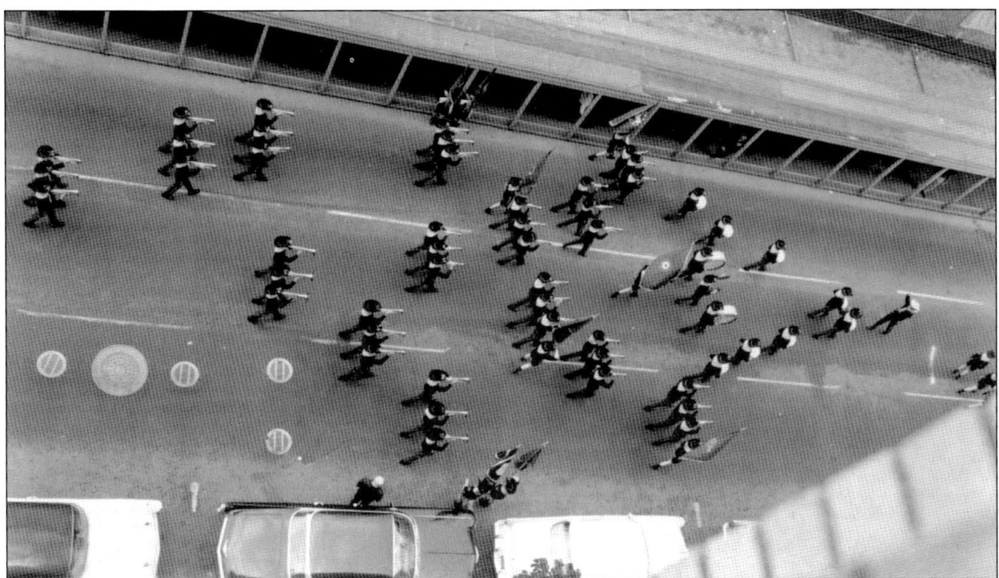

This bird's-eye view shows the Troopers marching in the Junior Rose Festival Parade in Portland, Oregon, on June 15, 1962. The caption in the *Casper Tribune-Herald* on June 18, 1962, read, "Troopers March: Casper Troopers Drum and Bugle Corps, led by a police escort, paraded up Broadway and down 6th Avenue, Portland's two major thoroughfares, Friday. They were greeted by heavy applause throughout their march." (Courtesy of the Troopers Archives.)

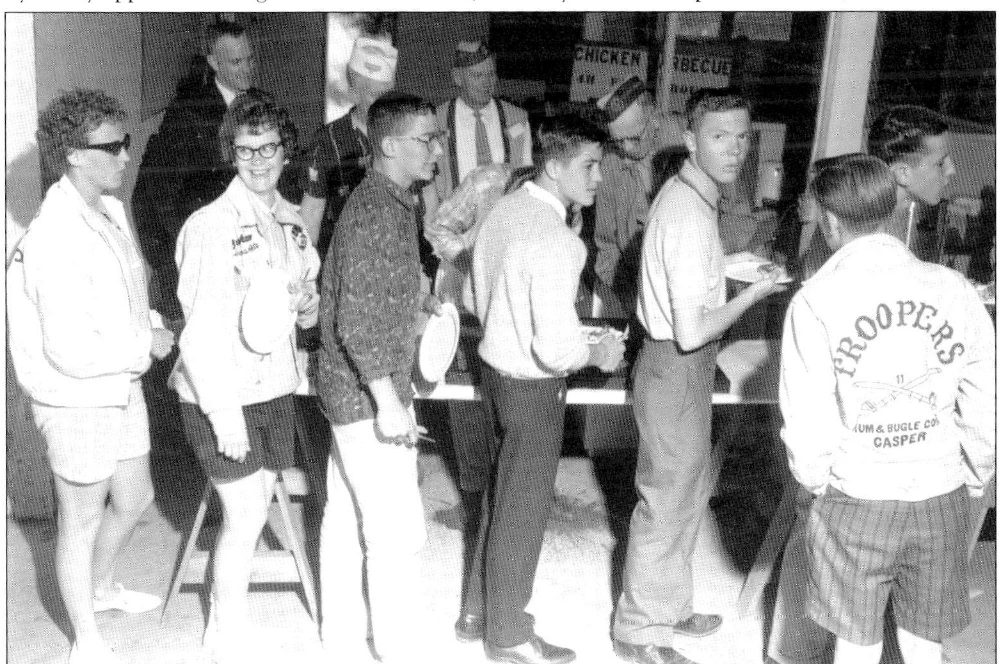

Troopers wait in line at a salmon barbecue in Astoria, Oregon. A similar photograph ran in the *Daily Astorian* on June 20, 1962, with the caption, "Special banquets for the Troopers are reported always well attended by the guests who haven't left much in the way of empty plates. Here the Troopers go through the chow line for a salmon barbecue in Astoria, Ore." (Courtesy of the Troopers Archives.)

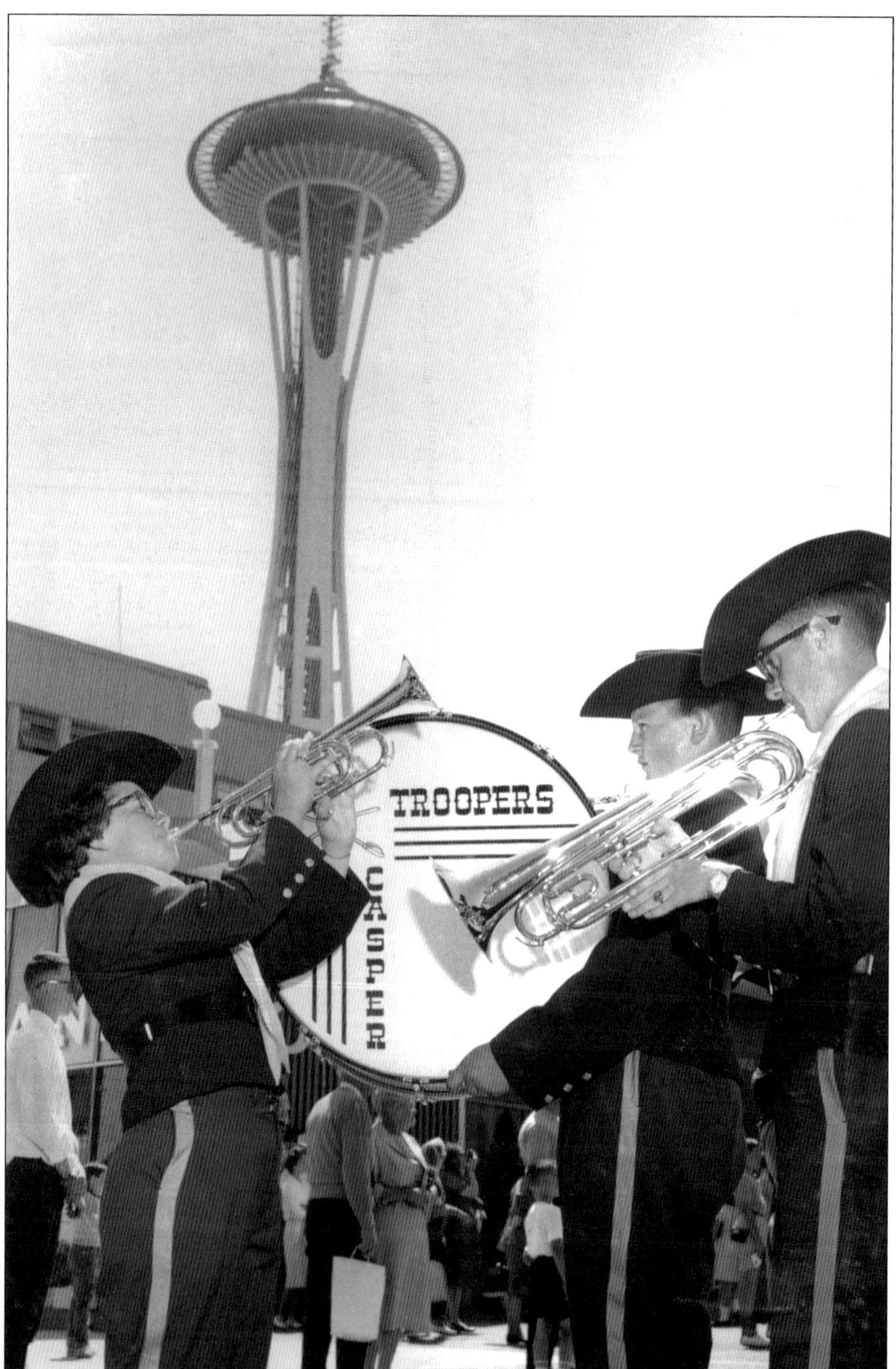

The Troopers pose for a publicity photograph in front of the Space Needle in Seattle, Washington, during the Century 21 World's Fair in 1962. From left to right are Donna Neeley, Jim McDaniels, and Ray Wilson. The Troopers' first West Coast tour in 1962 was due in large part to having been invited to participate in the Portland Rose Festival. They played at the World's Fair in Seattle and won the VFW competition in Walla Walla, Washington. (Courtesy of the Troopers Archives.)

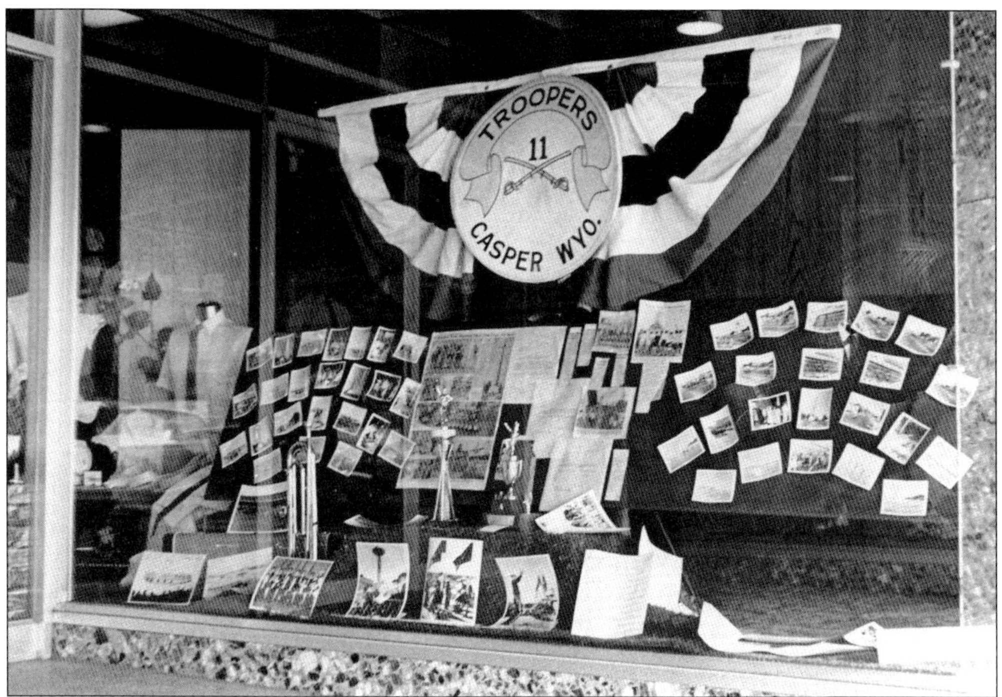

"Troopers Display at Yesness Store" was the title of this photograph when it ran in the *Casper Tribune-Herald* in July 1962. The caption went on to say: "Pictures, news clippings, letters and trophies are displayed in the window of the Harry Yesness Clothing Store at 133 South Center." The photographs and trophies were from the Troopers' recent trip to Oregon and Washington. (Courtesy of the Chuck Morrison Collection, Casper College Western History Center.)

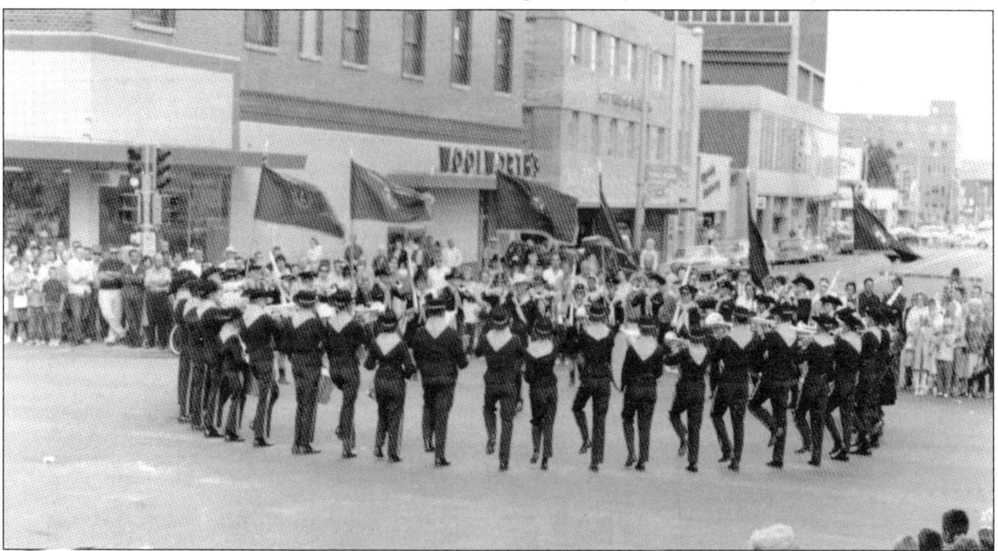

The Troopers perform at Crazy Daze in downtown Casper on July 14, 1962. They are wearing their new uniforms, which, according to an article in the May 2, 1962, *Casper Morning Star*, "is an authentic reproduction of garrison-dress uniforms worn by members of the 7th U.S. Cavalry regiment during the Indian-fighting days along the Western Frontier." (Courtesy of the Troopers Archives.)

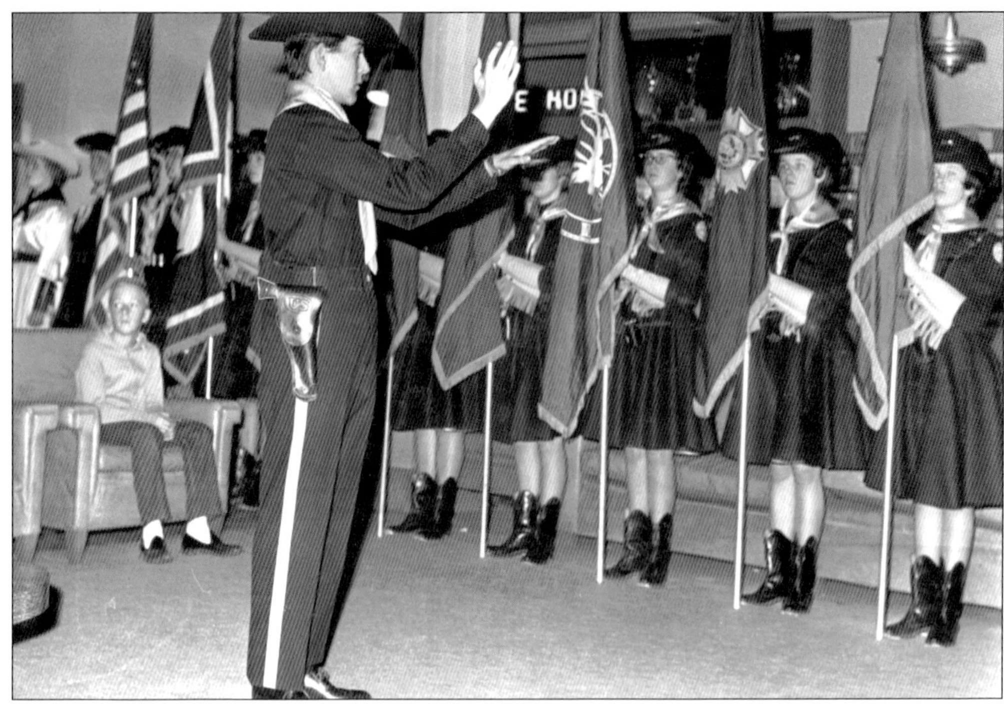

The Troopers were on hand to greet the American Legion national commander in the lobby of the Henning Hotel in Casper on February 4, 1963. Above, Troopers drum major Pete Emmons stands in front of the color guard leading the corps. Below, Troopers director Jim Jones talks with American Legion national commander James E. Davis and state commander Norman J. Guster of Sheridan. From left to right are an unidentified Troopers color guard member, Jones, Davis, Guster, and drum major Pete Emmons. Davis was in town to speak at the American Legion Regional Membership Conference. He said, "I hope the Troopers take first place next summer, because they certainly deserve it. Casper can be proud of these young people. They are Wyoming." (Both, courtesy of the Troopers Archives.)

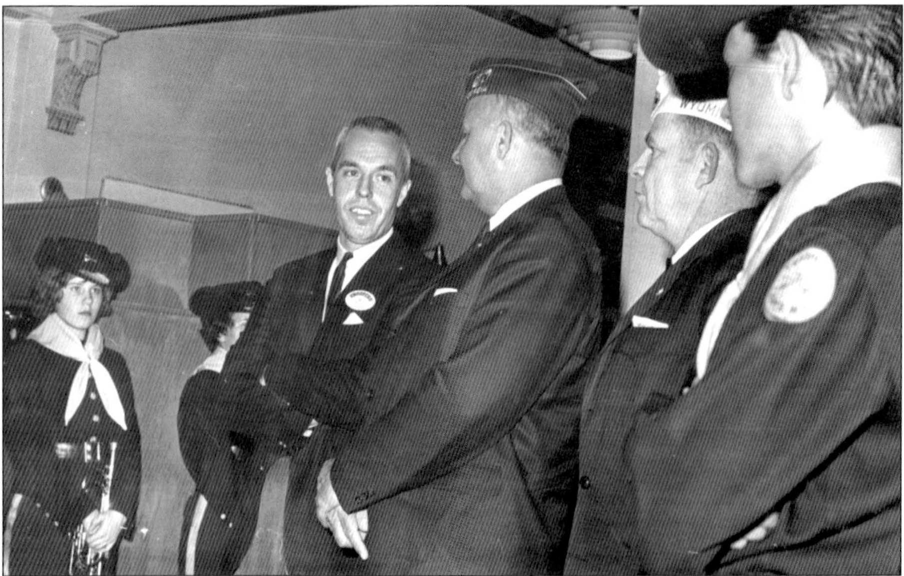

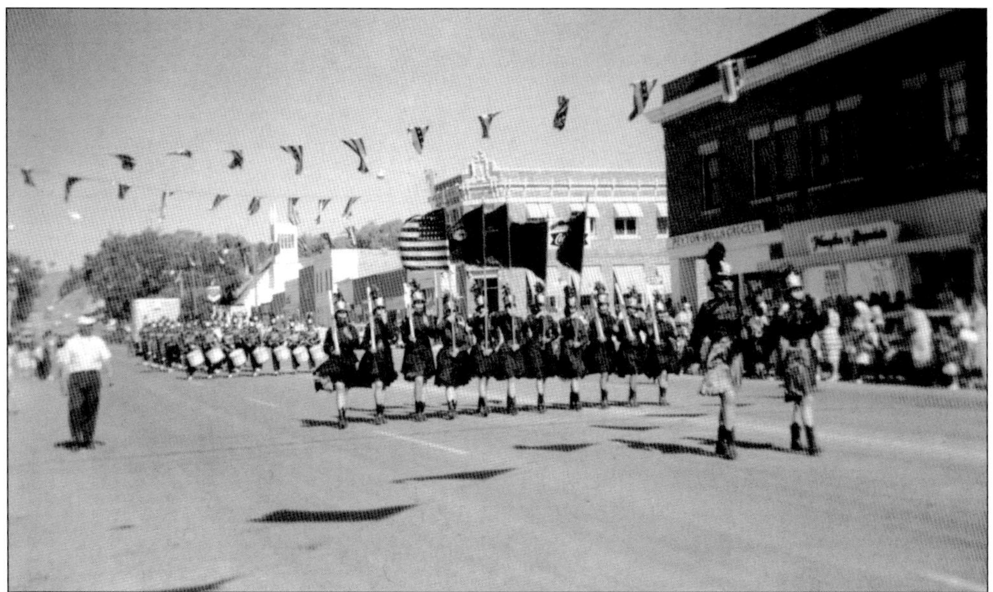

The Troopers Cadets Drum & Bugle Corps marches in the American Legion Parade in Douglas, Wyoming, in 1963. Due to the overwhelming popularity of the Troopers, Jim Jones started the Cadets or B corps in 1961. Many Troopers learned the basics of playing an instrument and marching in the B corps before moving up to the A corps. (Courtesy of the Troopers Archives.)

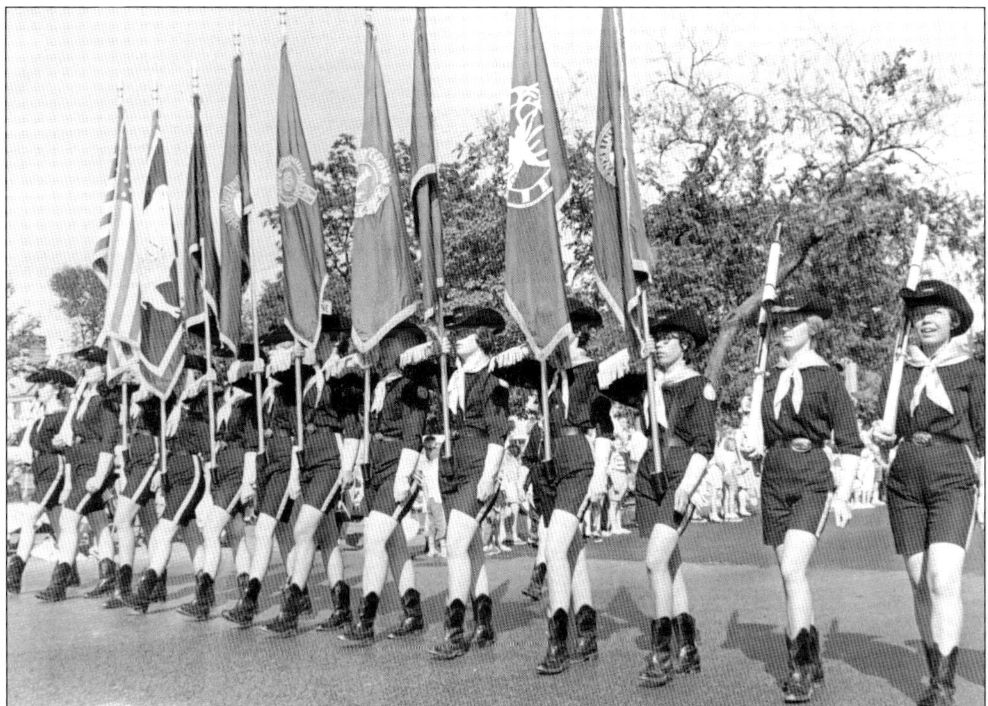

The Troopers color guard marches in the Wyoming State Fair Parade in Douglas in 1963. In the early 1960s, the color guard parade uniform included Bermuda shorts instead of skirts. The heavy wool skirts were very uncomfortable in the hot summer weather. (Courtesy of the Troopers Archives.)

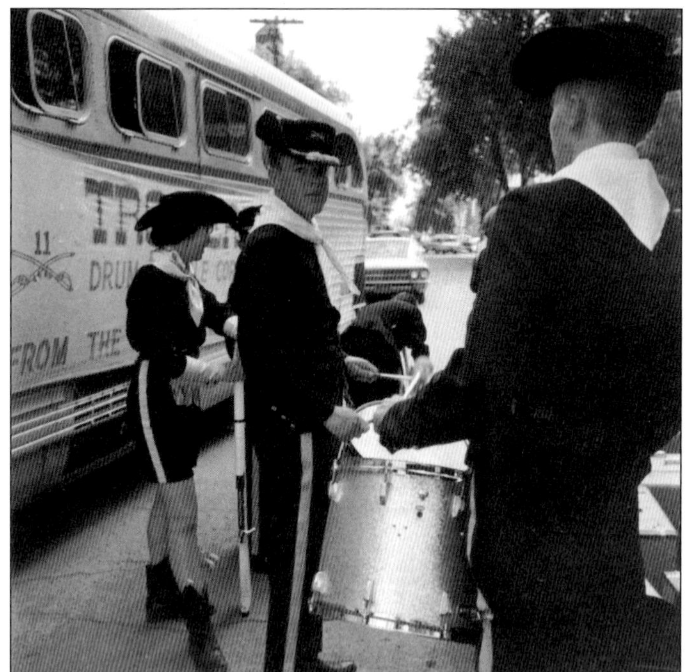

Several Troopers prepare for a parade in 1963. From left to right are Janet Ferrell (color guard), Fred Sanford (facing camera), and Bill Bailey (back to camera). Part of the score at VFW and American Legion contests included marching in a parade. In addition to performances throughout Wyoming that year, the Troopers competed in Wisconsin, Illinois, Kansas, and Washington. (Courtesy of the Troopers Archives.)

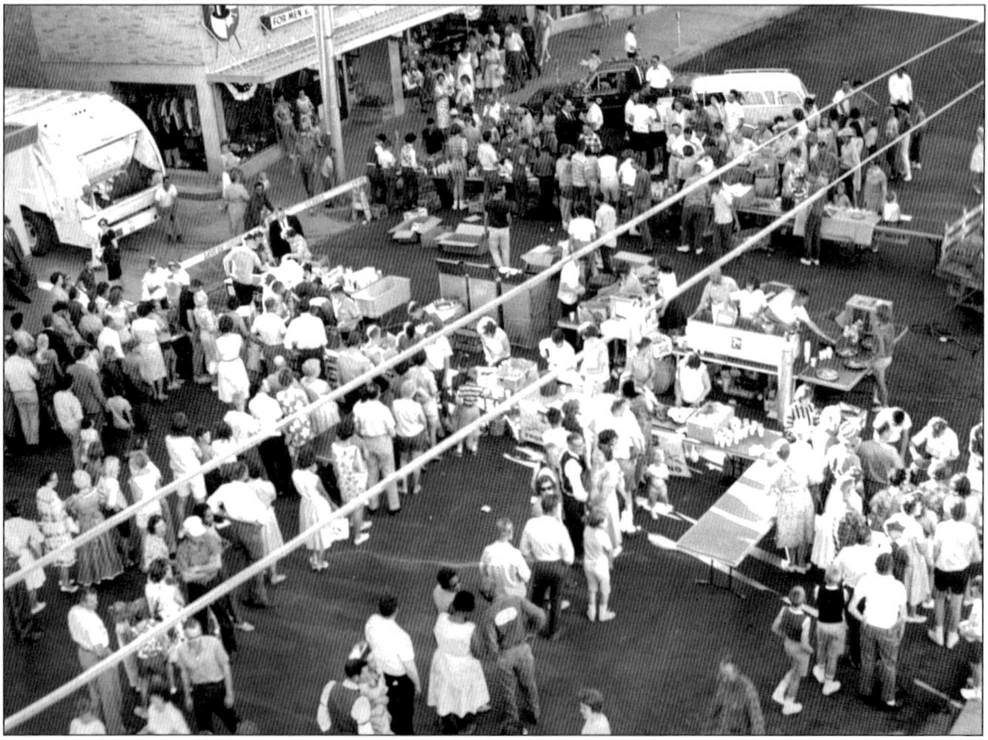

Crowds line up to buy a barbecued buffalo sandwich and a pop for 25¢ from the Troopers in downtown Casper in 1964. The buffalo was donated by Bud Basolo from the B Bar B Ranch near Wright, Wyoming. The Troopers served over 3,000 people that day. This was another of the many fundraisers that the Troopers have done over the years. (Courtesy of the Troopers Archives.)

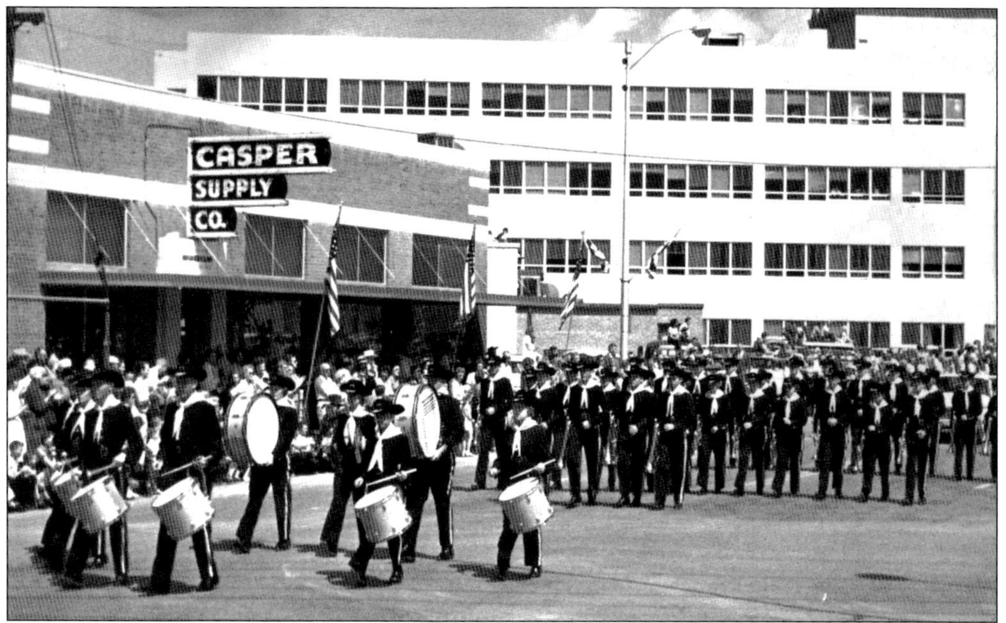

The Troopers march down South Center Street in the Central Wyoming Fair and Parade in Casper on July 29, 1964. That day, the fair program in the *Casper Tribune* had an advertisement that read: "Thursday, July 30, 7PM, Performance by The Troopers, Casper's national prize-winning drum and bugle corps." (Courtesy of the Troopers Archives.)

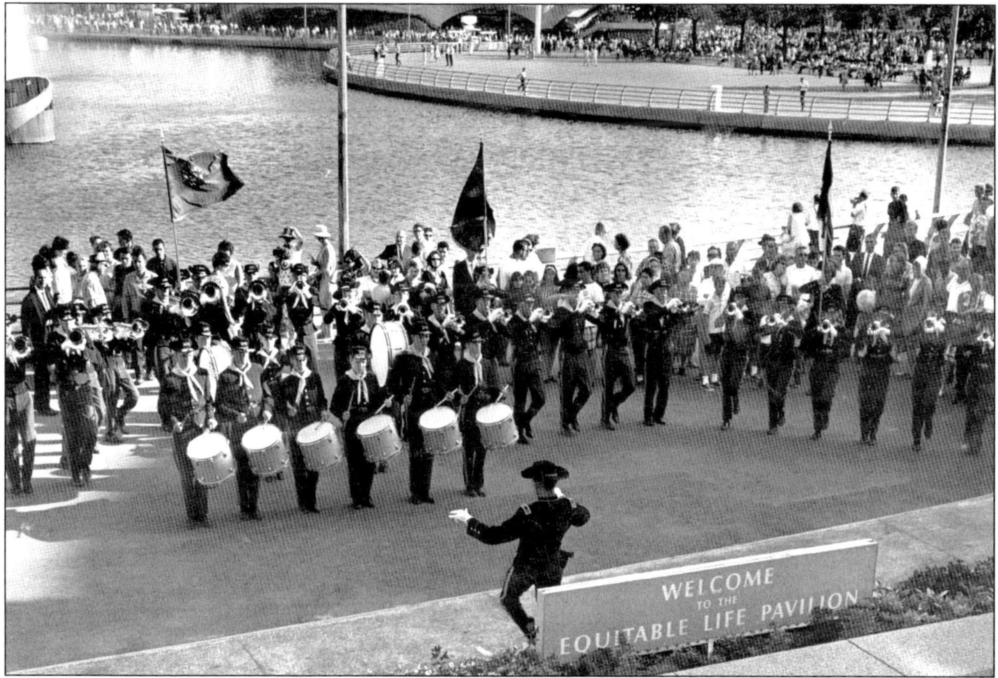

The Troopers gave a concert at the Equitable Life Pavilion during the New York World's Fair in 1964. Drum major Pete Emmons is seen leading them. The Troopers spent three days in New York City. While there, they took a boat trip, went shopping, visited Coney Island, and saw a Broadway show. (Courtesy of the Troopers Archives.)

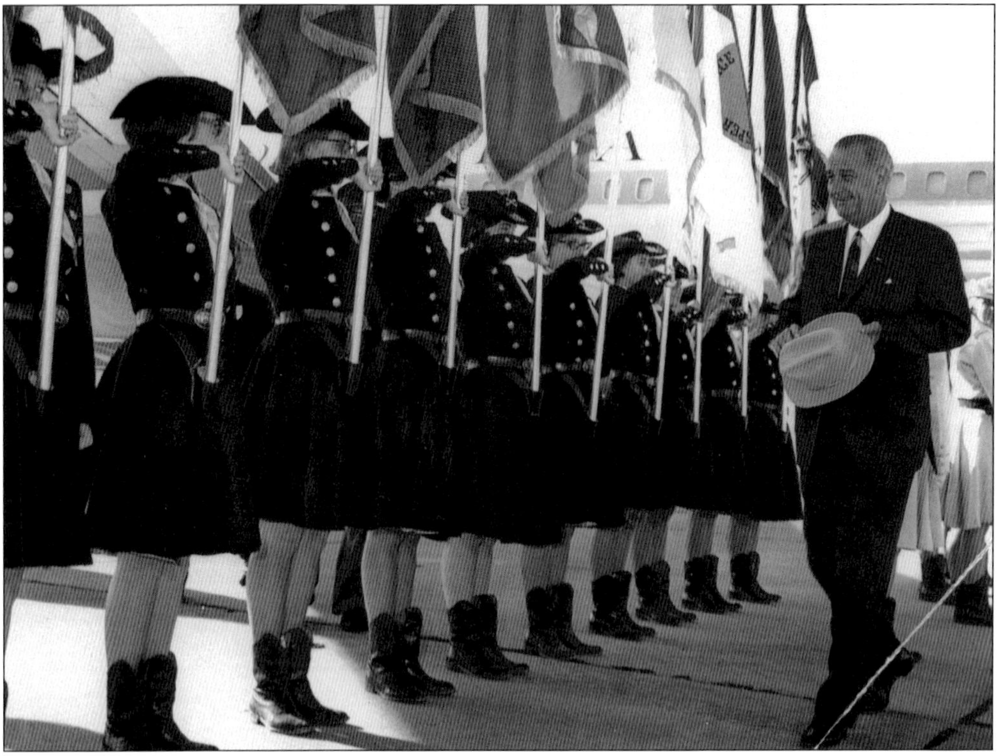

"Honor Guard" was the caption for this photograph that appeared in the *Casper Tribune* on October 13, 1964, the day after Pres. Lyndon Johnson made a campaign stop in Casper. He was greeted by the Troopers color guard upon his arrival at the Casper Air Terminal. The first three color guard members from the left are Susie Cunningham, Mary Shea, and Michelle Charbonneau. (Courtesy of the Chuck Morrison Collection, Casper College Western History Center.)

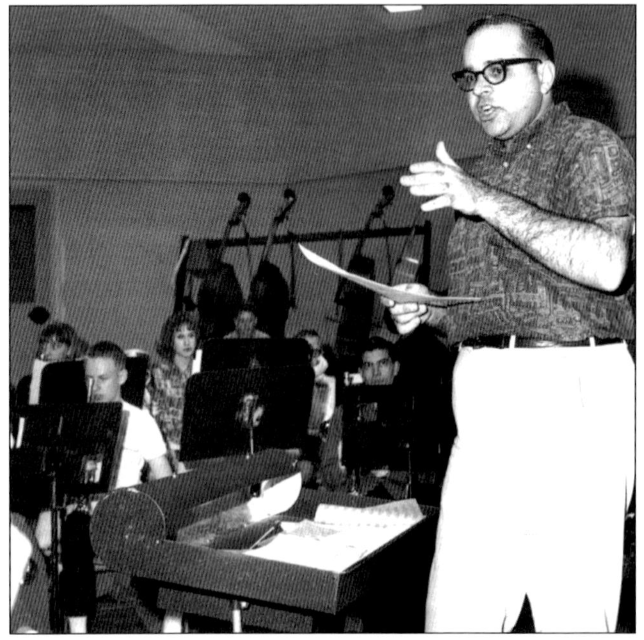

The Troopers brass section is shown working with Don Angelica in the Natrona County High School band room in Casper in 1965. Angelica, from New Jersey, was a well-known music instructor and arranger of corps music who worked with the Troopers in the 1960s. (Courtesy of Fort Caspar Museum.)

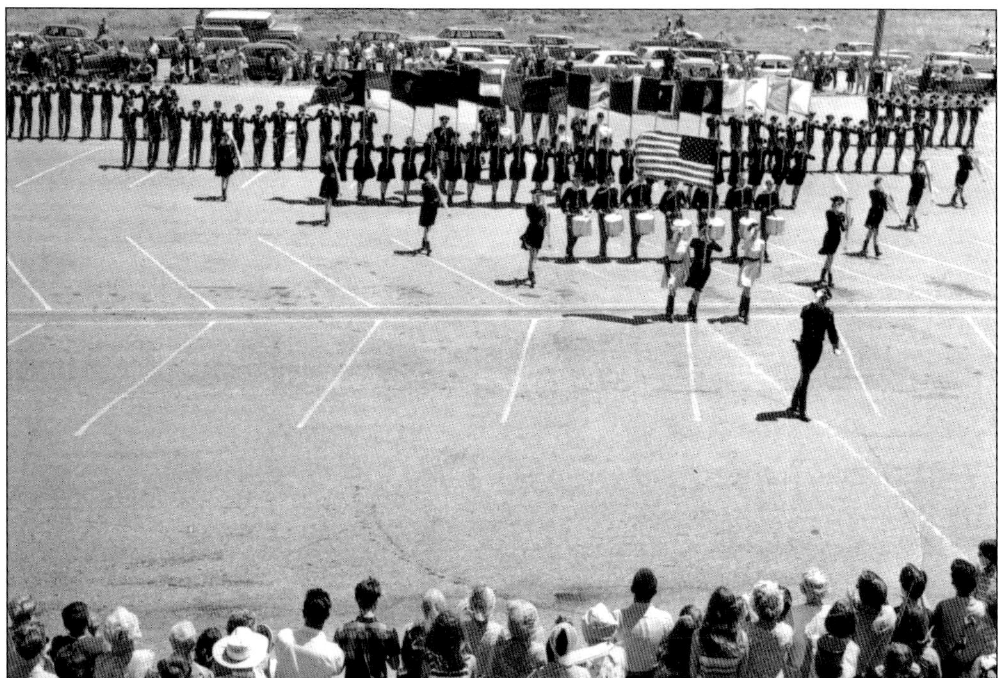

The Troopers perform in the parking lot of the Sunrise Shopping Center in Casper in July 1965. Later that day, an art auction was held as a fundraiser. Paintings and sculptures were donated by Wyoming artists for the event. The proceeds helped finance the eastern tour in August. (Photograph by Chuck Morrison, courtesy of Fort Caspar Museum.)

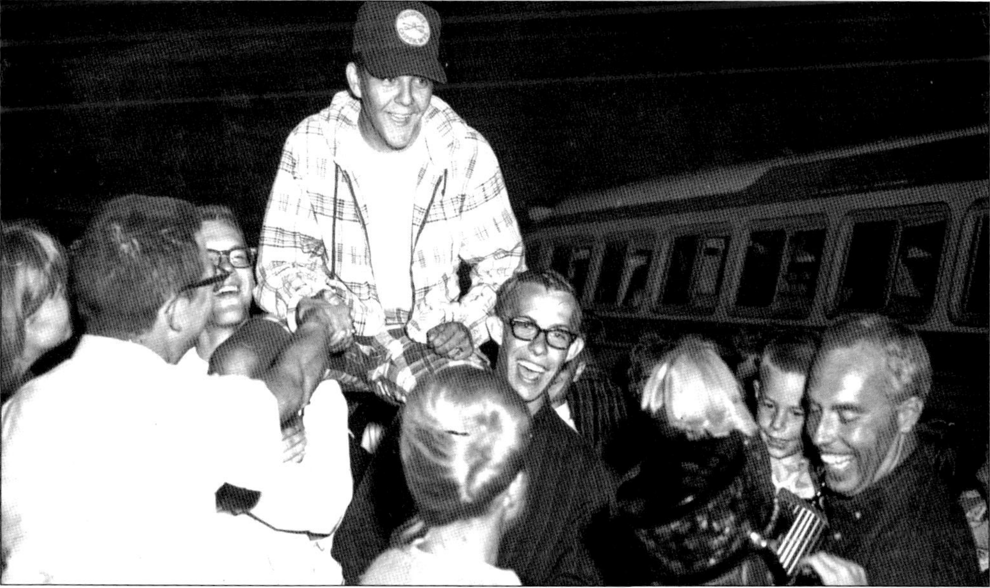

"Troopers Welcomed Home" was the title that ran with a similar photograph in the *Casper Star-Tribune* on July 9, 1965. The caption read: "Many Casperites gathered at Hilltop parking lot Wednesday evening to welcome the Troopers Drum and Bugle Corps back to Casper after they took first place in Streator, Ill. . . . Left to right: Mayor Pat Meenan, Jim Wade, Drum Major Pete Emmons, Nick Krause, and Jim Jones, director, holding son Jimmy." (Courtesy of the Troopers Archives.)

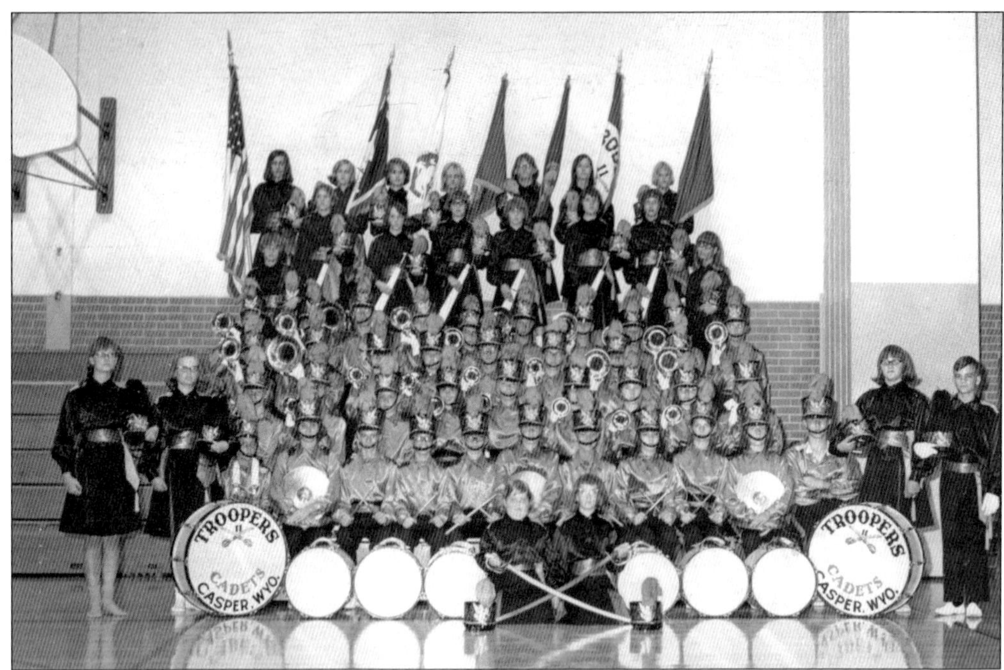

"Casper Trooper Cadets" was the title of this photograph when it appeared in the *Casper Star-Tribune* on August 15, 1965. The caption read, "The Trooper Cadets with their Color Guard make an imposing group of young people who give much time and effort toward making their unit a first class organization." (Photograph by Chuck Morrison, courtesy of Fort Caspar Museum.)

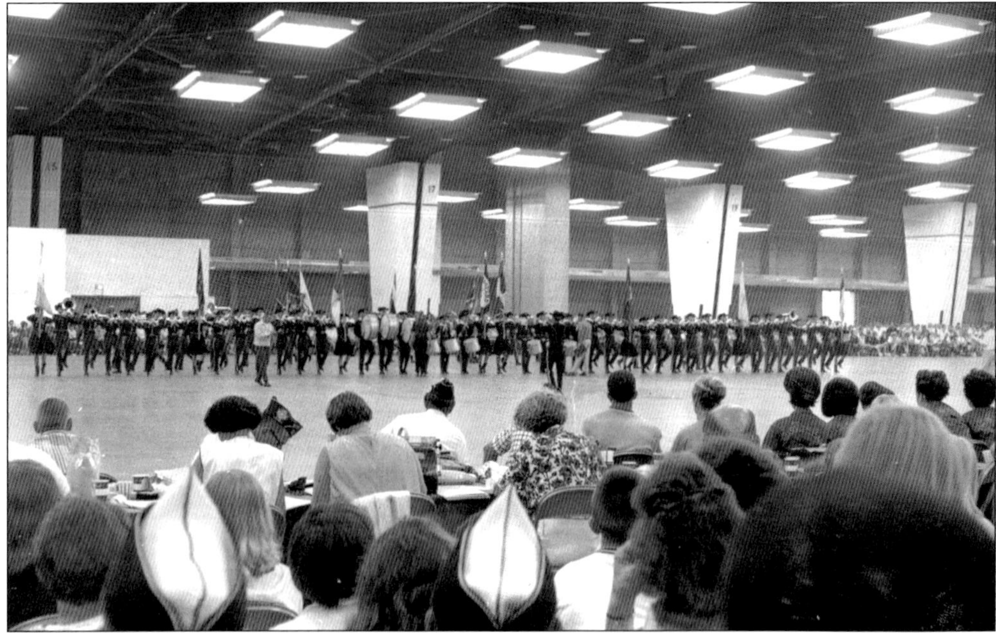

The Troopers perform at the VFW National Championships in Chicago, Illinois, on August 18, 1965. The competition was moved from Soldier Field to McCormick Place due to rain. The Troopers finished fourth that day but went on to win their first national championship at the World Open Finals in Bridgeport, Connecticut, three days later. (Courtesy of the Troopers Archives.)

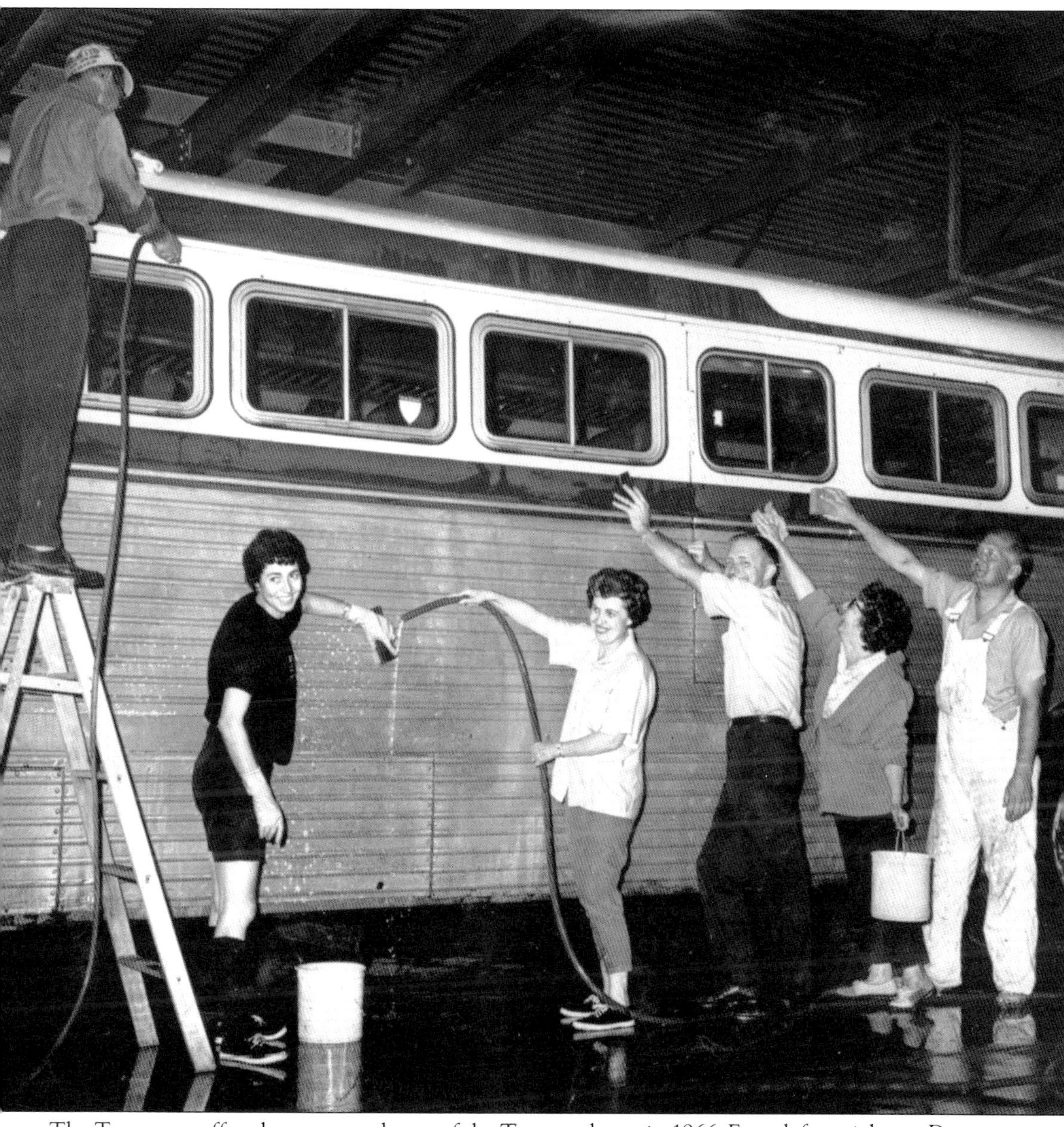

The Troopers staff and parents wash one of the Troopers buses in 1966. From left to right are Don Carr (drill instructor), Verna Campbell (parent), Gwendolyn Maxon (Bill Maxon's wife, known as "Mom Maxon"), Jim Campbell (parent), Veronica Kennedy (parent), and Bill Maxon (Cadets director). (Courtesy of the Troopers Archives.)

THE
AMERICAN LEGION
Presents
"YOUTH ON PARADE"

Drum and Bugle Corps
Contest

Featuring

- *Cavaliers of Chicago, Illinois*
- *Troopers of Casper, Wyoming*
- *Scouts of St. Paul, Minnesota*
- *Kilties of Racine, Wisconsin*
- *Sky Ryders of Hutchinson, Kansas*

Wilbur Dalzell Field
JULY 2
7:30 p.m.

TICKETS
Adult Advance Sale $1.50
Adult at Gate $2.00
Children .50¢

This show poster is from the American Legion competition Youth on Parade in Dubuque, Iowa, on July 2, 1966. The Troopers finished second to the Chicago Cavaliers in their first meeting of the year. The Troopers went on to win five times that year, including becoming the VFW National Junior Drum Corps champions by winning the Million Dollar Pageant of Drums in Jersey City, New Jersey, on August 24. (Courtesy of Fort Caspar Museum.)

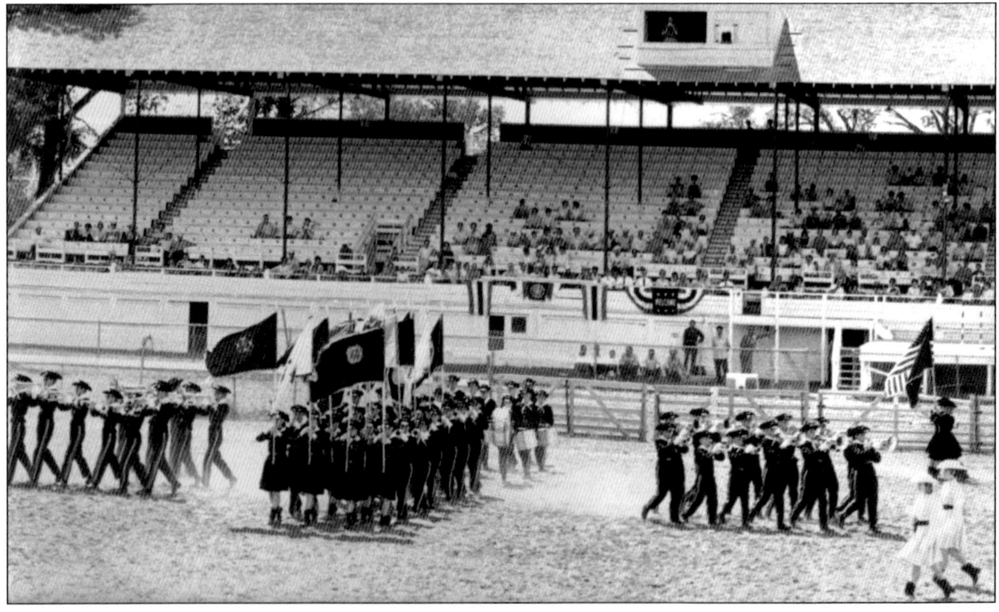

The Troopers perform at the Wyoming High School Rodeo in Douglas in 1966. That year, the drum major was Pete Emmons and the guard captains were Laurel Jones and Mary Shea. The Troopers played "How the West Was Won," "Battle Hymn of the Republic," "Bonanza," "Ghost Riders," and "Magnificent Seven" that year. (Courtesy of the Troopers Archives.)

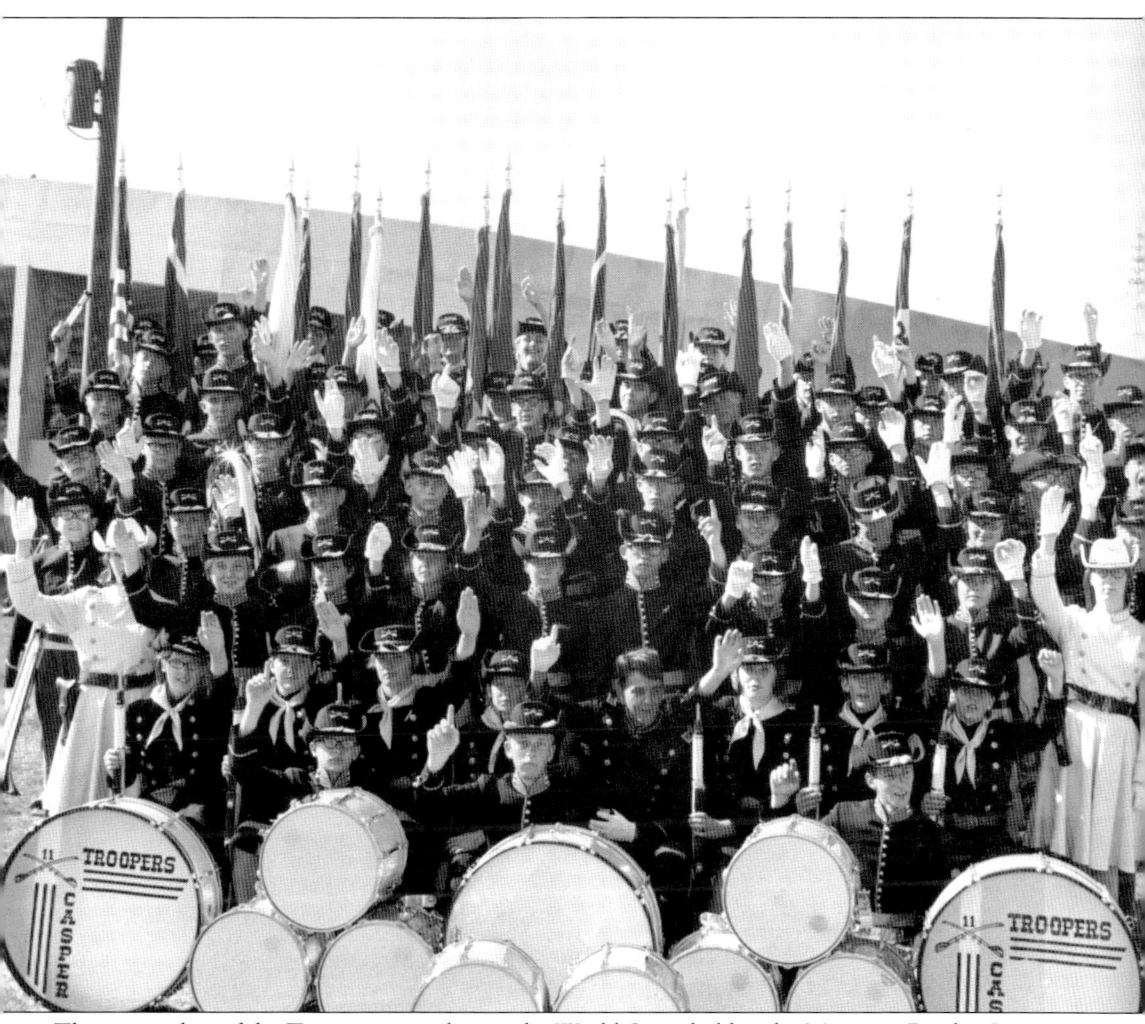

This group shot of the Troopers was taken at the World Open held at the Manning Bowl in Lynn on August 20, 1966. They had a busy couple of weeks on the East Coast. The Troopers competed in the World Open Contest, at the National Dream Contest in Jersey City on August 21, the VFW Nationals also in Jersey City on August 22 through 24, and the American Legion Nationals between August 27 and 29 in Washington, DC. (Courtesy of the Troopers Archives.)

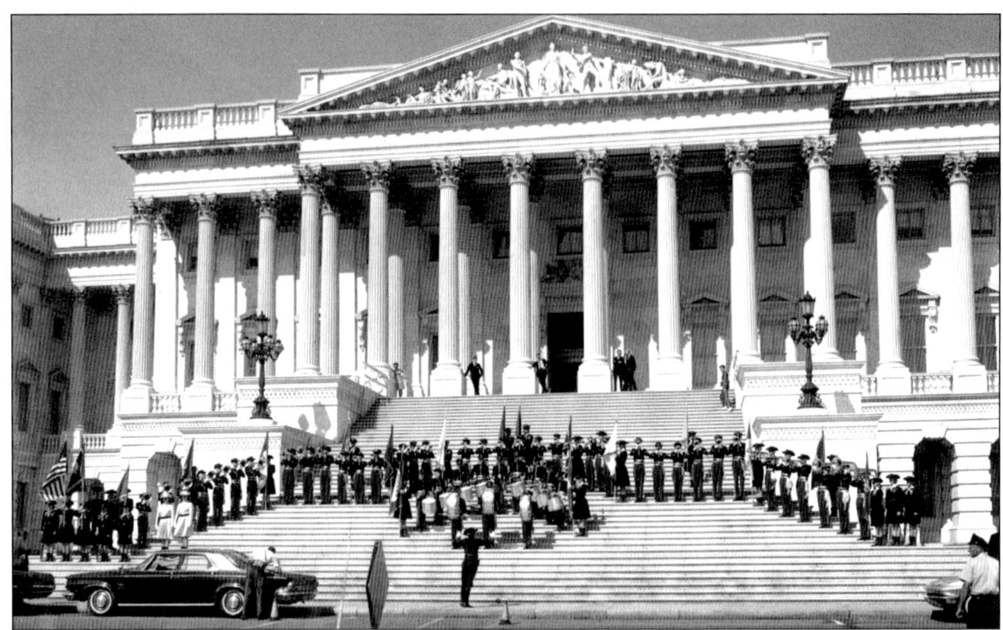

The Troopers perform on the steps of the Senate Wing of the US Capitol in Washington on August 26, 1966. According to the flyer: "Wyoming United States Senator Milward L. Simpson PROUDLY INVITES YOU AND YOUR STAFF. To attend a performance by the WORLD CHAMPION CASPER TROOPERS." The Troopers were in Washington for the American Legion National Championships. They finished in fourth place. (Courtesy of Fort Caspar Museum.)

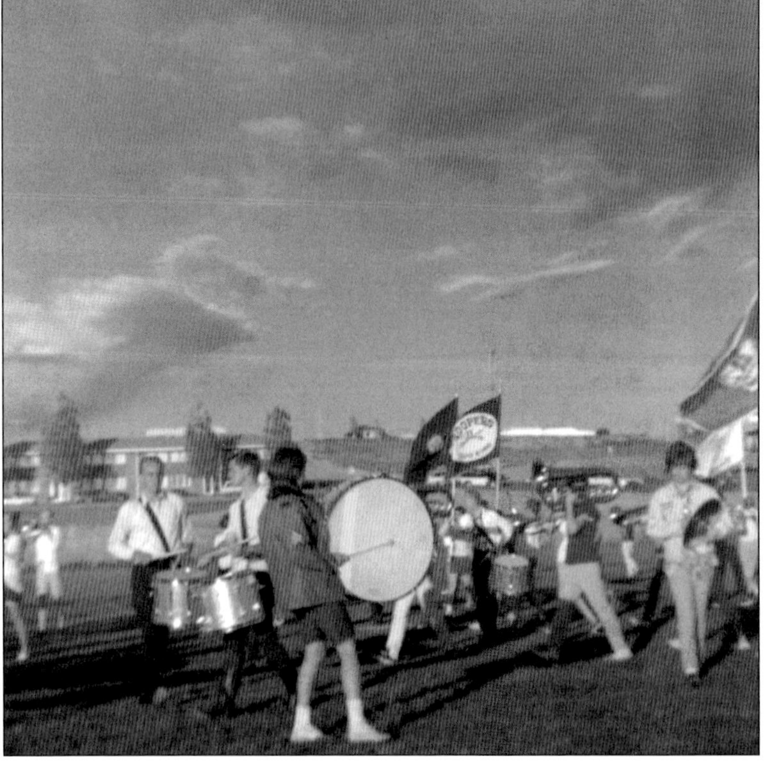

The Troopers practice next to East Junior High School in Casper in the spring of 1967. Percussion players are, from left to right, Bill Bailey and Eddie Bostwick (snares), Linda White (bass drum), Dennis Dusel (snare), and Renee McCarrel (cymbals). Director Jim Jones was a building contractor in Casper and had built the school. (Photograph by James White, courtesy of Linda Schulz.)

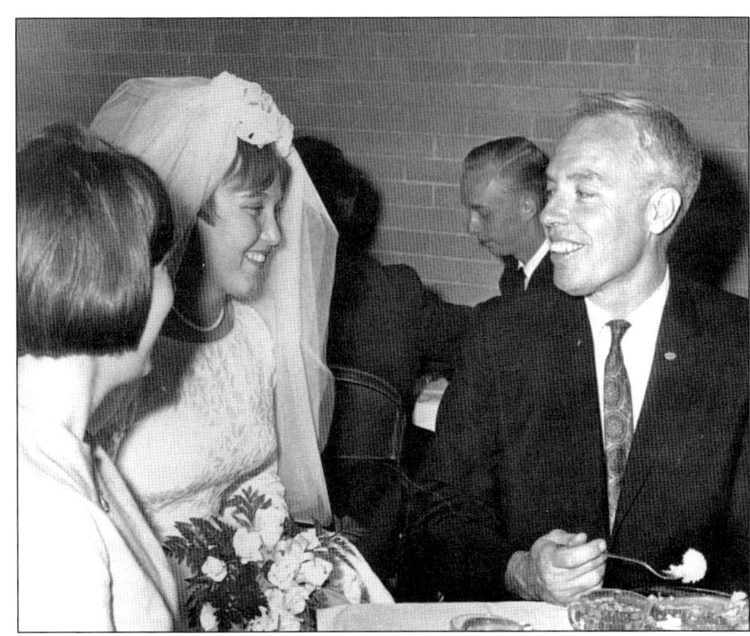

Troopers director Jim Jones (right) attended the wedding of Ruth Anne Smith and Robert Kosma in Casper on June 3, 1967. Smith, who played snare drum, was a charter member of the corps. The Troopers surprised the newlyweds as they left the church: the color guard formed an arch of flags for them to walk under, and the corps played several of the bride's favorite songs. (Courtesy of the Troopers Archives.)

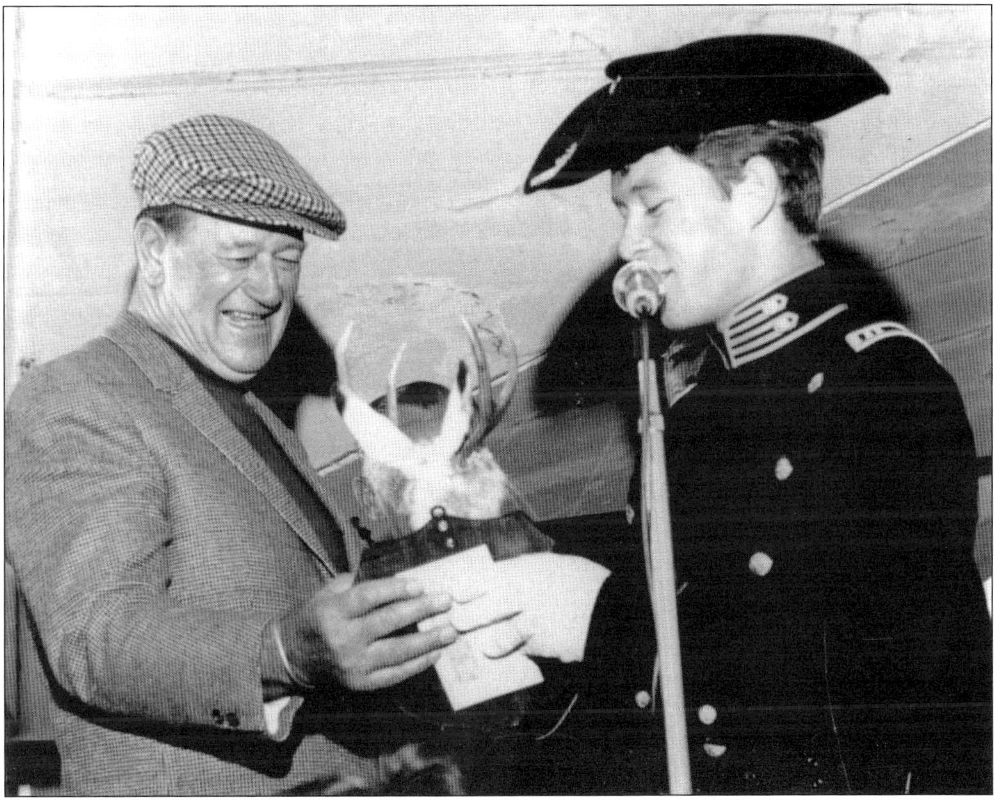

Troopers drum major Jim McIntyre presents a mounted jackalope to John Wayne after a public performance at the Holiday Inn in Casper in 1968. Wayne was in Casper filming *Hellfighters*. He told the crowd that he had been "deeply moved" by the Troopers and called them the "best I've ever seen." (Courtesy of Jim and Suzette McIntyre.)

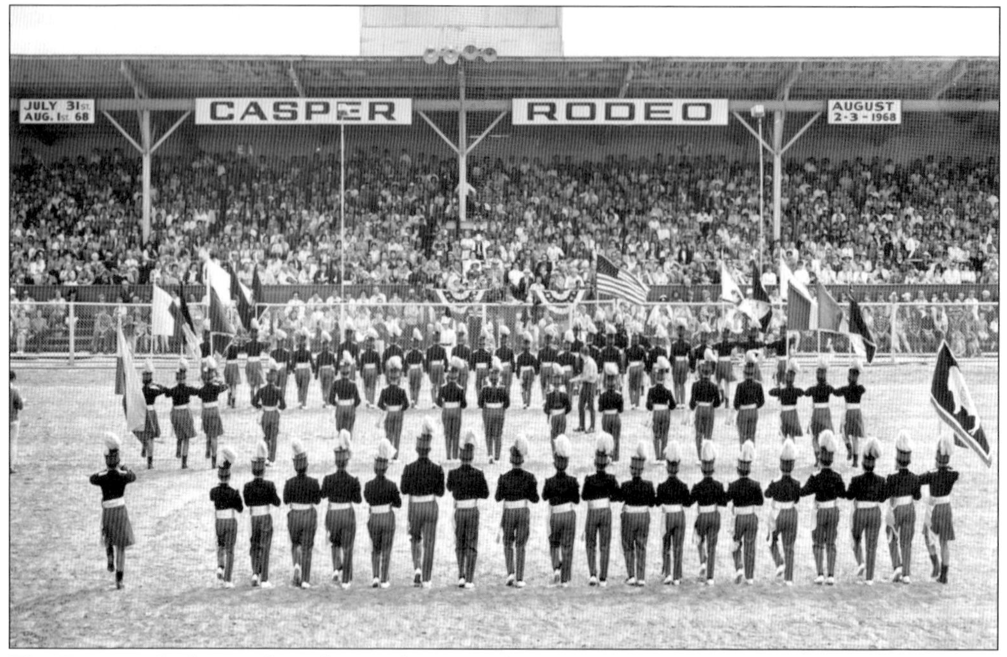

The Troopers Cadets perform during the Central Wyoming Fair and Rodeo at the Casper Rodeo on Wednesday, July 31, 1968. The staff for the Cadets that year included Bill Maxon, director; Jim Jones, manager; Jake Putnam, color guard; Bob Kalkofen, Dennis Dusel, and Gary Shockey, drums; John Aanestad and Warren Schaeffer, bugles; and Don Carr, Dick Jones, Tom Harvey, Leonard Sisco, and Gene Salzman, music and marching. (Courtesy of Fort Caspar Museum.)

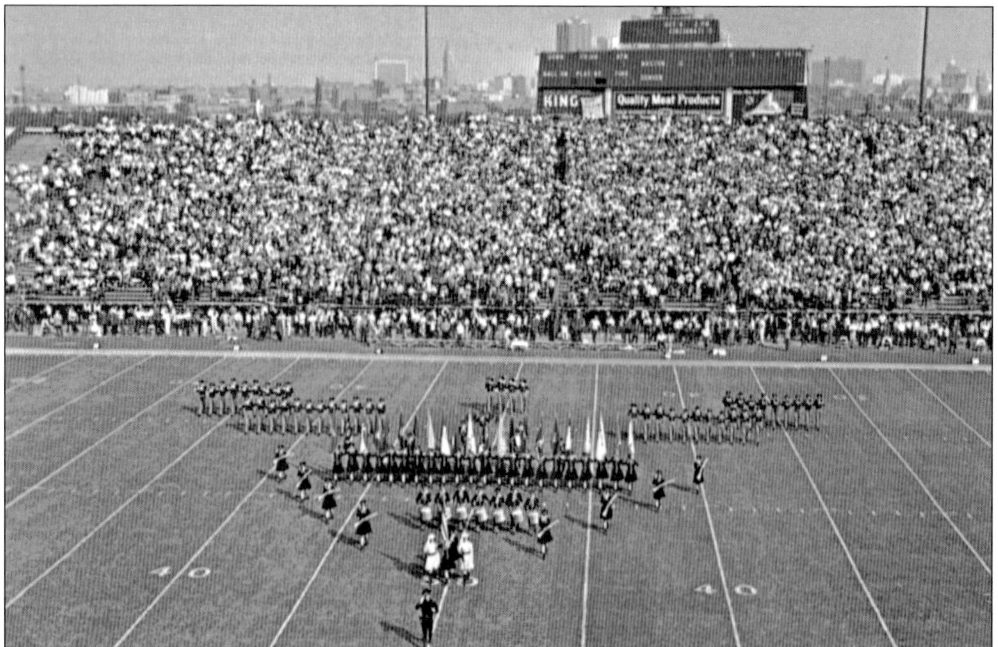

This Troopers souvenir postcard shows them performing at halftime at a Denver Broncos game against the Boston Patriots on Sunday, September 29, 1968, in Denver. Postcards like this were sold out of the Troopers' souvenir stand, an old sheep wagon. (Courtesy of Fort Caspar Museum.)

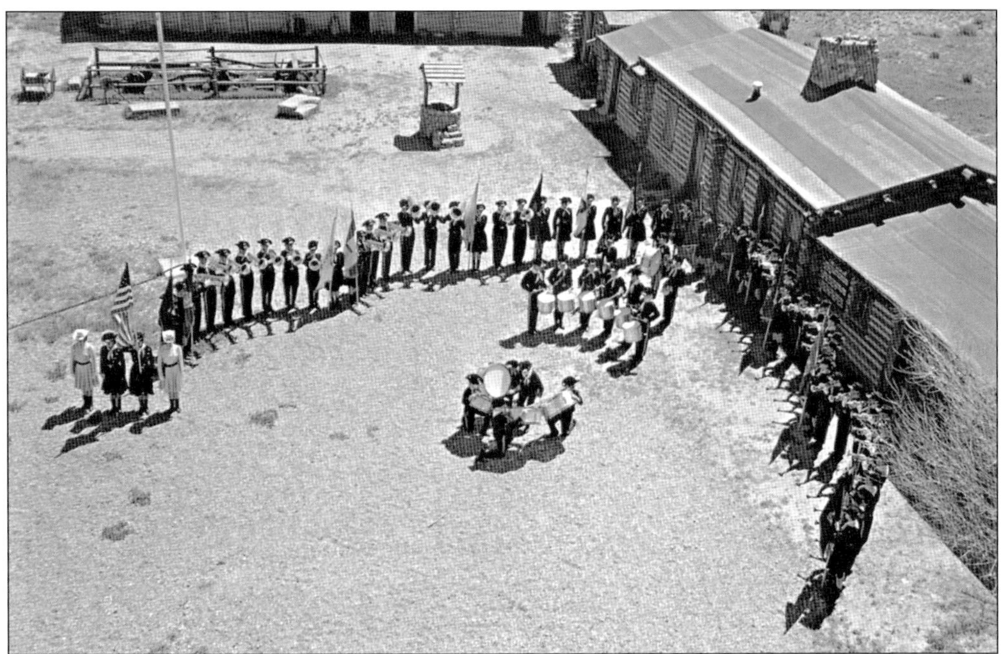

This 1969 photograph of the Troopers at Fort Caspar Museum was made into an oversized souvenir postcard. The city was named after the fort, which was named for Lt. Caspar Collins, who died here on July 26, 1865. (Courtesy of Fort Caspar Museum.)

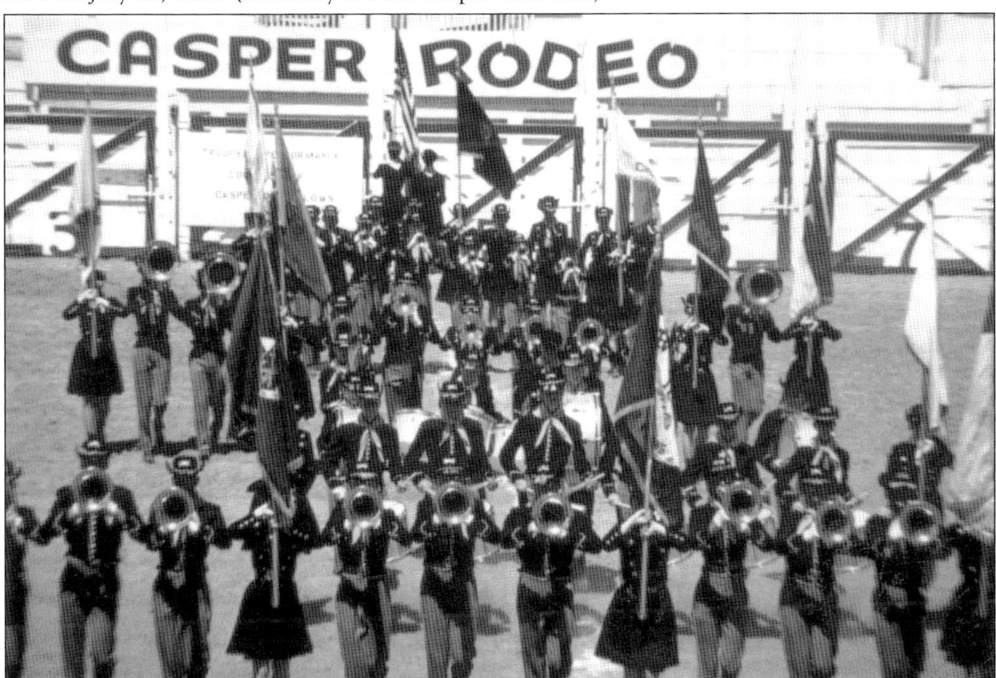

The Troopers perform at the Central Wyoming Fair and Rodeo in Casper in 1969. That year, they won the CYO National Championship and the World Open Championship, while the color guard was the Midwest Color Guard champions, the VFW National Color Guard champions, and the American Legion Color Guard champions. (Courtesy of the Troopers Archives.)

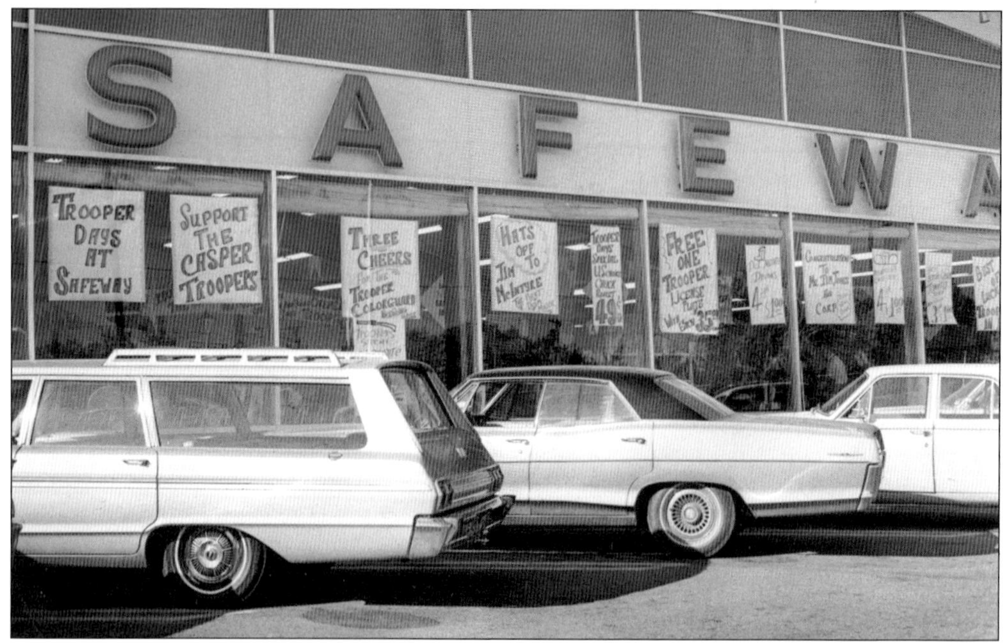

"Trooper Days at Safeway" proclaims one of the signs in the front window of the Safeway store at 1375 CY Avenue in Casper on August 13–16, 1969. Safeway pledged to donate a percentage of the sales from those four days, which totaled $2,604. This kind of donation demonstrates one of the ways local businesses support the Troopers. (Courtesy of the Troopers Archives.)

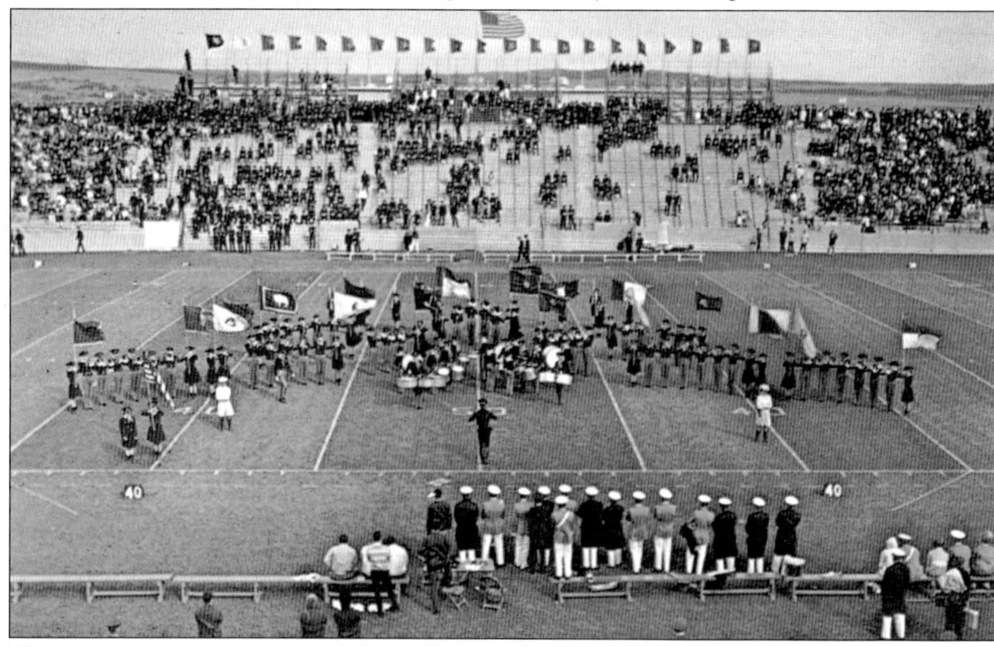

This Troopers souvenir postcard shows them performing at halftime during the US Air Force Academy–University of Wyoming football game in Colorado Springs, Colorado, on September 27, 1969. The Wyoming Cowboys won a close game, 27-25. In the audience that night was a member of the Air Force Academy Drum and Bugle Corps, Jim Wade, a charter member of the Troopers. (Courtesy of Fort Caspar Museum.)

Three

1970s

A New Direction, Drum Corps International

For the Troopers Drum & Bugle Corps, the new decade started off with a bang. They won the VFW National Championship, the CYO National Championship, the North American Championship, and the World Open Championship in 1970. Casper welcomed home the Troopers with 6,000 parents, friends, and residents packing the stadium at Natrona County High School. Among the people there to greet the corps was Wyoming governor Stan Hathaway and Casper mayor Bill Muller.

Throughout the 1950s and 1960s, several organizations held national championships: the American Legion, VFW, CYO, and others. Each group had different rules and criteria for judging performances and crowned its own champion. This led to several national championships being won each year, which proved to be confusing. Jim Jones and the Troopers, along with 12 other corps, founded Drum Corps International (DCI) in 1972 and established one set of rules and one national championship.

The apex for the Troopers in terms of winning national championships was 1970. Since that year, the corps has not won a championship, although they did finish second at the DCI finals in 1973. However, the color guard continued to win in the 1970s, and brought home the Continental Divide Color Guard Championship in 1973, 1974, 1975, and 1977.

While the Troopers may not have brought home another championship after 1970, their popularity has never waned. Their distinctive US Cavalry–inspired uniforms, outstanding marching and maneuvering, friendliness, and esprit de corps made them fan favorites everywhere they went. The Troopers were invited to perform for the halftime show at Denver Broncos football games in 1971 and 1975, and played at a Kansas City Chiefs game in 1972.

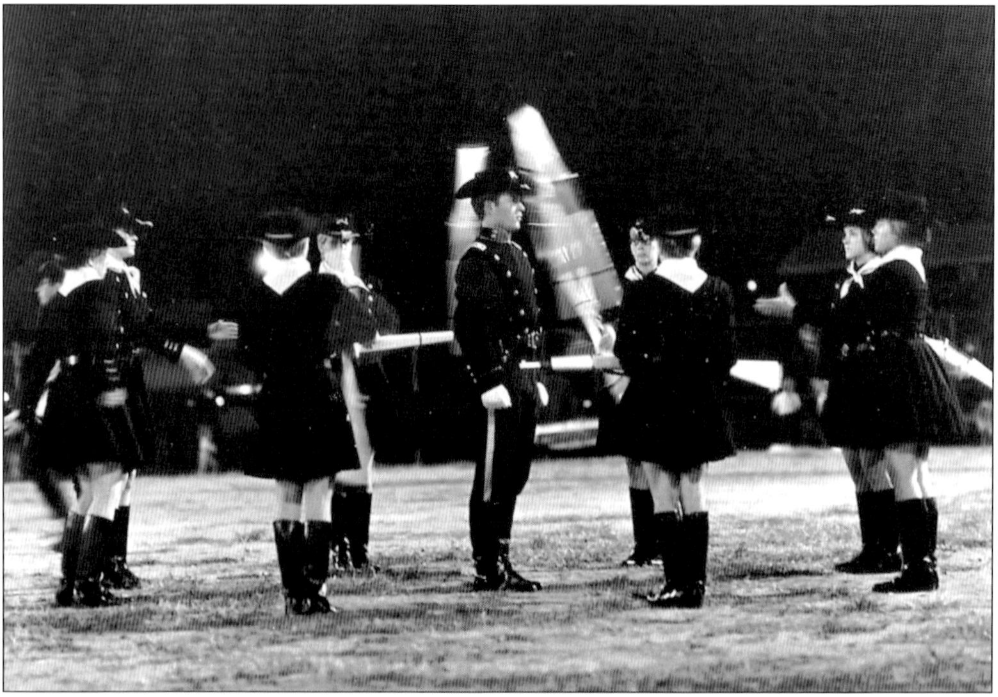

The Troopers perform the suicide toss in 1970. Drum major Jim McIntyre stands in the center of a circle, and 10 color guard members toss their rifles across the circle, just missing him, to be caught by the person on the opposite side. (Courtesy of Jim and Suzette McIntyre.)

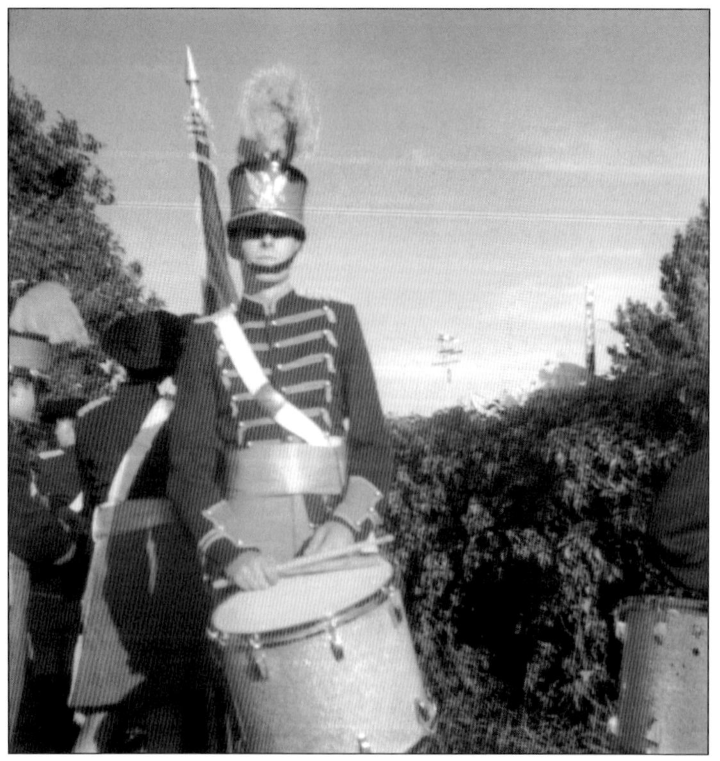

Troopers Cadet snare drummer David Rake is pictured before a parade in Alliance, Nebraska, in July 1970. The Cadets took part in the Drums on Parade in Chadron, Nebraska, on July 25, 1970, sponsored by the American Legion. A flyer for the show read: "Don't miss the big parade featuring drums and bugle corps, drill teams and high school bands also competing for trophies." (Courtesy of the Troopers Archives.)

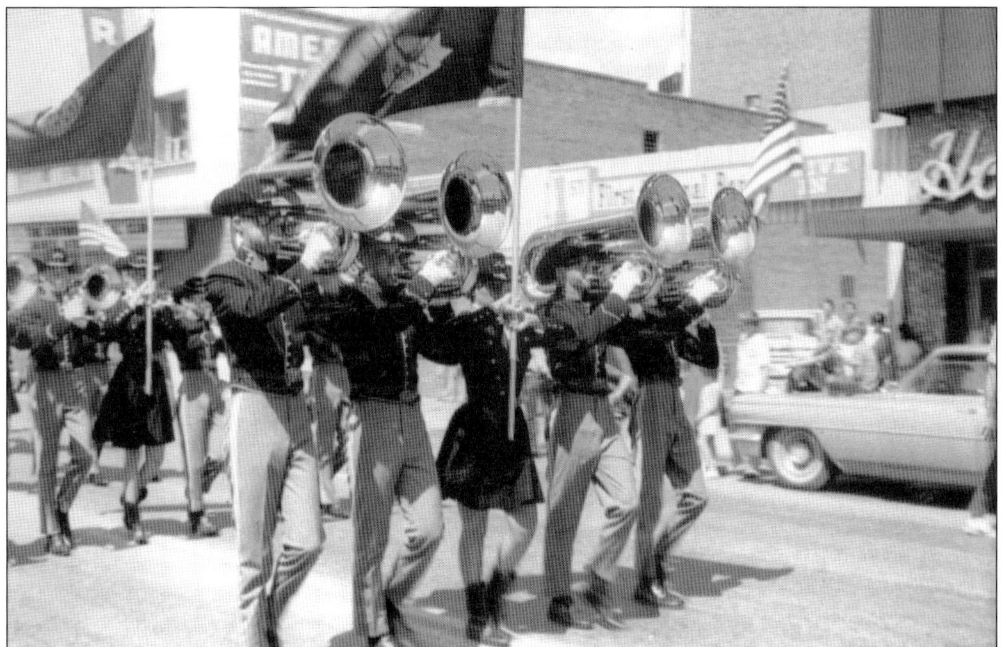

The Troopers march down South Center Street in the Central Wyoming Fair and Rodeo Parade in Casper on July 29, 1970. From left to right are (first row) Warren Schafer, Glenn Schoenberg, Kathy Fraser, Pat Dye, and Rick Jones; (second row) Brett Hede, Karen Norgaard, and Cary Johnson. (Courtesy of the Troopers Archives.)

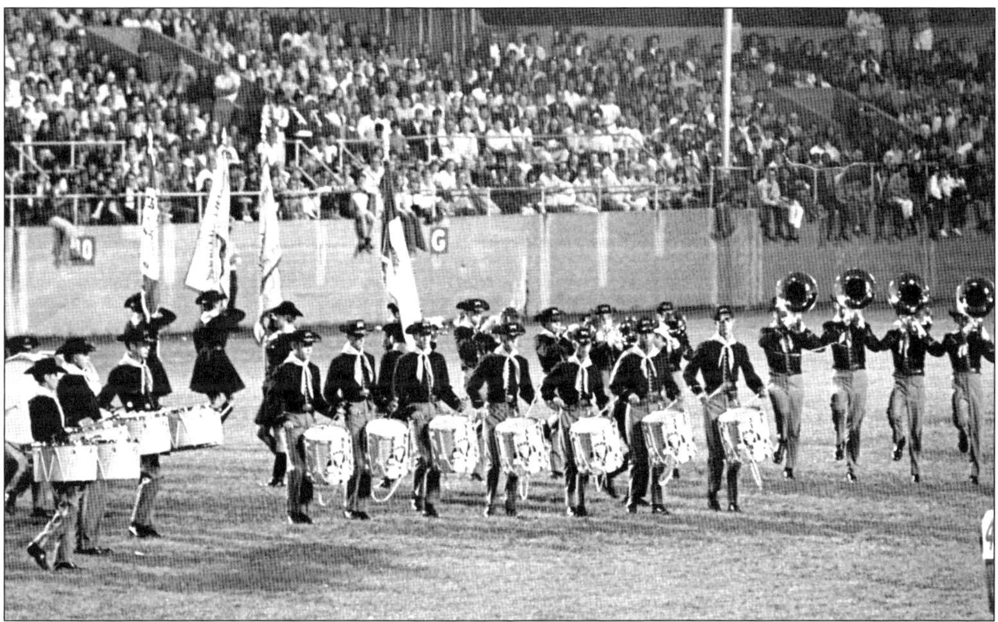

The Troopers perform at the World Open Finals in Lynn on August 22, 1970. That year, they brought home the championship trophy from the World Open as well as from the VFW National Championships in Miami Beach, Florida, the CYO National Championships in Boston, Massachusetts, and the North American Invitational in Toronto, Canada. (Courtesy of the Troopers Archives.)

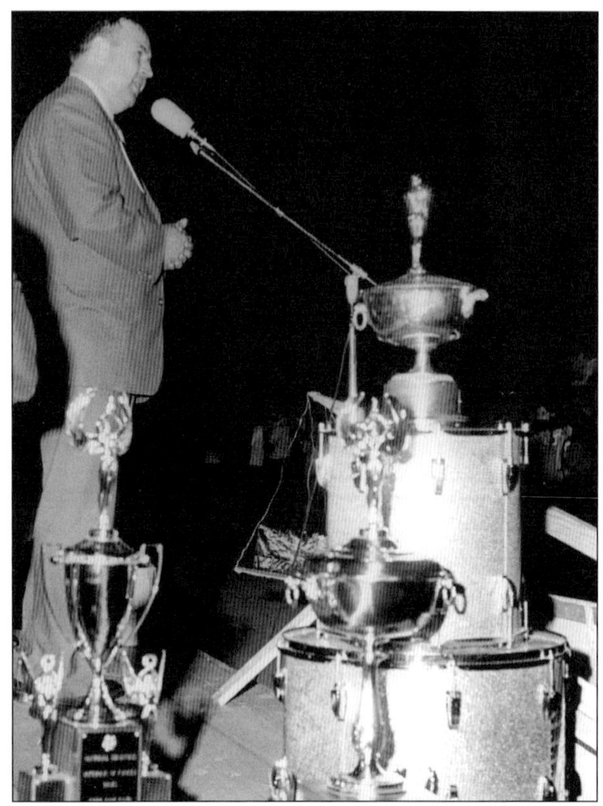

Wyoming governor Stanley Hathaway (left) gives a speech to the Troopers at their Welcome Home Celebration Ceremony on September 1, 1970. Below, Hathaway shakes hands with Troopers drum major Jim McIntyre. With them are Dick Jackson (center), president of the Casper Chamber of Commerce, and Bill Muller, Casper mayor. The celebration was held at the Natrona County High School stadium in Casper after winning the World Open, the VFW Championships, the CYO Championships, and the North American Invitational. Hathaway and his wife came up from Cheyenne, Wyoming, to attend the gigantic celebration in Casper, which included 6,000 parents and friends. (Both, courtesy of the Chuck Morrison Collection, Casper College Western History Center.)

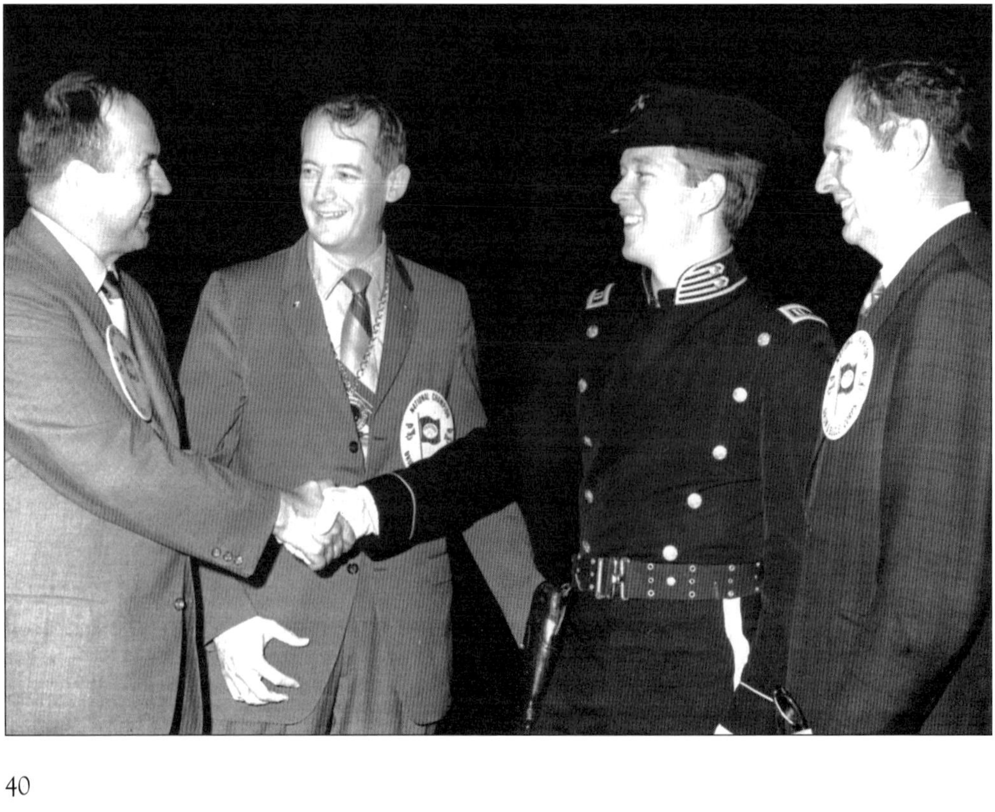

The Troopers Cadets (right) and the color guard (below) march out of the Safeway parking lot on East Collins Drive in Casper to start a parade in 1971. Bill Maxon formally became the Cadets director in 1965, a position he held until the mid-1970s. According to the *Troopers Profile*, published in the early 1970s, "Being a Cadet doesn't offer much in the way of thrills. They do get to do a little traveling but it's in family car-caravans and generally for short distances. The Cadets represent the Corps around the State of Wyoming and travel into Nebraska and Colorado." (Both, courtesy of the Troopers Archives.)

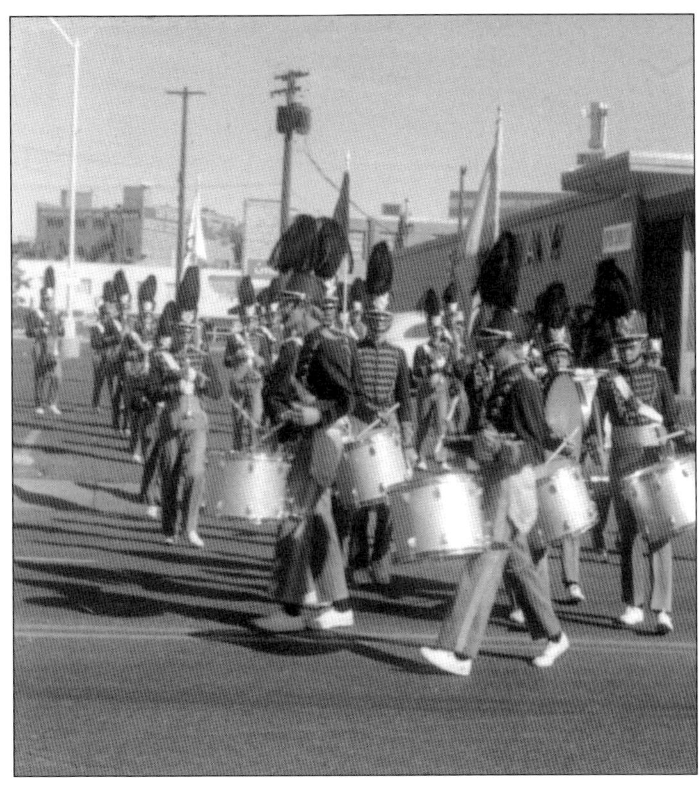

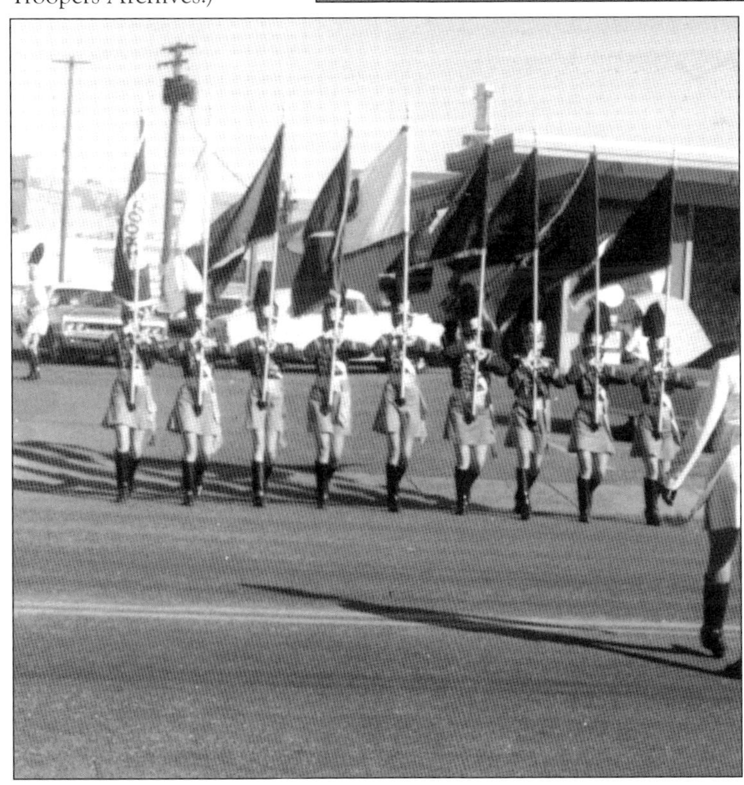

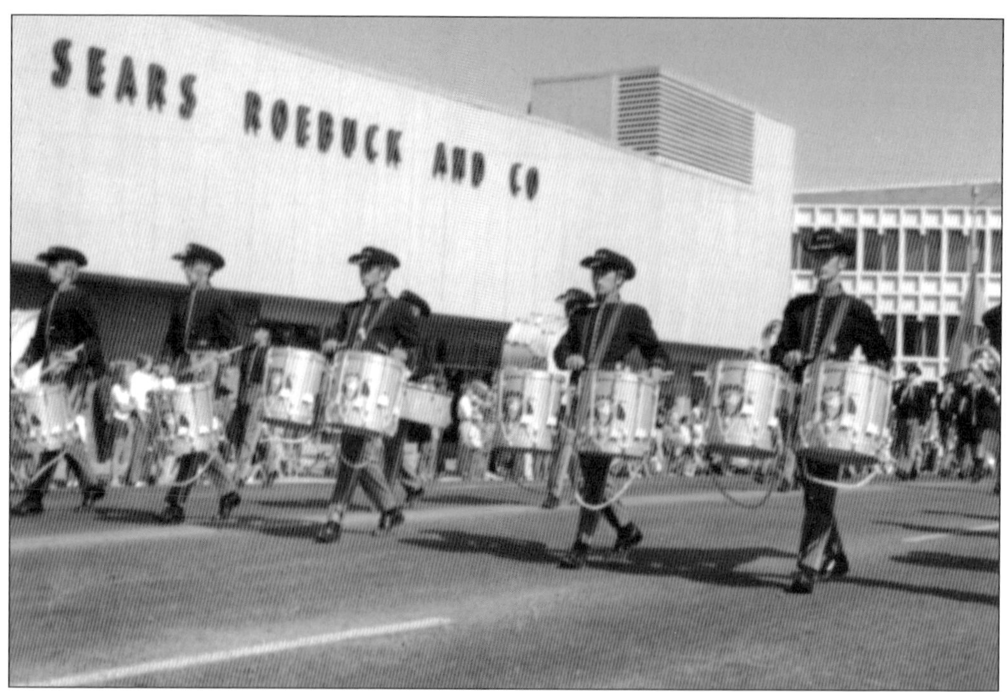

The Troopers drum line marches down South Center Street (above) in the Central Wyoming Fair and Rodeo Parade in Casper on July 29, 1971. They also had a performance in the rodeo arena (below) and opened the rodeo at Central Wyoming Fair that year. For many years, the Troopers planned their summer touring schedule in two parts. First, they traveled to either the East or West Coast in late June and early July, and in August, they headed east for the national championships. This allowed them to be in Casper for the Central Wyoming Fair and Rodeo in late July and early August. (Both, courtesy of Vickie Weber.)

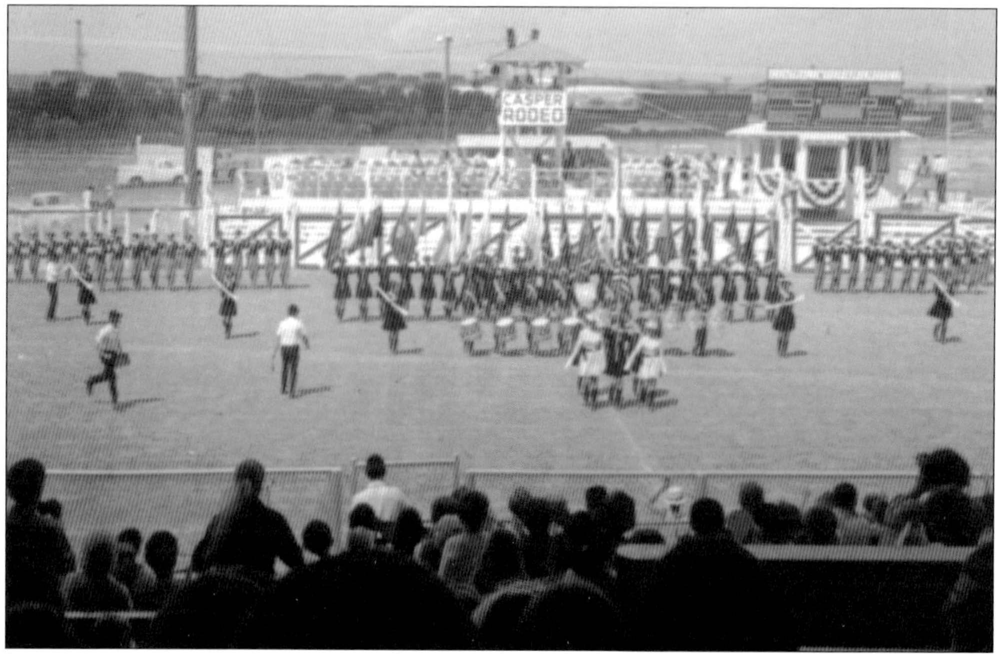

Troopers color guard commanders Erna Lindahl (center) and Gail Jones (right) present Alvin Flanagan of Mullins Broadcasting Company with the Honor Award for the company's support of the Troopers in 1971. Mullins Broadcasting Company was based in Denver and owned the ABC affiliate station (Channel 9) there. The company became a sponsor in 1970. In addition to the plaque, the Troopers carried a flag with the company logo in parades and at competitions. (Courtesy of the Troopers Archives.)

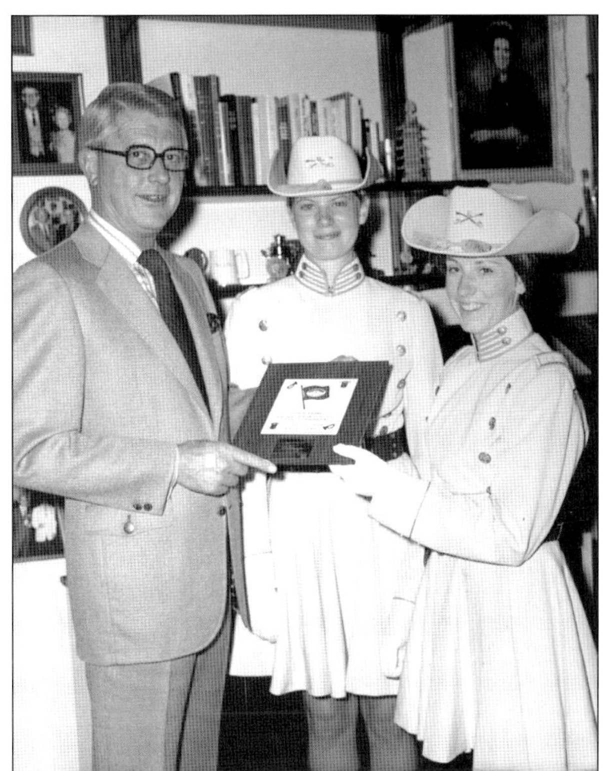

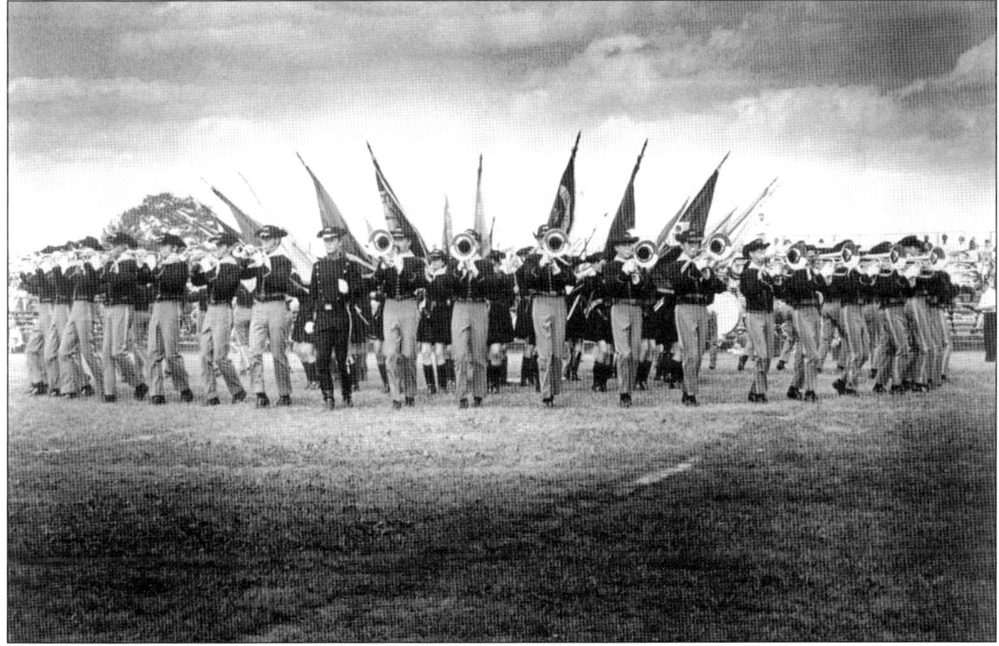

The Troopers perform their signature circle formation (also called the sunburst or wagon wheel) at the Mid-America Open in Overland Park, Kansas, on August 14, 1971. They were on their way to the VFW National Championships in Dallas, Texas. The Troopers finished second in Dallas. Drum major Jim McIntyre is at front just left of center. (Courtesy of Pat Chagnon.)

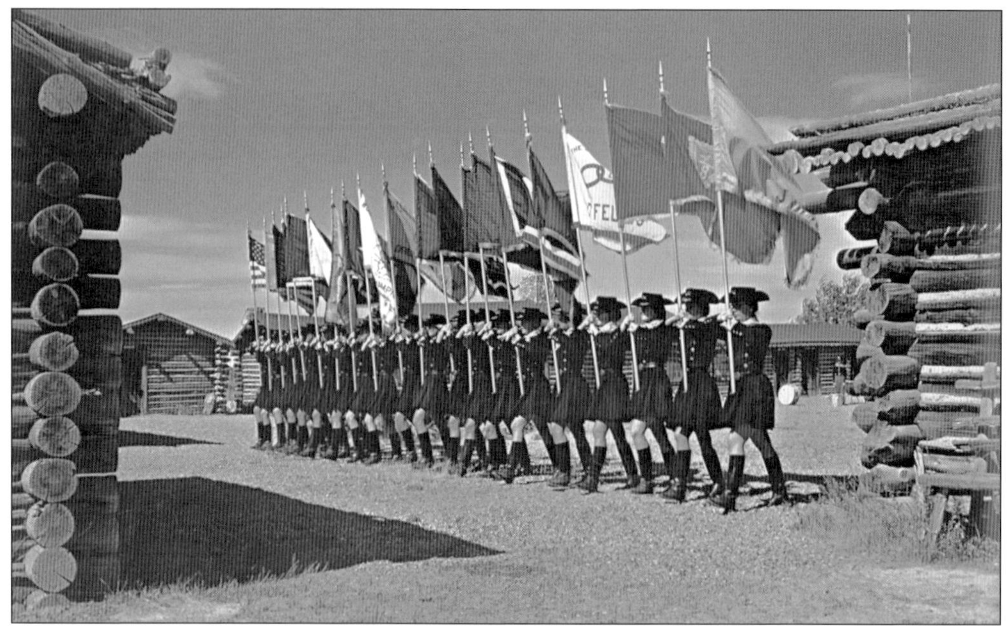

This photograph of the Troopers color guard at Fort Caspar Museum was used on a 1972 calendar put out by Mountain States Lithographing. The Casper printing company used photographs of the Troopers on many of its promotional calendars in the 1970s. Mountain States used the calendars as an advertising vehicle, distributing them free to local businesses. This is yet another way that local businesses have supported the Troopers. (Courtesy of the Troopers Archives.)

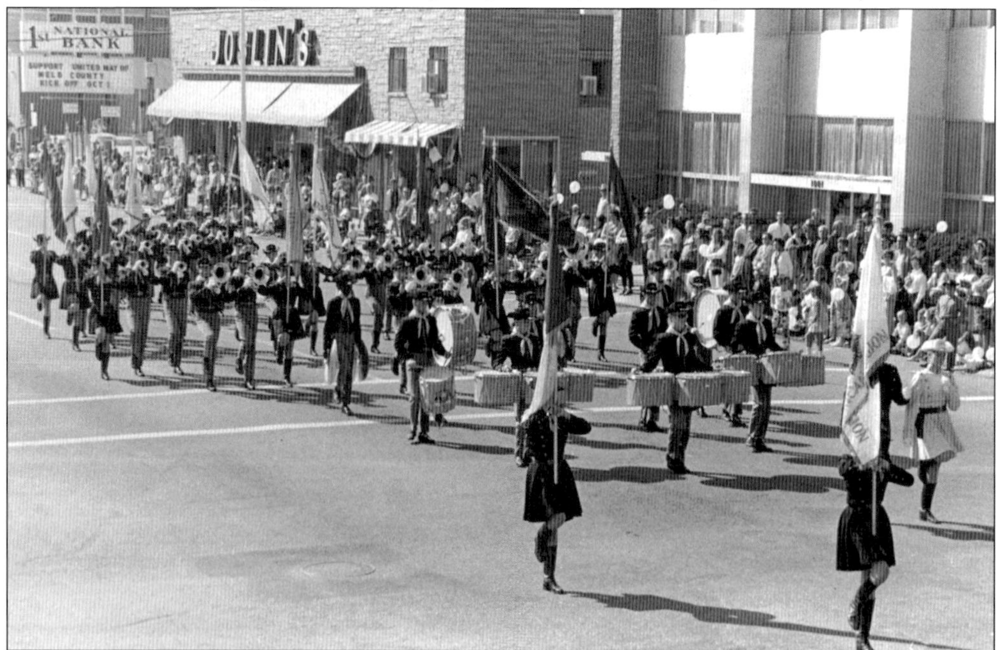

The Troopers march in the Greeley Independence Stampede Parade on July 4, 1972, in downtown Greeley, Colorado. That year, the Fourth of July parade was televised regionally. This was not the first time the Troopers had been on television; they had been performing at halftime for National Football League games since 1968. (Courtesy of the Troopers Archives.)

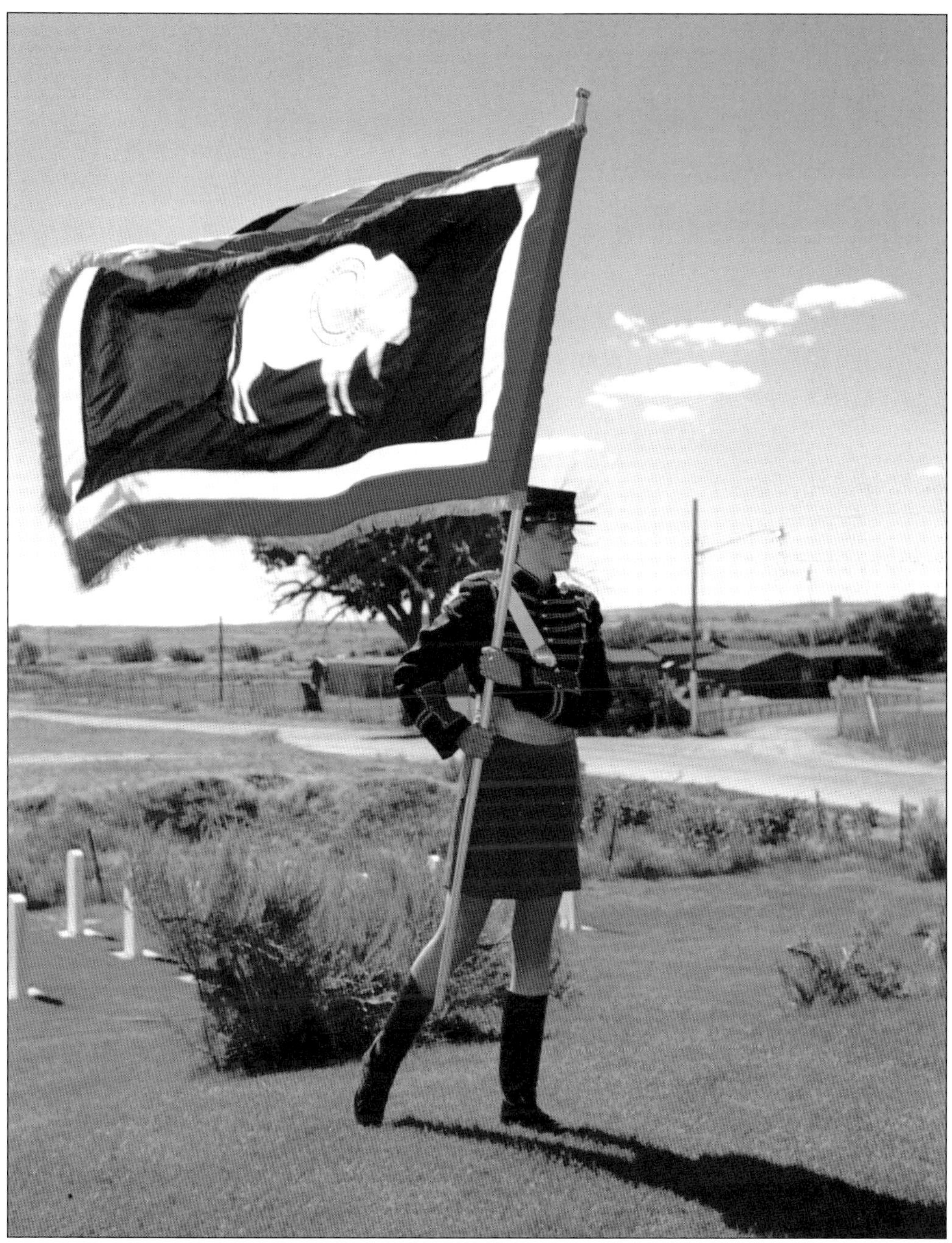

Troopers Cadet color guard Shelly Soffe holds the Wyoming state flag on a hill to the east of Fort Caspar Museum in 1973. This image was used for promotional purposes by the Troopers. (Courtesy of the Chuck Morrison Collection, Casper College Western History Center.)

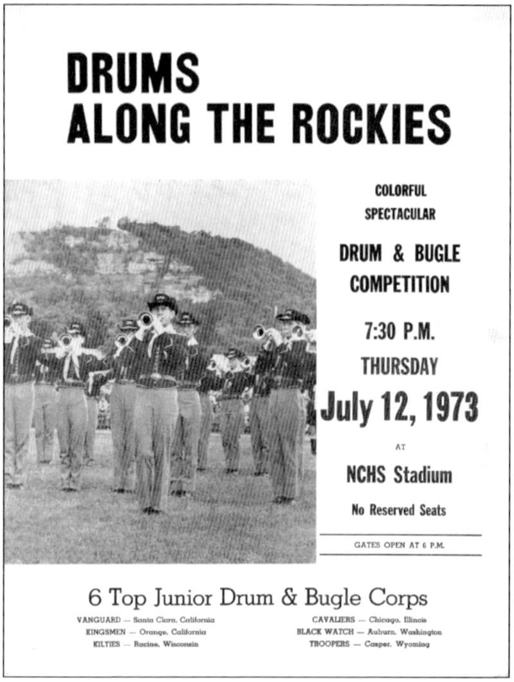

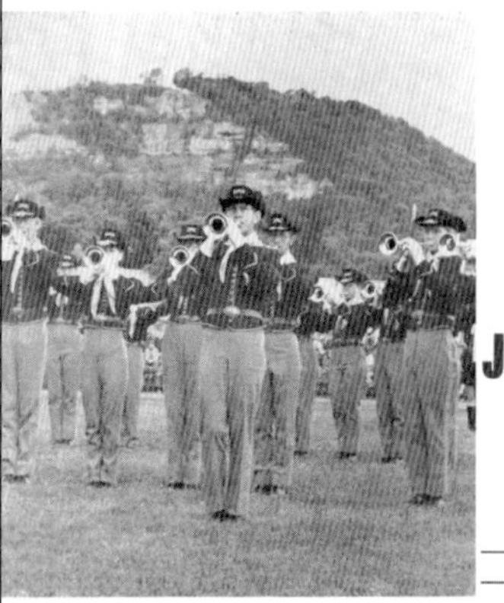

A poster advertises the Drums Along the Rockies competition, held in Casper on July 12, 1973. The event's program stated, "Welcome to the Casper edition of the finest drum and bugle corps series in the nation. This is the third annual staging of one of the most exciting and spectacular forms of entertainment available to the public." The Troopers finished second behind the Santa Clara Vanguard. (Courtesy of Fort Caspar Museum.)

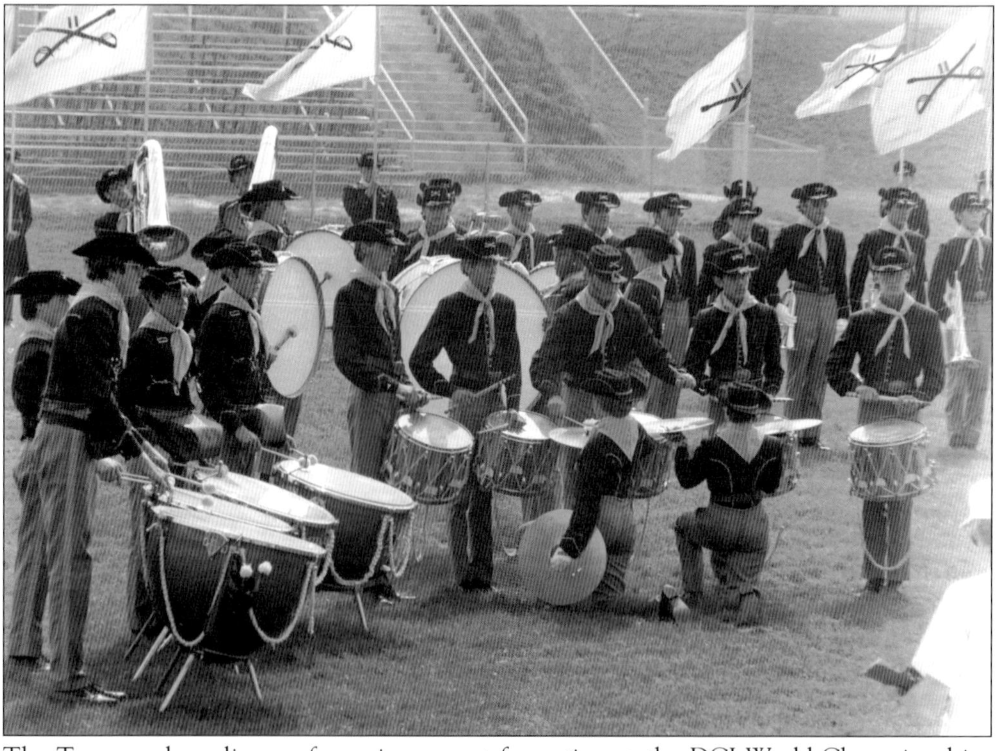

The Troopers drum line performs in concert formation at the DCI World Championships Preliminaries in Whitewater, Wisconsin, on August 16, 1973. They finished second in both the preliminaries and finals that year. This is the highest the Troopers have ever finished at the DCI World Championships. (Courtesy of Pat Chagnon.)

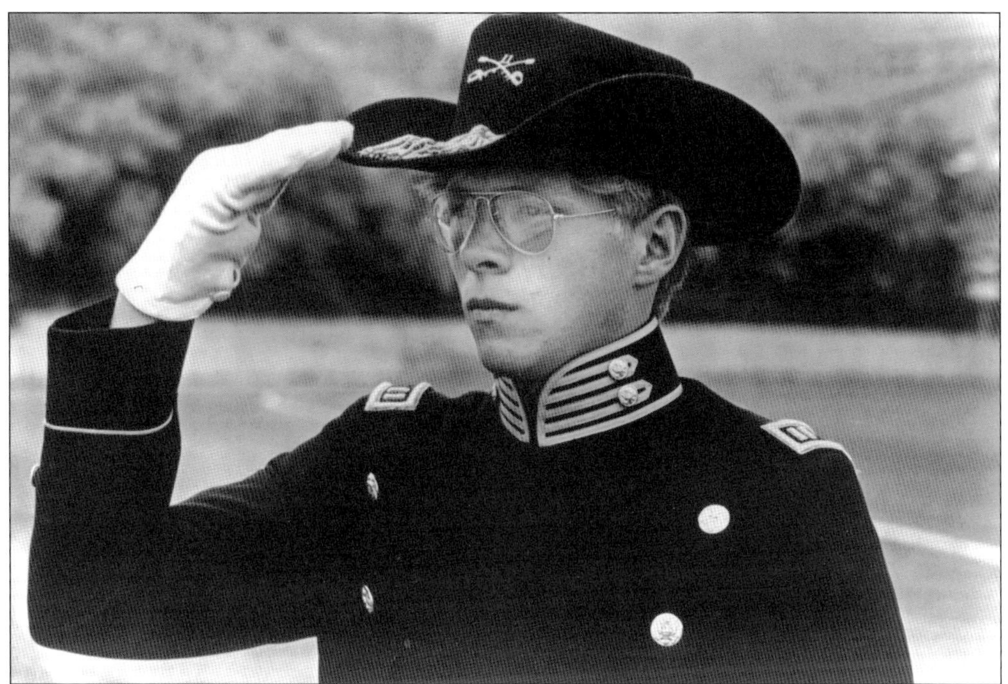

Michael DePaemelaere was the Troopers drum major between 1972 and 1975. He is shown here in 1974. Drum majors lead the corps. They need to be proficient musically, have great leadership skills on and off the field, be conductors, and inspire their fellow corps members. (Courtesy of Pat Chagnon.)

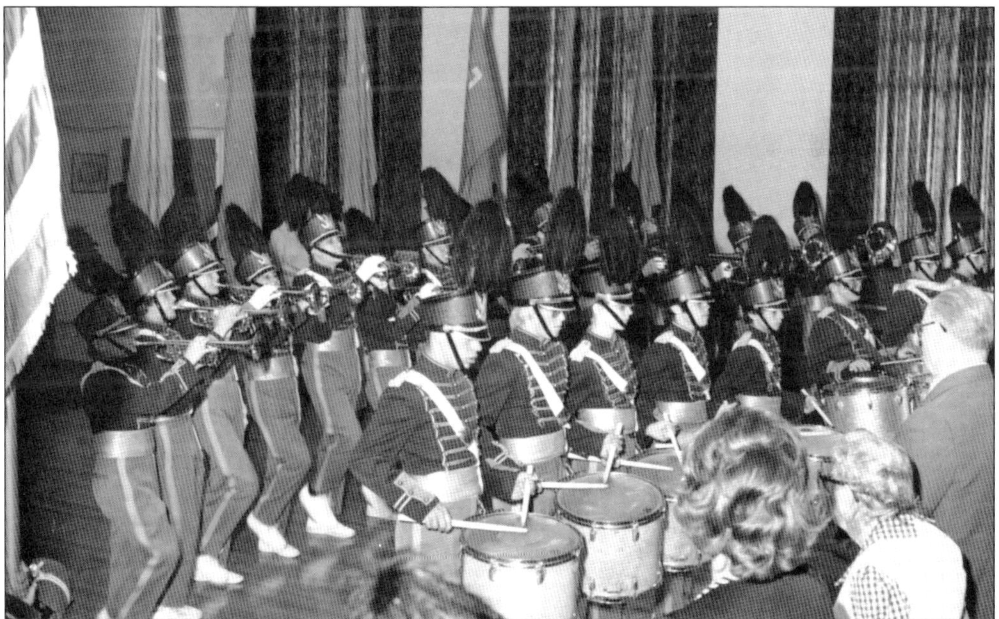

The Cadets play during the Citizenship Day ceremony in the 1970s at the Elks Lodge in Casper. Between 1972 and 1976, the Cadets performed the presentation of colors and during the ceremony. Cadet corps members were between the ages of 12 and 15. In 1972, the Cadets had 72 members: 27 in color guard, 14 on drums, 24 sopranos, and 7 baritones. (Courtesy of Fort Caspar Museum.)

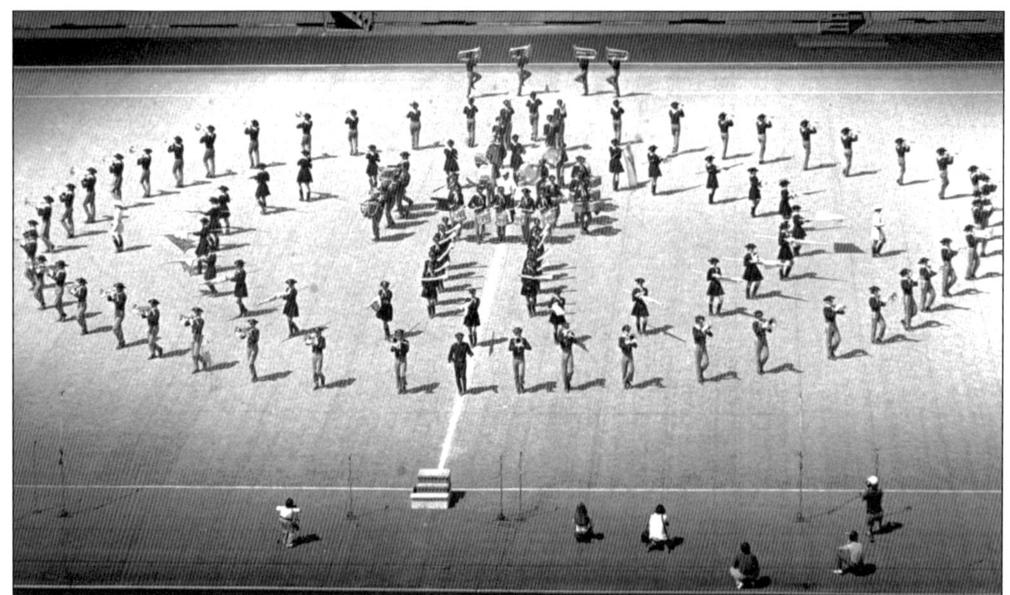

The Troopers perform the circle formation at the DCI World Championships Preliminaries at Cornell University in Ithaca, New York, on August 16, 1974. They placed fifth in both the preliminaries and the finals that year. The song selections that year were all Western and patriotic: "Ghost Riders in the Sky," "Yankee Doodle Medley," "Yellow Rose of Texas," "The Virginian," "Prayer of Thanksgiving," and "Battle Hymn of the Republic." (Courtesy of Troopers Archives.)

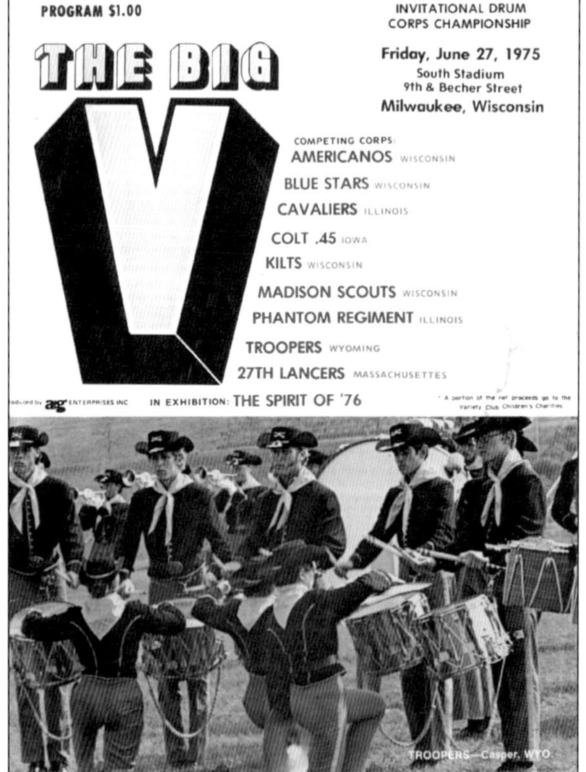

The Troopers were on the cover of the Big V program for the Invitational Drum Corps Championship in Milwaukee, Wisconsin, on June 27, 1975. The Big V was put on by the Variety Club of Milwaukee, with a portion of the proceeds going to the Variety Club Children's Charities. The Troopers finished seventh. (Courtesy of Fort Caspar Museum.)

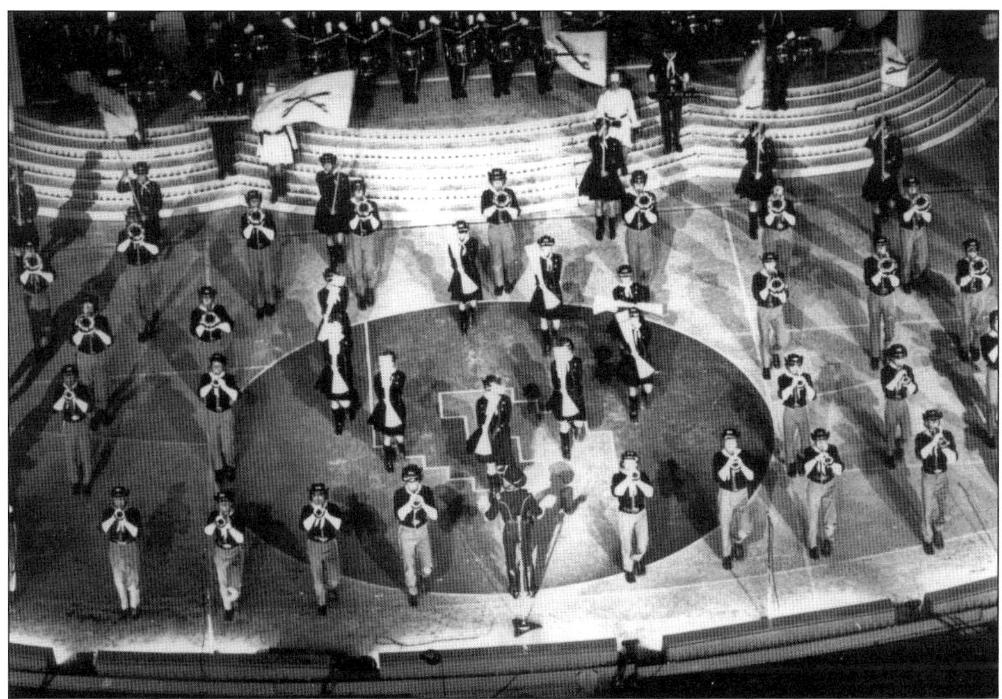

The Troopers were one of the groups that performed at the Calgary Stampede in Calgary, Canada, on July 9–18, 1976. They performed nightly (above) on the main stage and several times at the rodeo grounds. Below are several members of the horn line. From left to right are Jon Grussendorf, Mike Glenn, unidentified, and Joe Busby. The *Official Souvenir Program and Guide to the Calgary Exhibition & Stampede* described them this way: "The Casper Troopers: Proud we are to have this tremendous group of young musicians to perform their Bicentennial production. 128 strong they are indeed the national champion drum and bugle corps of the United States." (Below, photograph by Larry Hollister; both, courtesy of Drum Corps World Archives.)

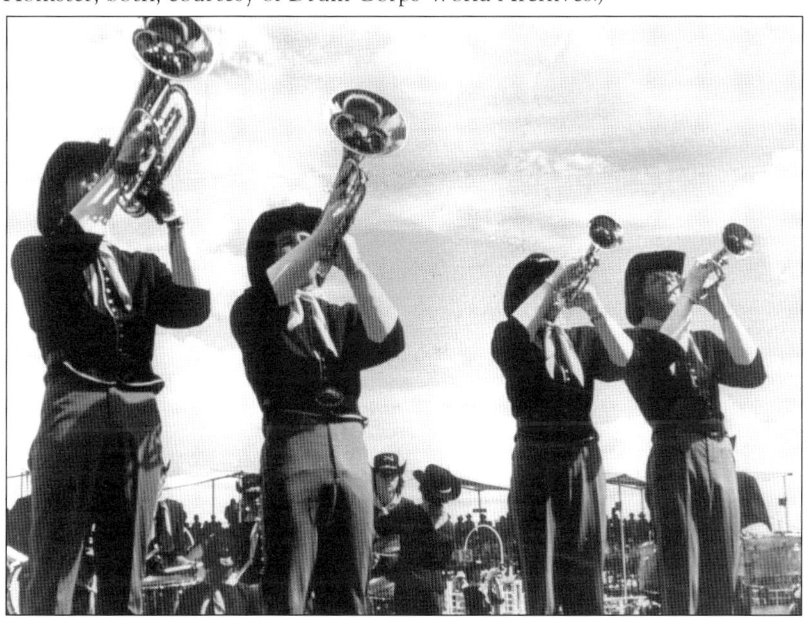

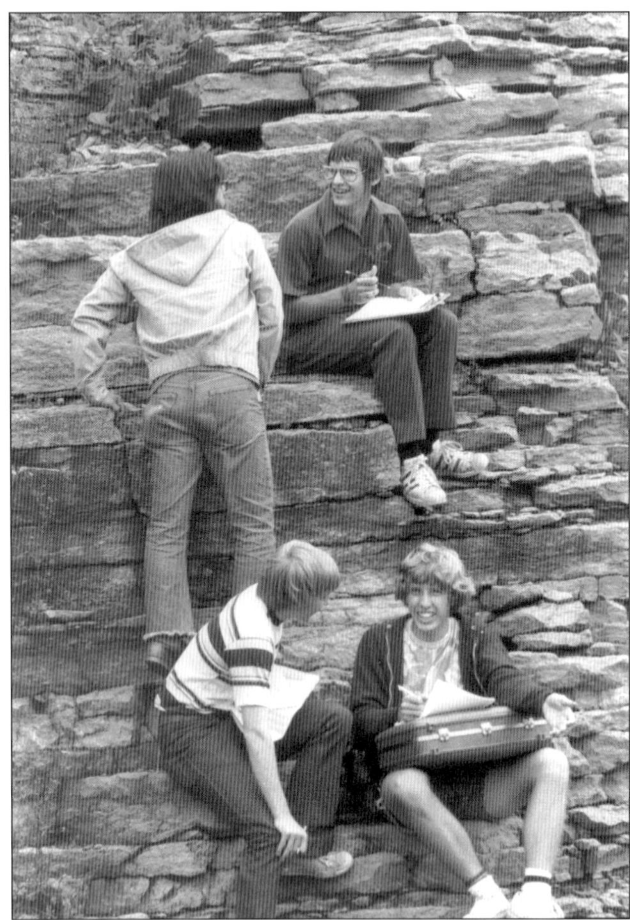

One of the Troopers' buses broke down traveling across New York State in 1976. While they waited for it to be fixed, the Troopers relaxed and practiced. Some members (left) sat and talked on rocks; from left to right are (first row) unidentified and Frank Archer; (second row) Nick Simon and Scott Barella. The snare drummers practiced in a field (below); from left to right are Les Bowron, Rich Hermann, Gary McIntosh, Gabe Luchetta, John Greenwald, unidentified, and Eric Fernelius. The Troopers spent most of August in the Northeast. They performed at contests in Ohio, New York, Quebec, Massachusetts, and Pennsylvania between August 11 and 22. (Both, courtesy of Drum Corps World Archives.)

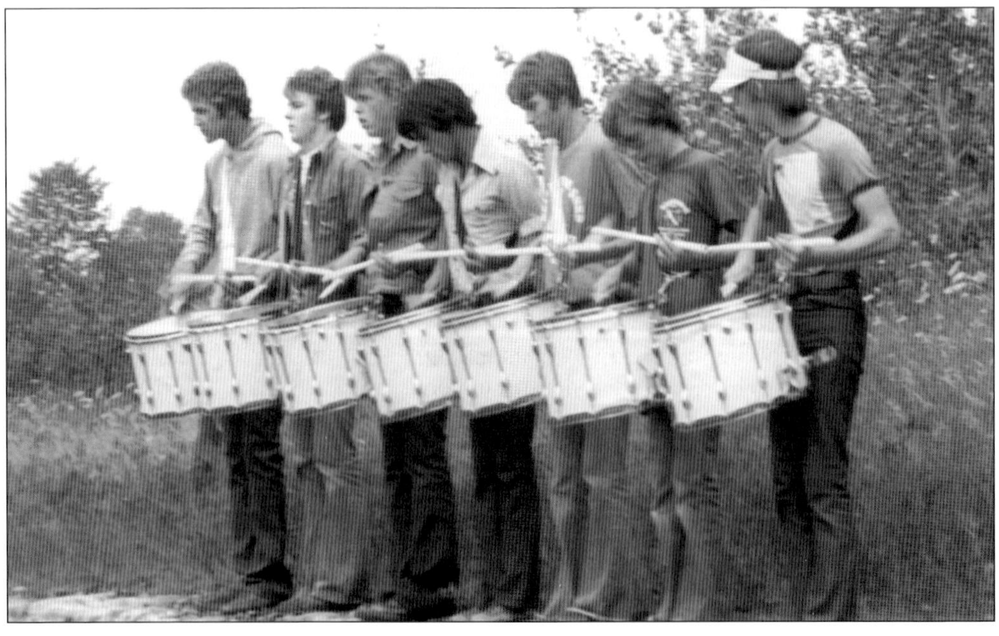

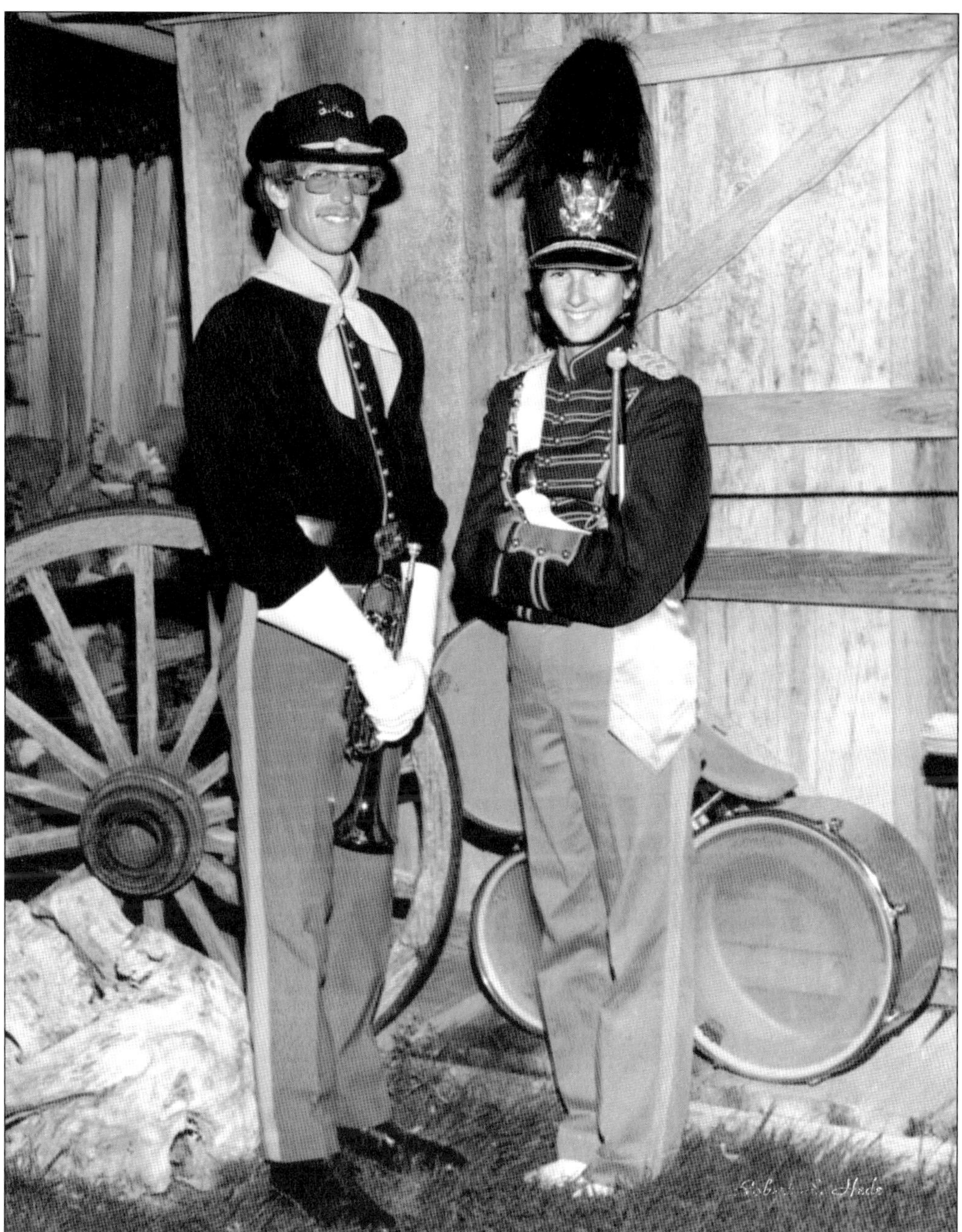

Siblings Joey and Dona Hunter are shown in their uniforms in 1975. Joey is in his Troopers uniform, and Dona is in her Cadets uniform. Joey played soprano bugle in the A corps from 1974 to 1976. Dona played percussion in the B corps from 1975 to 1979 and in the A corps in 1980 and 1981. This photograph was taken in Bob Hede's backyard. (Courtesy of June Hunter.)

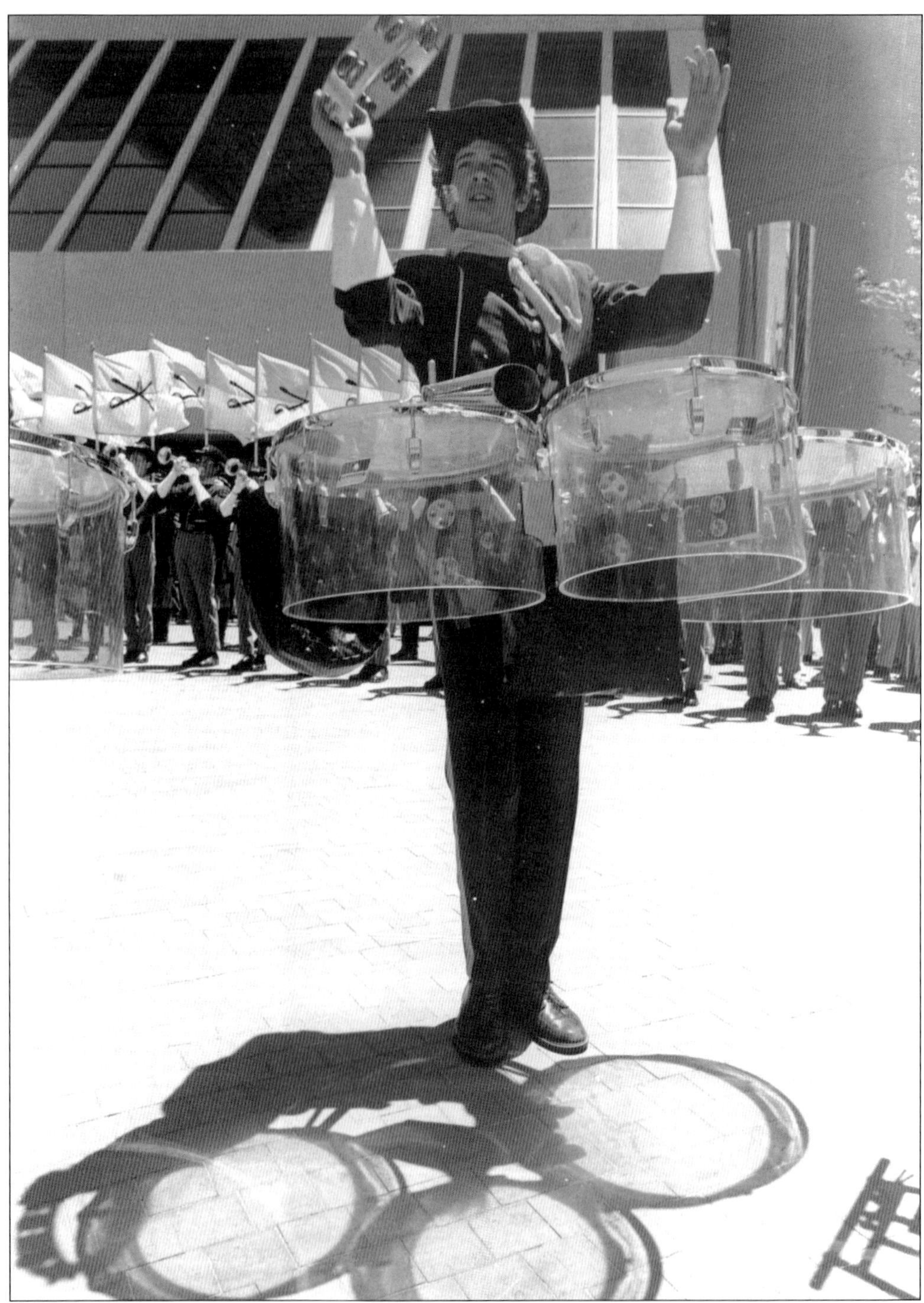

Ken Ross of the Troopers multi-tenor drummers is playing the tambourine in 1976. The music selections for that year were varied: "Dirty Dingus Magee" and "Alabama Jubilee" were lesser-known Western songs; "Land of Make Believe" by Chuck Mangione had a DCI arrangement; and "Looking for Space" and "Jet" were contemporary songs by John Denver and Paul McCartney, respectively. (Photograph from the Jones family, courtesy of Pat Chagnon.)

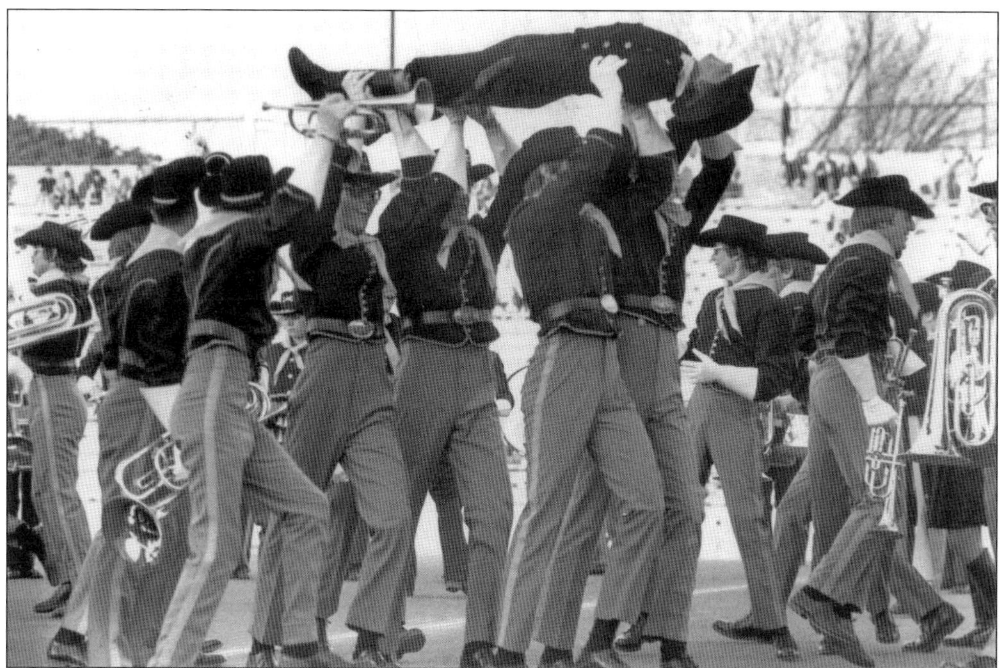

The Troopers horn line carries color guard member Ronda Renick during the drum solo in "Death of Billy the Kid" by Aaron Copland in 1977. Part of the performance included a shoot-out. Renick played Billy the Kid and after being killed was carried away. She had pants under her skirt and would take off the skirt behind the bass drums and buckle on her double holster to perform the shoot-out. (Courtesy of Drum Corps World Archives.)

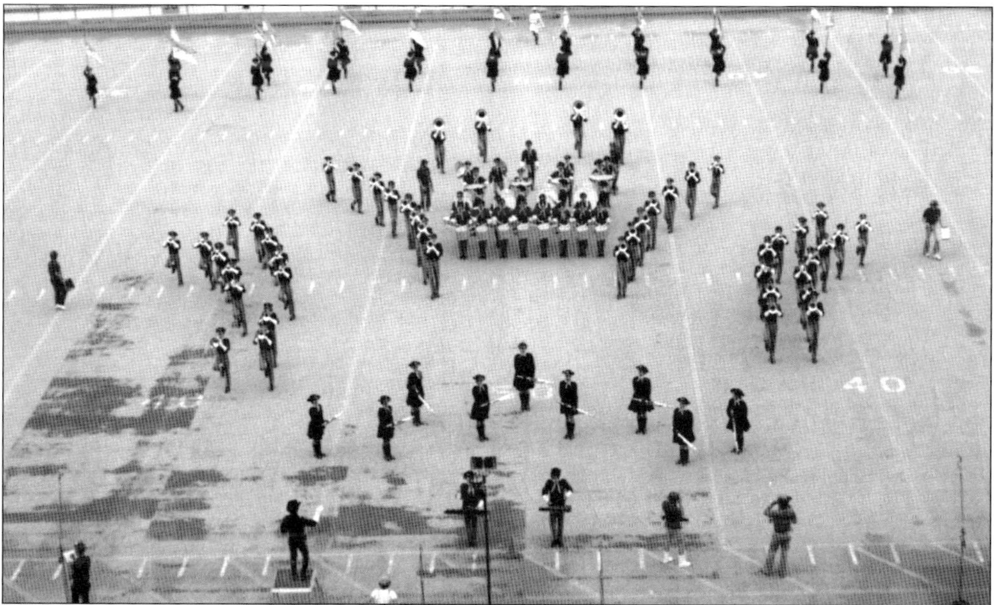

The Troopers perform at the DCI World Championships Preliminaries in Boulder, Colorado, on August 18, 1977. Drum major Dave Dundas is on the podium at bottom left. He was drum major in 1976 and 1977. The Troopers placed 20th at the DCI Championships that year. (Photograph from the Troopers Archives, courtesy of Pat Chagnon.)

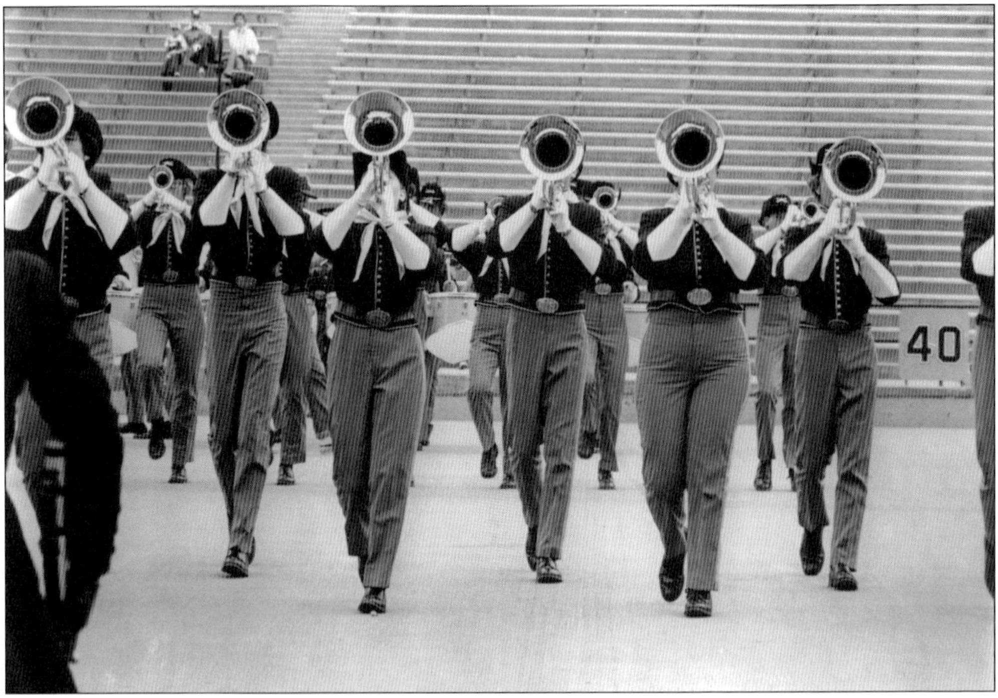

The Troopers horn line performs at the DCI World Championships Preliminaries in Boulder on August 18, 1977. From left to right are Mike Glenn, Rob Miracle, Laurie Hall, unidentified, Melana Lachelt, and unidentified. Music that year was comprised of portions of 10 songs, including "Hang 'Em High," "When Johnny Comes Marching Home," "Shenandoah," and "Wild, Wild West." (Photograph from the Jones family, courtesy of Pat Chagnon.)

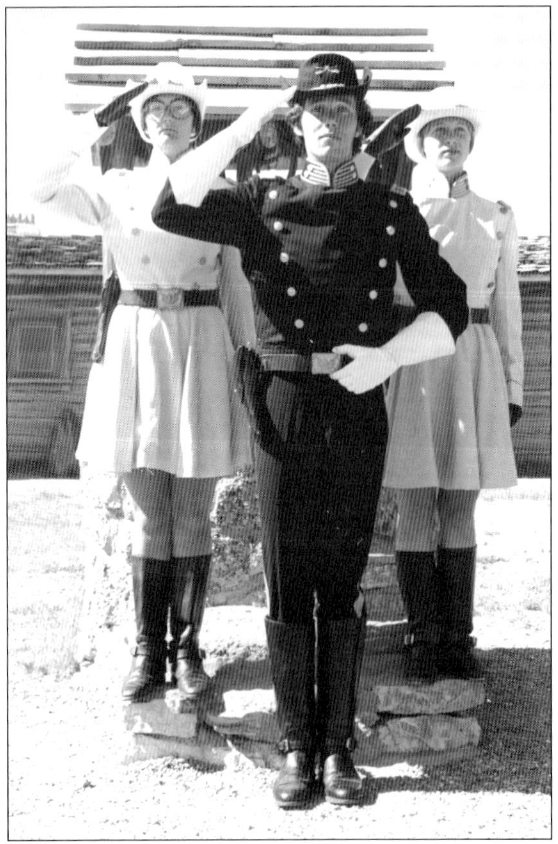

This publicity photograph of the Troopers commanders was taken at Fort Caspar Museum in 1978. Drum major Casey Smith stands in front of color guard commanders Marsha Emmons (left) and Bonnie Smith. Casey Smith was the drum major for only one year. Both Emmons and Bonnie Smith were color guard commanders from 1977 to 1979. (Photograph from the Jones family, courtesy of Pat Chagnon.)

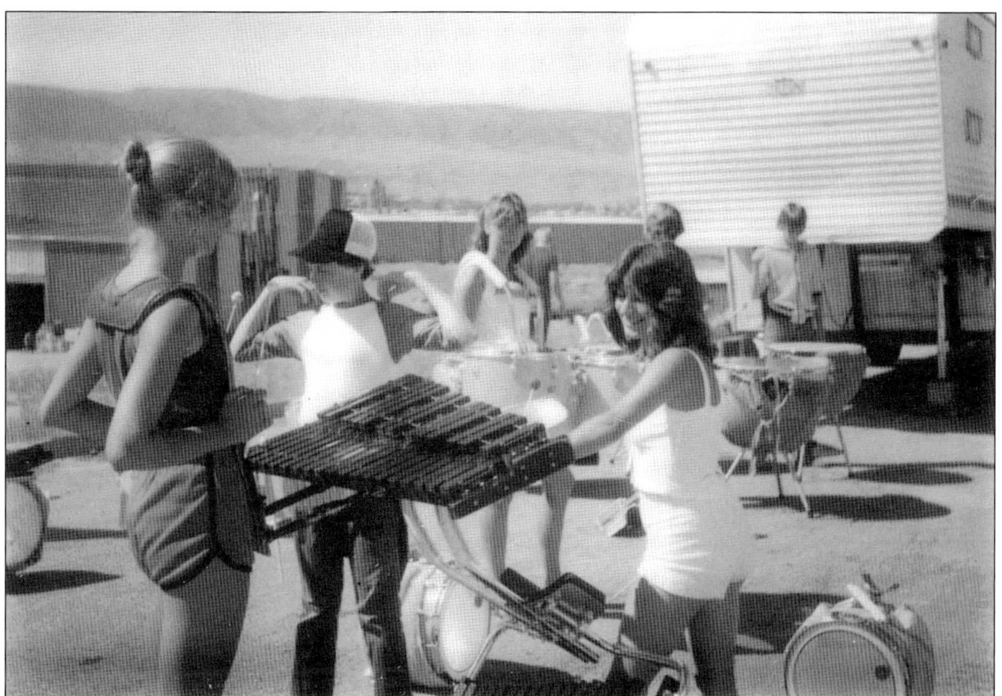

This Polaroid photograph captures the Troopers in the Natrona County School District bus garage parking lot on June 26, 1979. From left to right are Stephanie Adams, unidentified, Dona Hunter, and Sharon Geati. The Troopers often practiced in the parking lot. (Courtesy of June Hunter.)

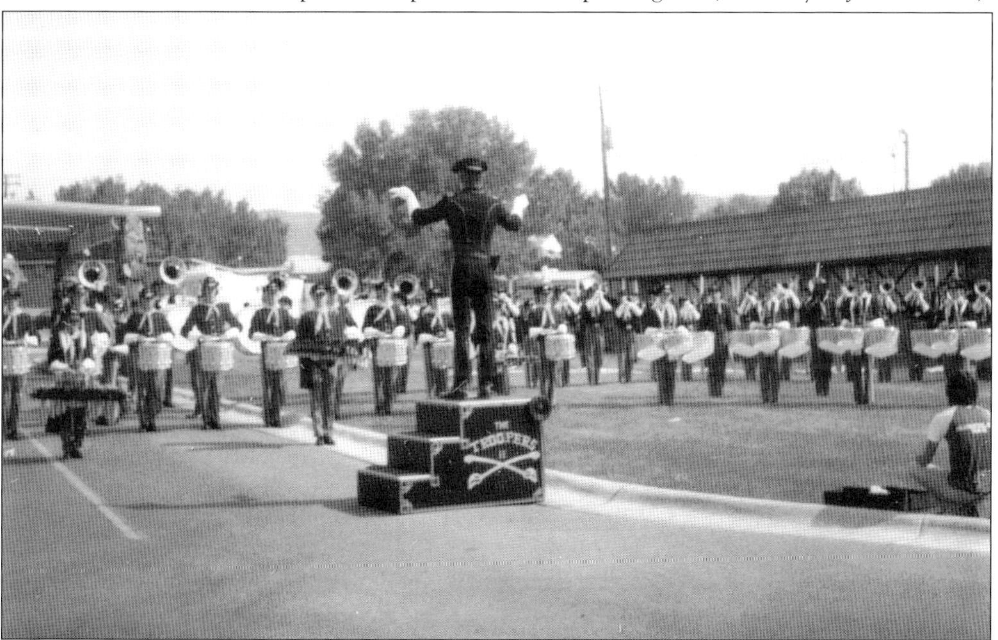

This Polaroid photograph shows the Troopers as they perform for Trooper Day in Casper on July 21, 1979. They are next to the Western National Bank building at the corner of CY Avenue and Boxelder Street, another building that Jim Jones built. Drum major John Masterson is standing on steps conducting the corps. (Courtesy of June Hunter.)

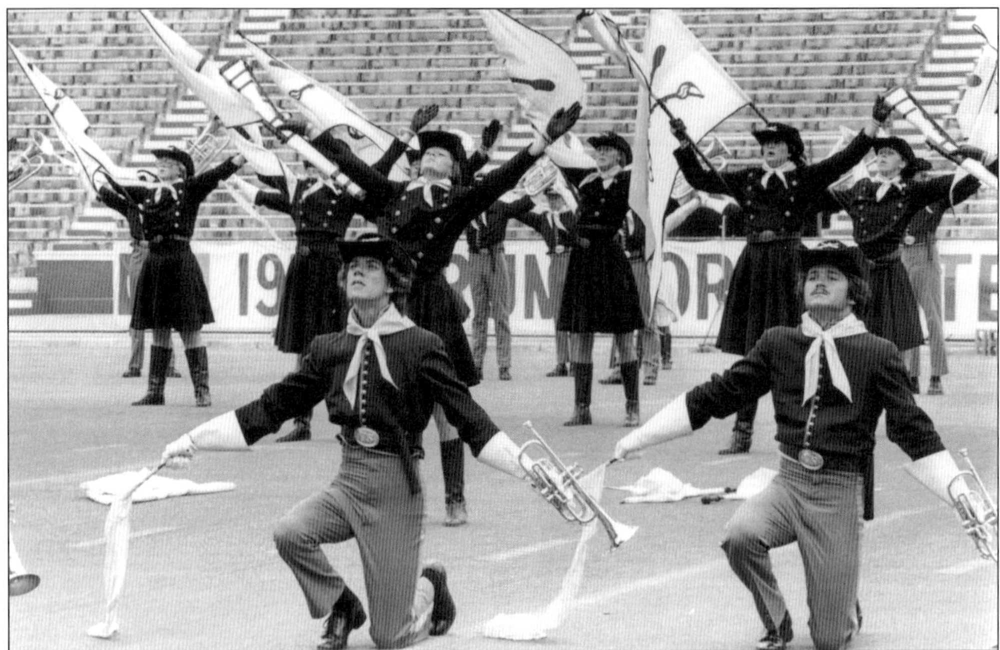

The Troopers perform at the DCI World Championships Preliminaries in Birmingham, Alabama, on August 17, 1979. They placed 12th in both the preliminaries and finals that year. The trumpet players kneeling are Steve Woodward (left) and Daryl Goff. (Photograph by Dick Deihl, courtesy of Drum Corps World Archive.)

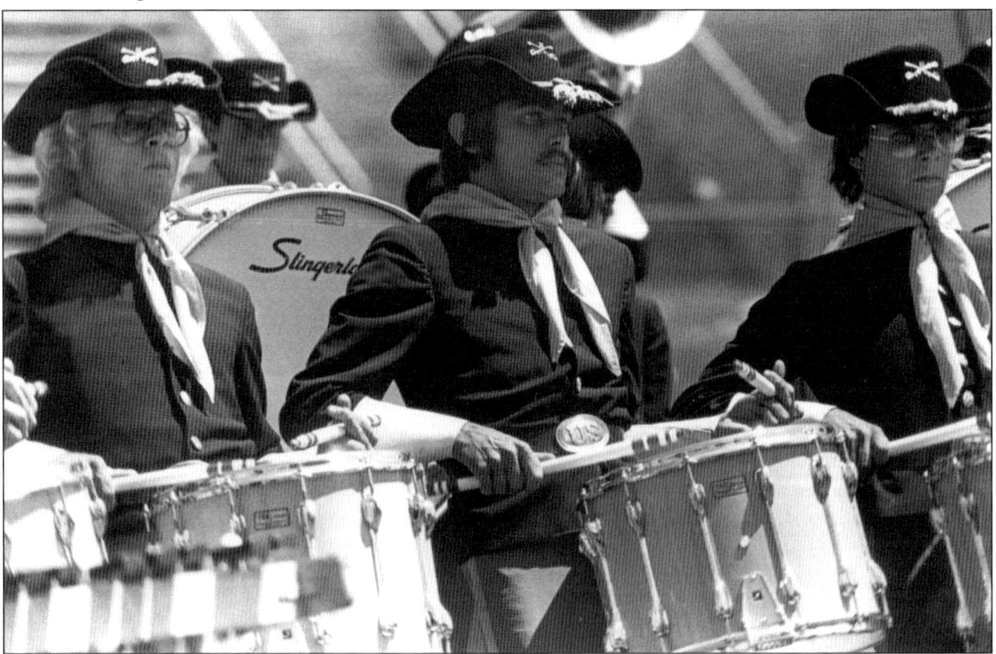

Troopers snare drummers are shown at a performance in 1979. From left to right are Vic Baker, Gabe Luchetta, and Eric Fernelius. That year, the Troopers traveled to contests in New York, Michigan, Wisconsin, Wyoming, Nebraska, Indiana, Ohio, Kentucky, Mississippi, Alabama, and Ontario, Canada. (Photograph by Dick Deihl, courtesy of Drum Corps World Archive.)

Four

1980s

America's Corps

Competitively, the Troopers struggled, only scoring in the top 12 three times in the 1980s. They finished 12th in 1981, 9th in 1985, and 11th in 1986. Some of the highlights from the 1980s include the Troopers performing at halftime for the Denver Broncos–Dallas Cowboys game in Denver on September 14, 1980, and at the halftime show of the first USFL championship game in Denver on July 17, 1983. They marched in the Rose Bowl Parade in Pasadena, California, on January 1, 1985, which was a great honor, since they were the first drum and bugle corps to be invited to the parade.

The Troopers Drum & Bugle Corps were first known as "Casper's Corps." After they were named "Wyoming's Musical Ambassadors," they became "Wyoming's Corps." Over the years, they have become "America's Corps" due in part to their US Cavalry–inspired uniforms, their frequent use of music with a Western or patriotic theme, and their popularity with the crowds.

After leading the Troopers for 30 years, Jim Jones retired as director in 1987. When he started the corps in 1957, Jones thought it would be nice to make it to the American Legion Championships, but he never dreamt of winning. Jones made the comment: "It's nice to win but trying to win is the name of the game." For him and for the Troopers, being highly motivated, disciplined, and well-mannered are what it is all about. He taught kids how to succeed, and to do that, they had to work hard, pay attention, and immerse themselves in the experience. Jones was not just teaching them how to march in drum corps but how to live their lives.

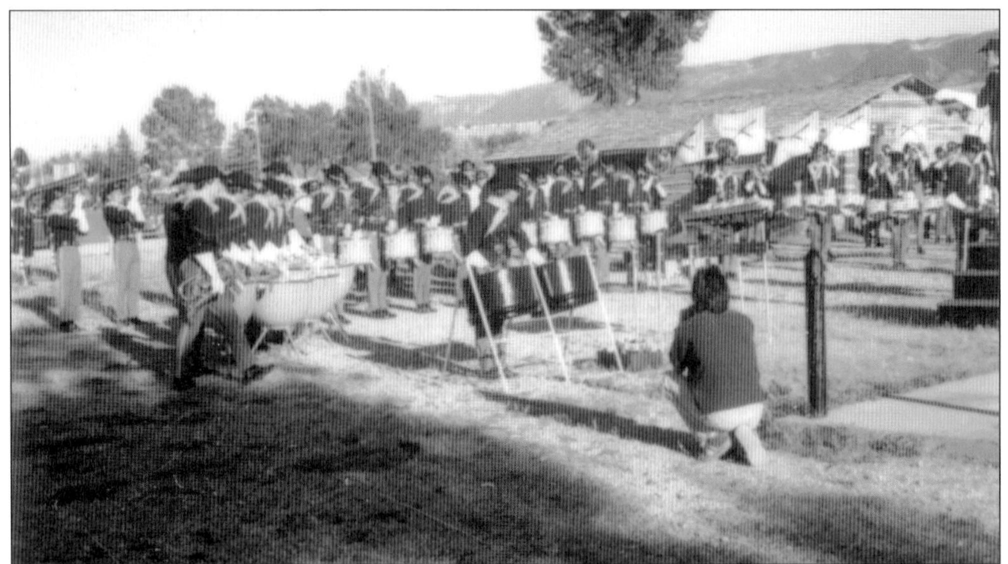

Another Polaroid photograph shows the Troopers performing on the grounds of Fort Caspar Museum in 1980. Dona Hunter is playing the steel drums. This was the first year the Troopers had a stationary percussion ensemble, otherwise known as the front ensemble or "pit." The pit included the steel drums and two xylophones. (Courtesy of June Hunter.)

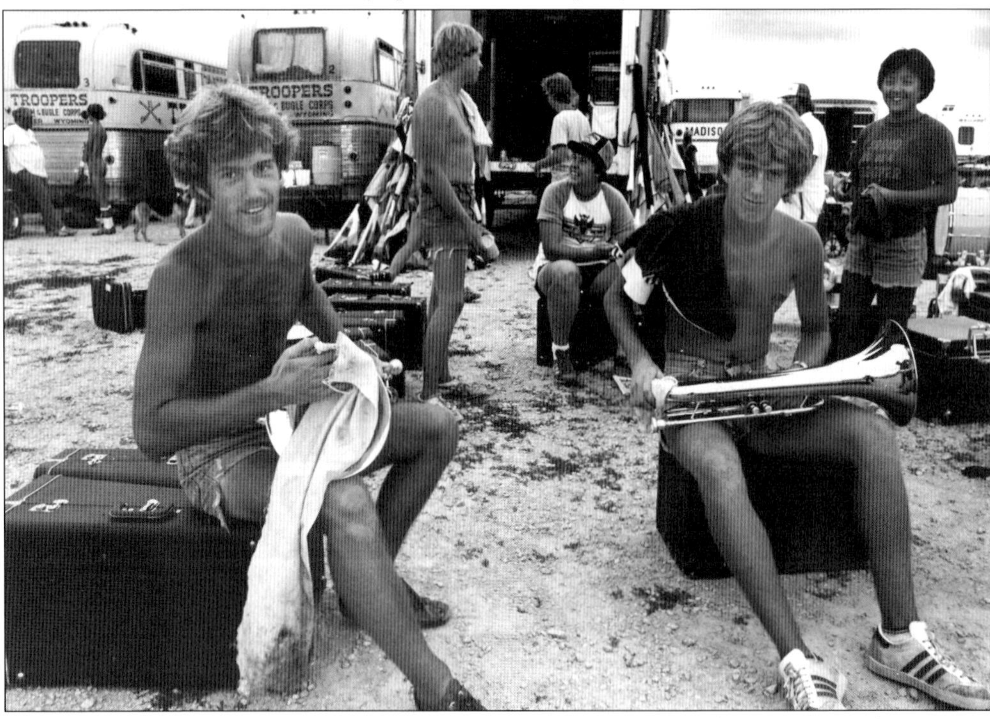

The Troopers are pictured after the DCI Midwest Preliminaries in Whitewater on July 12, 1980. From left to right are (first row) Ron Jones and Andy Winters; (second row) Blaine Heckart, John McCoy, and Nancy Freeman; (third row) unidentified, Eric Fernelius, unidentified, and Larry Hollister. Sheba the German shepherd is behind Jones's right shoulder. Sheba was the Troopers' unofficial mascot. (Photograph by Art Luebke, courtesy of Drum Corps World Archive.)

The Troopers march off the field at the DCI World Championships Preliminaries in Birmingham on August 15, 1980. They finished 14th that year. All of the music they played in 1980 was pure Western: "Cowboys," "Shenandoah," "Turkey in the Straw," "Ecstasy of Gold," and "Ghost Riders in the Sky." (Photograph by Art Luebke, courtesy of Pat Chagnon.)

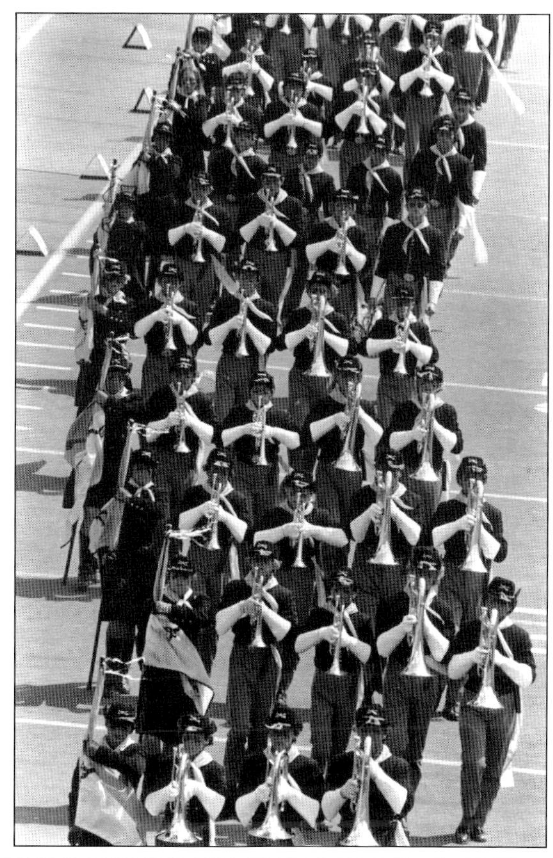

The Troopers color guard rehearses in the Natrona County High School gymnasium in 1981. Director Jim Jones is on the right, and Larry Hollister, color guard instructor, is behind Jones. Color guard members are, clockwise starting at the far left, Megan McKnight, Amanda Anderson, Tammy Beaumont, and Kim Hull. (Courtesy of Drum Corps World Archives.)

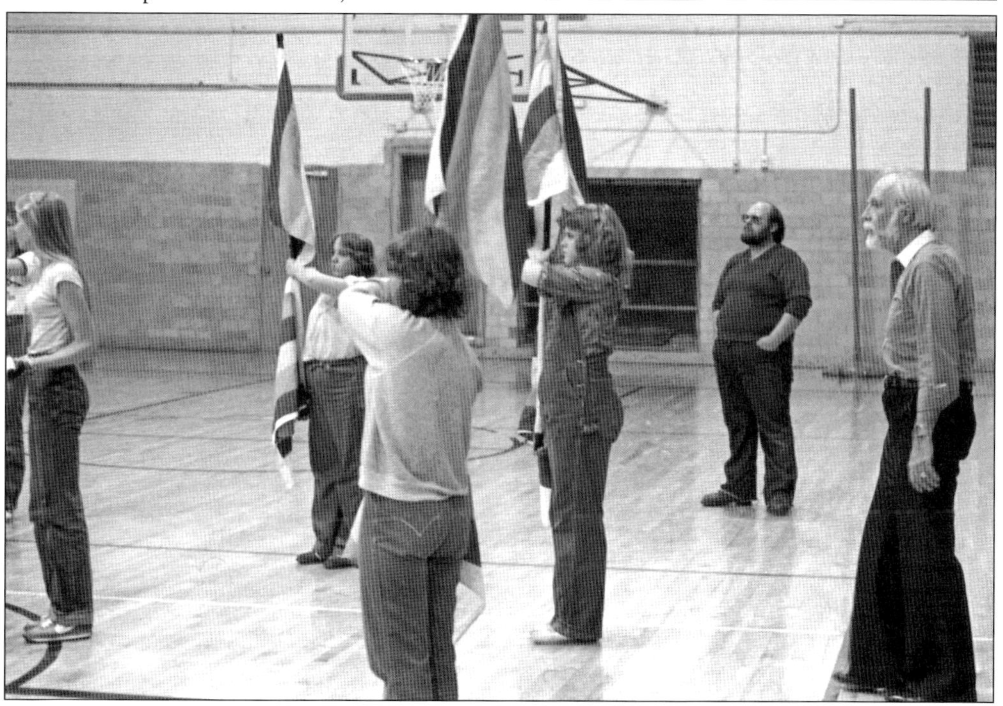

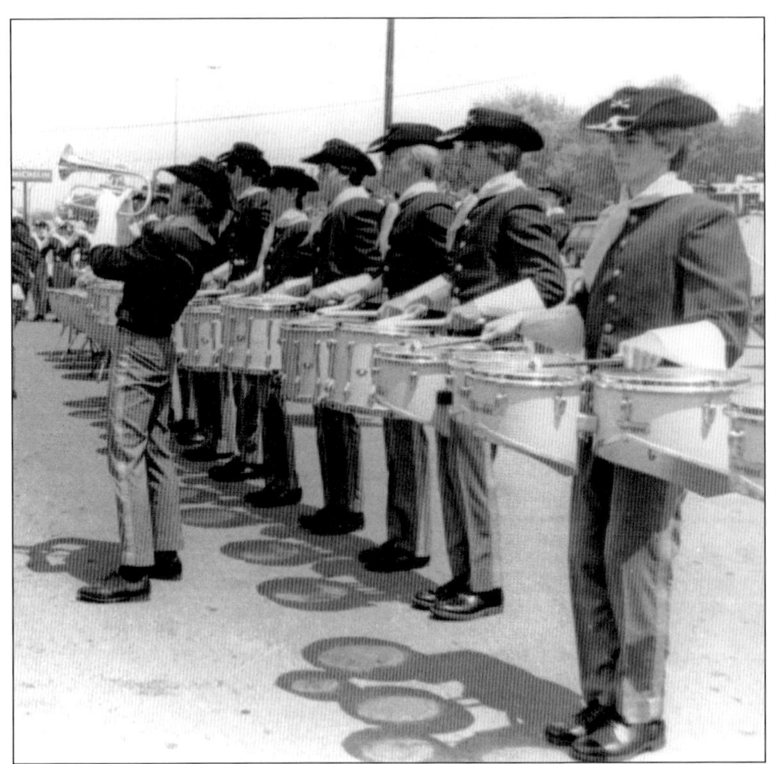

The Troopers play in Casper in 1981. From right to left are David Haining on multi-tenor drums; Ken Lancaster, Dick O'Hearn, John McCoy, Eric Fernelius, and Jon VanZandt on snare drums. Justin Olson is on the flugelhorn in the front. (Courtesy of the Casper Journal Collection, Casper College Western History Center.)

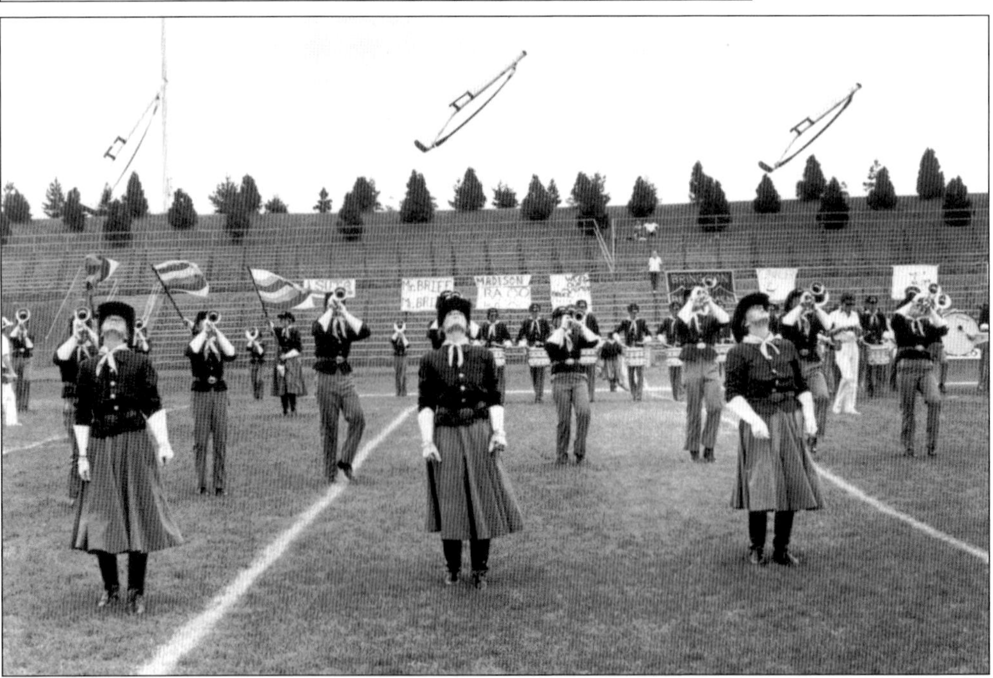

The Troopers perform at the DCI Midwest Preliminaries or Finals in Whitewater on August 8, 1981. Color guard members throw their rifles overhead in unison. Shawn Mulligan is in front at left. The color guard instructors that year were Ric Basil, Larry Davis, Larry Hollister, Gary Johnson, and Casey Smith. (Photograph by Dick Deihl, courtesy of Drum Corps World Archive.)

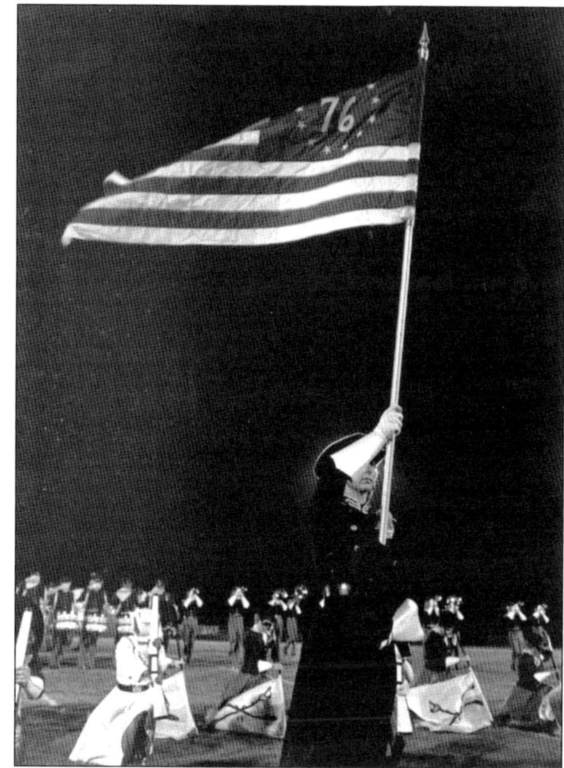

Dona Hunter was the Troopers assistant drum major at the homecoming celebration in 1981. The assistant drum major has several responsibilities, including picking up things on the field during a performance, serving as the "back conductor," and filling in where needed. Hunter was the assistant drum major in 1981. (Courtesy of June Hunter.)

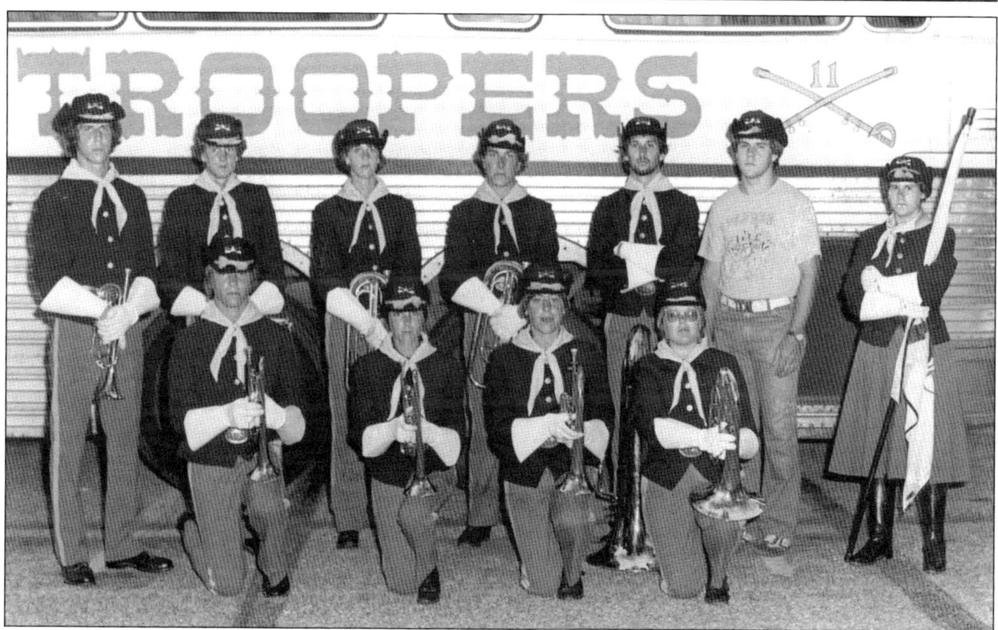

The "Ohio 11" pose at Drums Along the Rockies in Denver on July 10, 1982. After General Putnam's Men, a corps in Ohio, disbanded in 1982, eleven of them joined the Troopers. From left to right are (first row) Kim Beck, Jennifer Gordon, Jan Gossell, and Betsy Gordon; (second row) Craig Hedden, Mike Bailey, Teresa Hassell, Stewart Graham, Bill Mills, Don Brickner, and Elizabeth Graham McBee. (Courtesy of Drum Corps World Archives.)

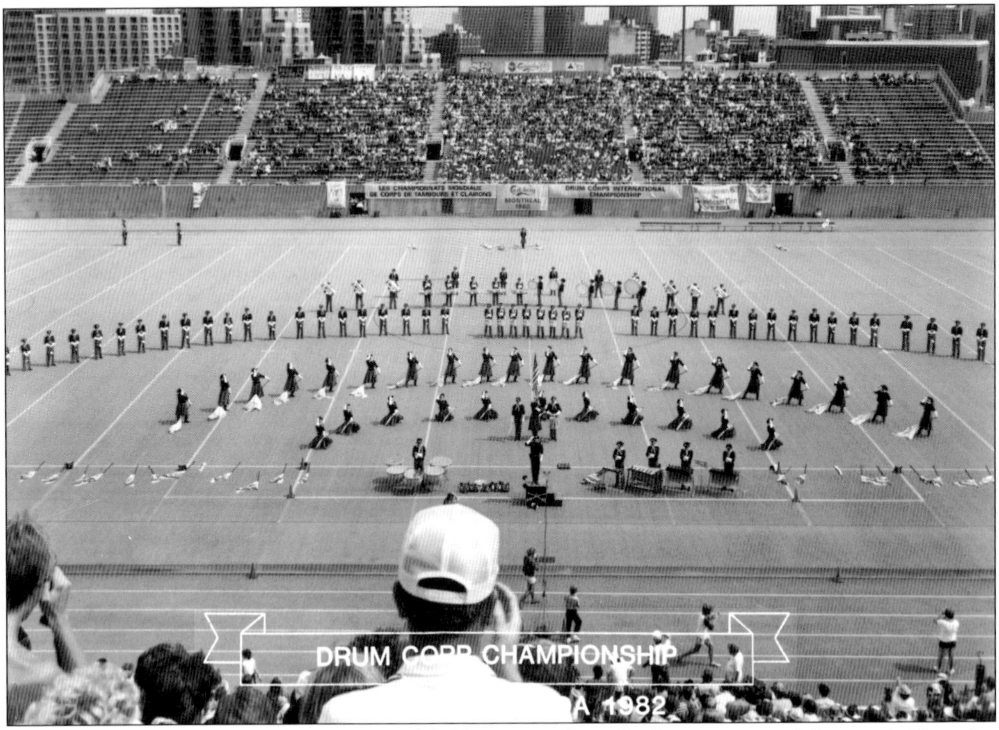

The Troopers perform at the DCI World Championships Preliminaries in Montreal, Canada, on August 20, 1982. This was drum major Tom Walsh's first year, and he led the Troopers to a 14th-place finish, only two spots short of making it to the finals. Walsh was drum major until 1985. (Photograph from the Troopers Archives, courtesy of Pat Chagnon.)

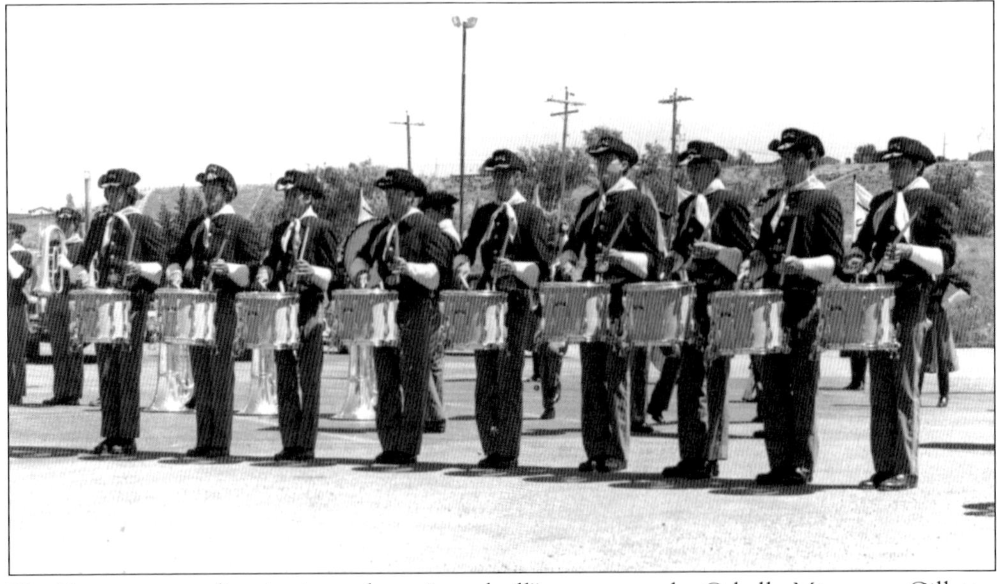

The Troopers snare line is pictured at a "standstill" concert at the Caballo Mine near Gillette, Wyoming, in 1983. From left to right are Chris George, Steve Bakker, "Tex," Randy Dobbs, Paul Hilderbrant, Richard Seckinger, Mike Bailey, Al Sanderson, and Dave Ogran. (Photograph from the Troopers Archives, courtesy of Pat Chagnon.)

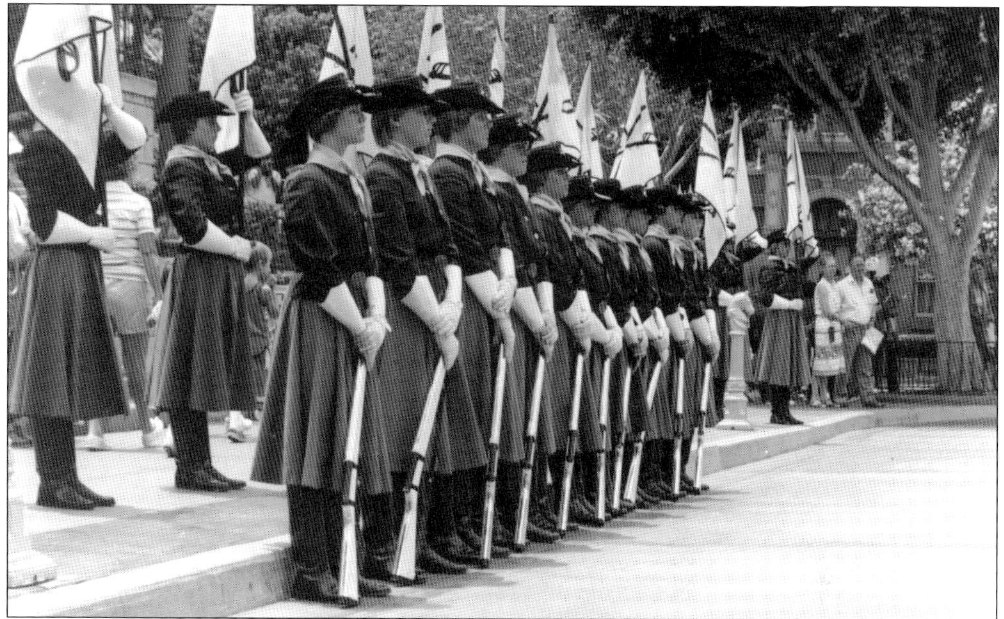

The Troopers color guard stands in formation at Disneyland in Anaheim, California, in 1983. The Troopers played in Disneyland many times. The first time was on July 25, 1972. Since then, they have performed there in 1973, 1974, 1978, 1981, 1982, 1983, 1994, 1998, and 2010, and they played in Disney World in 1998. (Photograph from the Jones family, courtesy of Pat Chagnon.)

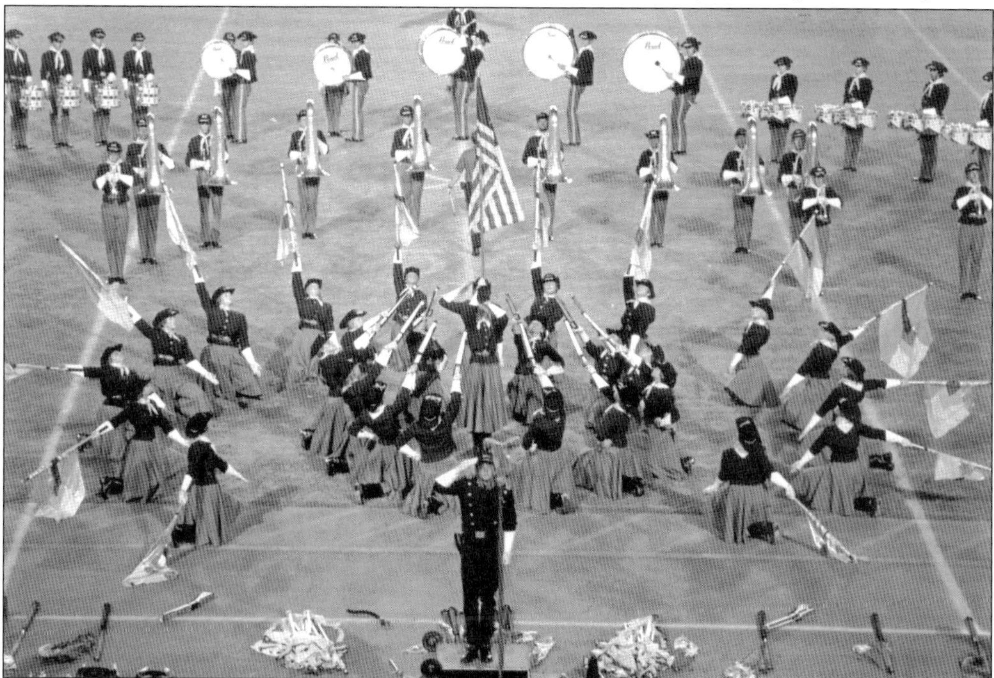

The Troopers are captured in their final position at the end of their performance at the Orange Bowl during DCI Finals Week in Miami, Florida, in August 1983. They celebrated their 25th anniversary that year and the corps numbered 126 members. The drum major was Tom Walsh and the guard captains were Sue Barella and Lisa Broz. (Courtesy of Drum Corps World Archives.)

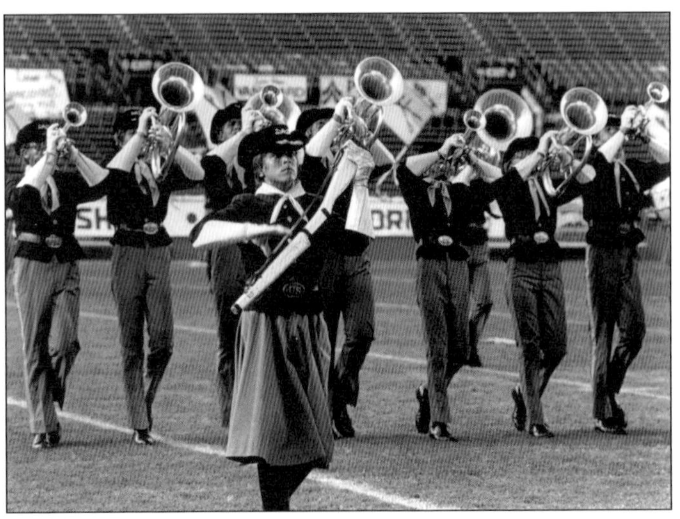

The Troopers perform at the DCI World Championships Quarter- or Semifinals in Miami on August 18 or 19, 1983. The Troopers finished third in the quarterfinals and placed 15th in the semifinals. Color guard member Jill Pesceone holds a rifle in front. The horn line is, from left to right, Alex Clegg, Teresa Hassell, Jon Beerman, three unidentified, and Craig Hedden. (Courtesy of Drum Corps World Archives.)

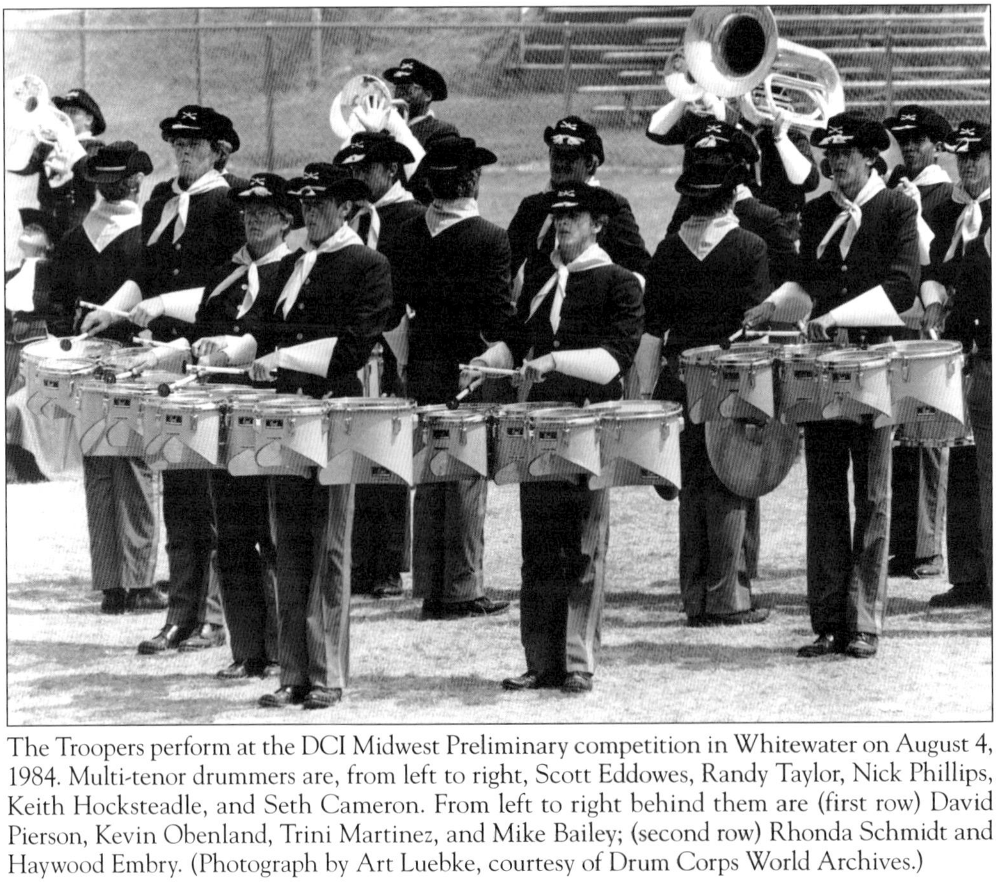

The Troopers perform at the DCI Midwest Preliminary competition in Whitewater on August 4, 1984. Multi-tenor drummers are, from left to right, Scott Eddowes, Randy Taylor, Nick Phillips, Keith Hocksteadle, and Seth Cameron. From left to right behind them are (first row) David Pierson, Kevin Obenland, Trini Martinez, and Mike Bailey; (second row) Rhonda Schmidt and Haywood Embry. (Photograph by Art Luebke, courtesy of Drum Corps World Archives.)

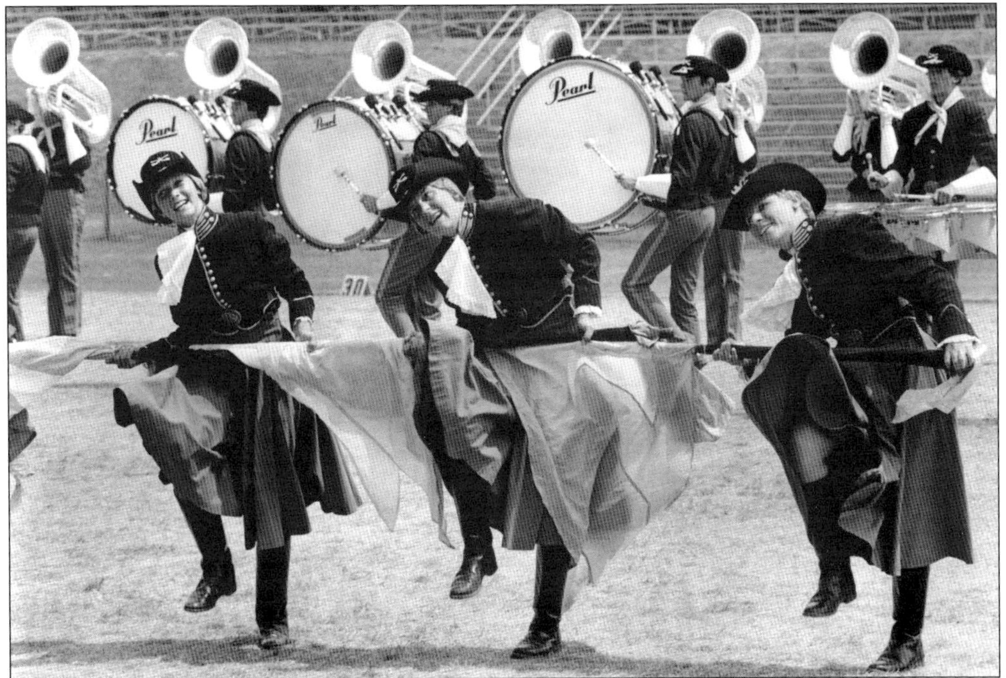

The Troopers perform at the DCI Midwest Preliminaries in Whitewater on August 4, 1984. The color guard is, from left to right, Cindy Jammerman, Suzanne McGary, and Bonnie Swanson. The drummers are, from left to right, Lance Waldorf, Doug Mitchell, Marty Stroh, and Bob Dietz on bass drums, with Seth Cameron on the multi-tenor drums. (Photograph by Art Luebke, courtesy of Drum Corps World Archives.)

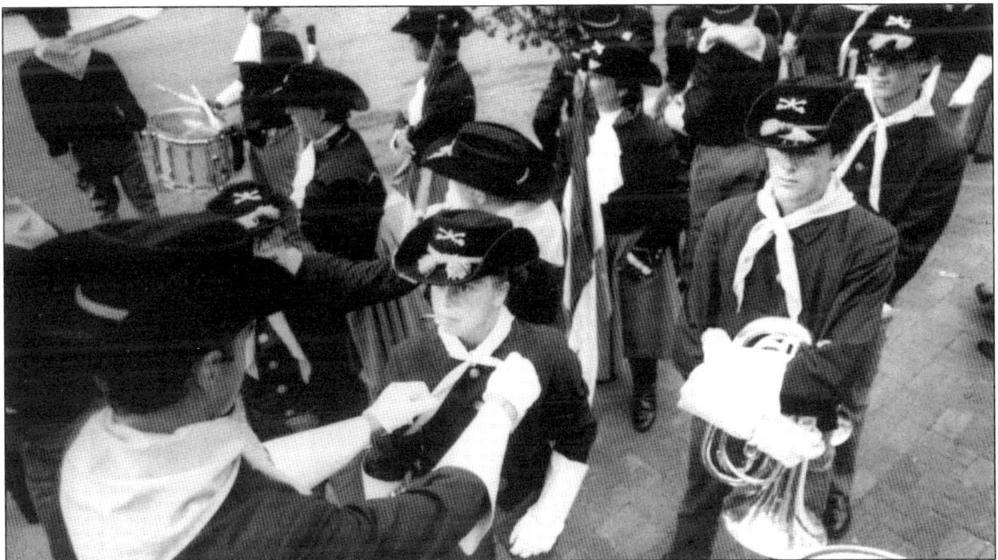

The Troopers line up for a uniform check before they perform at the DCI World Championships Quarter- or Semifinals in Atlanta, Georgia, on August 16 or 17, 1984. Julie Past is getting her scarf adjusted by an unidentified member while her hat is being straightened by Betsy Gordon. Ross Hocksteadler is waiting in line behind Past, and Brian Grussendorf is behind him. (Photograph by Orlin Wagner, courtesy of Drum Corps World Archives.)

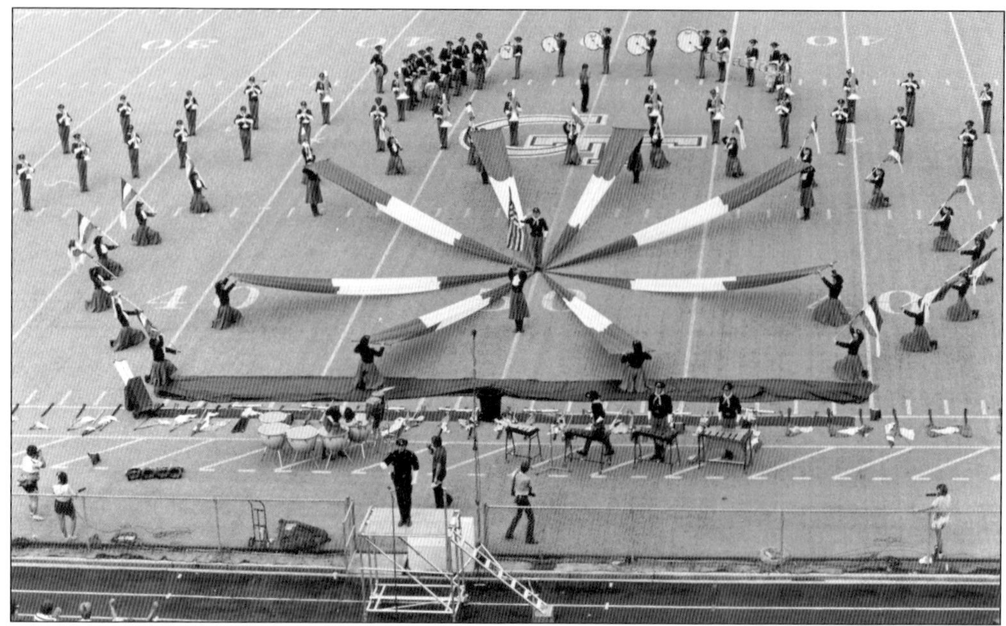

The Troopers perform at the DCI World Championships Quarter- or Semifinals in Atlanta on August 16 or 17, 1984. Drum major Tom Walsh stands on the scaffolding. In front, the pit had grown to include a set of timpani drums and four xylophones. The Troopers finished second in the quarterfinals and 13th in the semifinals. (Photograph by Ed Fergusson, courtesy of Drum Corps World Archives.)

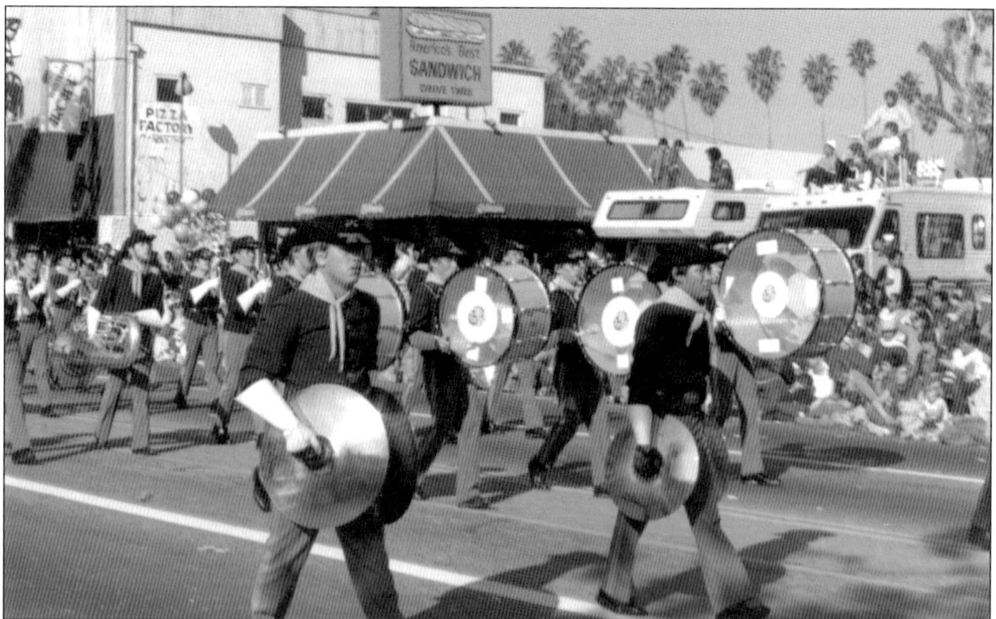

The Troopers march in the Rose Bowl Parade in Pasadena on January 1, 1985. Praise from a California resident in a letter to the mayor of Casper noted: "In this years' parade your Troopers Drum & Bugle Corps from Casper, WY, was far superior to any other marching unit." The Troopers were the first corps from DCI to march in the Rose Bowl Parade. (Photograph by Glenn E. Hall, courtesy of the Troopers Archive.)

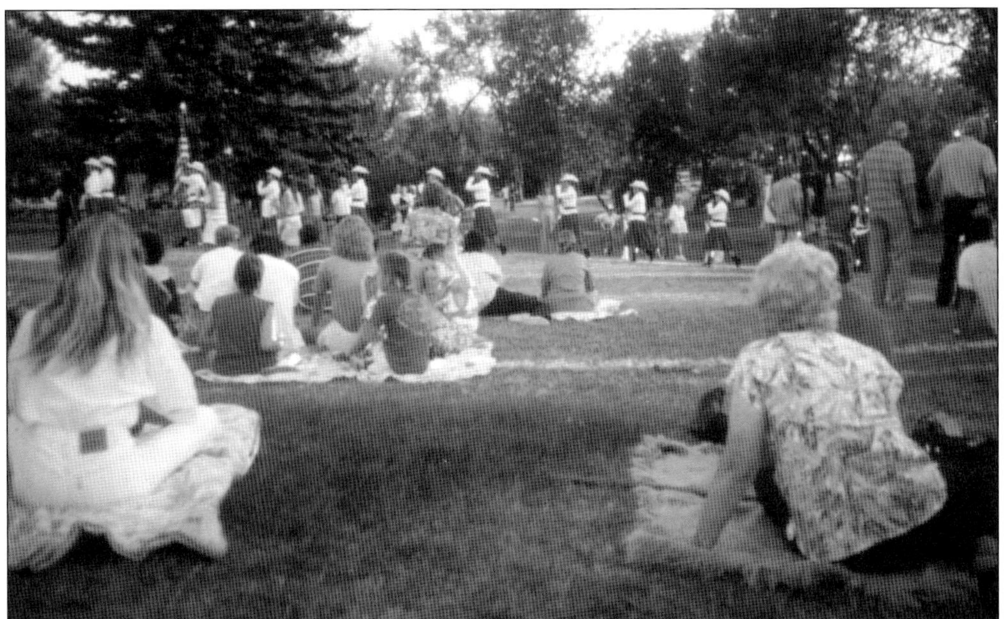

The Troopers color guard marches through the crowd at Washington Park in Casper in June 1985. Drum major Tom Walsh is at the head of the column. They performed with the Casper Municipal Band that evening. The musical selections that year were a bit more classical but still Western in nature: "Symphonic Dance" by Clifton Williams, "Copland Sampler," "Buckaroo Holiday," and "Red Pony." (Courtesy of Fort Caspar Museum.)

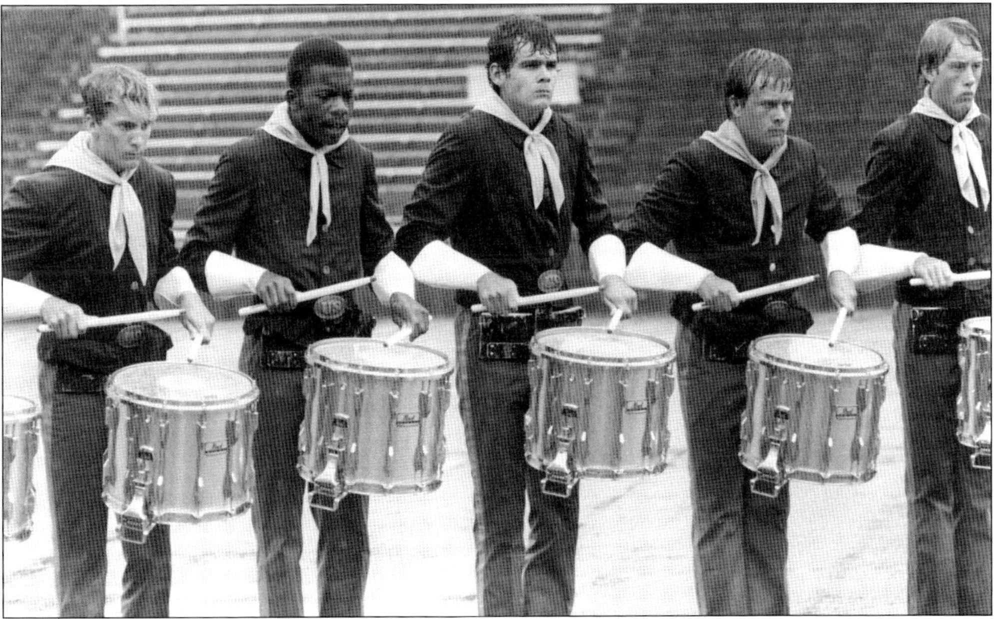

The Troopers snare drummers perform in the pouring rain at the DCI South Preliminaries competition on July 6, 1985. From left to right are Mike Bailey, J.J. Johnson, Pat Amann, Kevin Obenland, and Nick Phillips. Because the preliminary performance was in the afternoon, they had to wear their wet wool uniforms that evening when they competed in the finals. (Photograph by Art Luebke, courtesy of Drum Corps World Archives.)

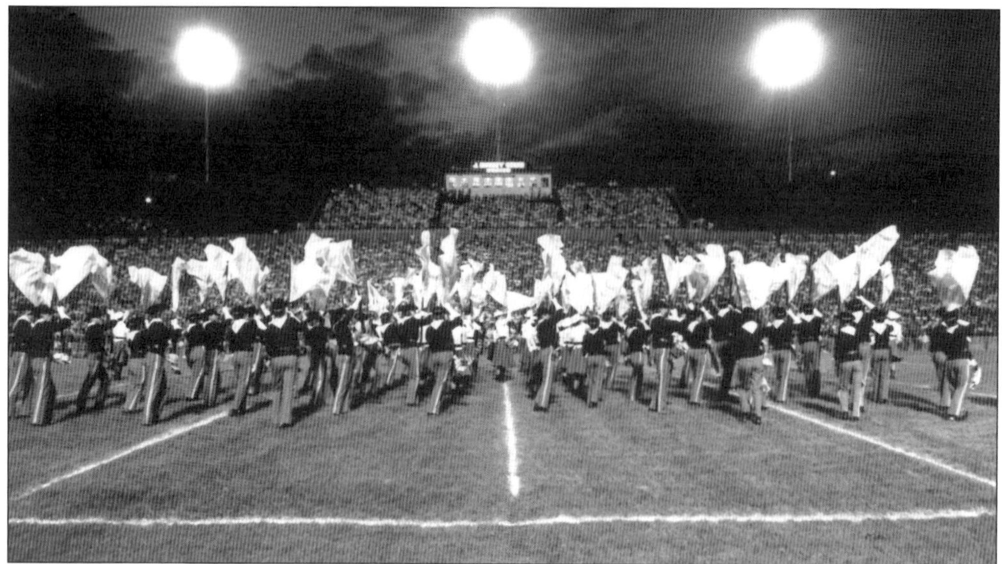
The Troopers perform at the DCI East Preliminaries competition in Allentown, Pennsylvania, on August 3, 1985. They finished 10th in the preliminaries and 12th in the finals. Troopers founder and director Jim Jones was inducted into the DCI Hall of Fame that year. Jones was one of the founding directors of DCI in 1972, and 1985 was the inaugural year of the hall of fame. (Photograph by Roy Ives, courtesy of Drum Corps World Archives.)

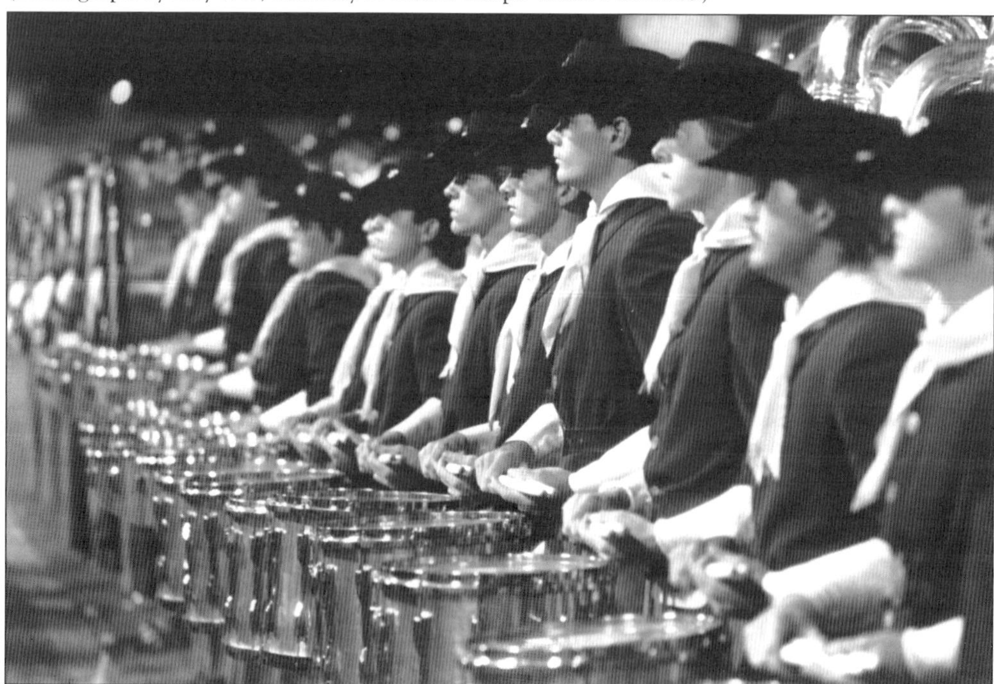
The Troopers drum line stands at rest in 1986. From right to left are Keith Hocksteadler, Kent Barton, Nick Phillips, Pat Amann, Mike Bailey, Mark Trautman, Dan Cavaliere, unidentified, Becky Blink, and Pete Simpson. The musical repertoire that year was titled *A Western Weekend*, with the Troopers playing "American Salute," "Silverado," "Prayer of Thanksgiving," "Red Pony," and "Battle Hymn of the Republic." (Courtesy of Drum Corps World Archives.)

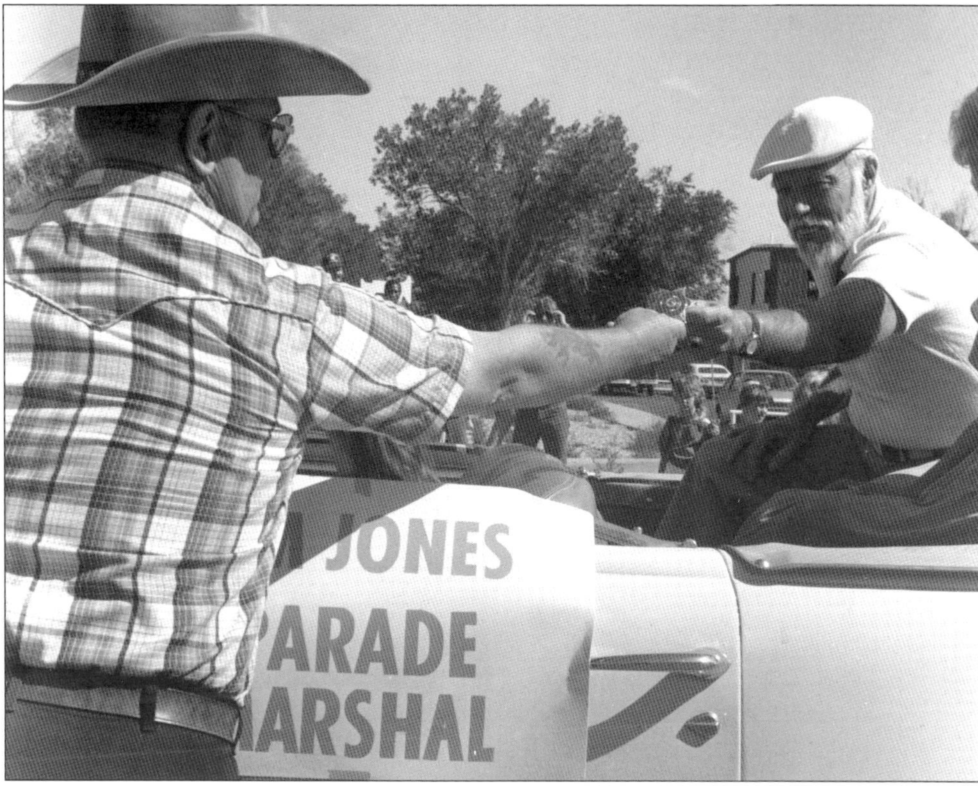

Troopers director Jim Jones was the parade marshal for the Central Wyoming Fair and Rodeo Parade in Casper in 1986. Above, he is receiving the official marshal badge at the start of the parade. The Troopers (below) were the first unit behind the parade marshal's car. (Both photographs from the Jones family, courtesy of Pat Chagnon.)

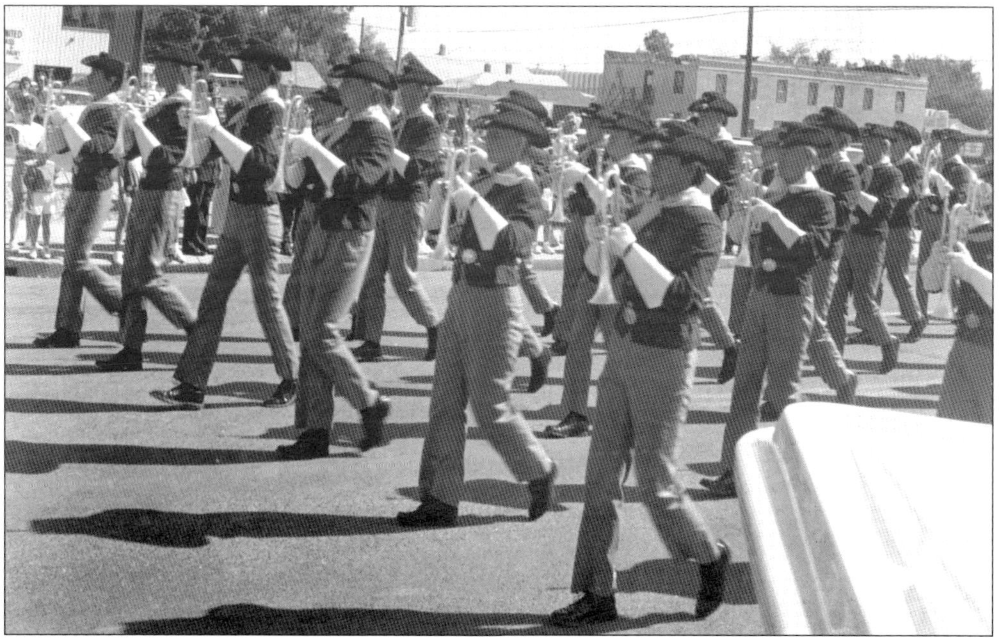

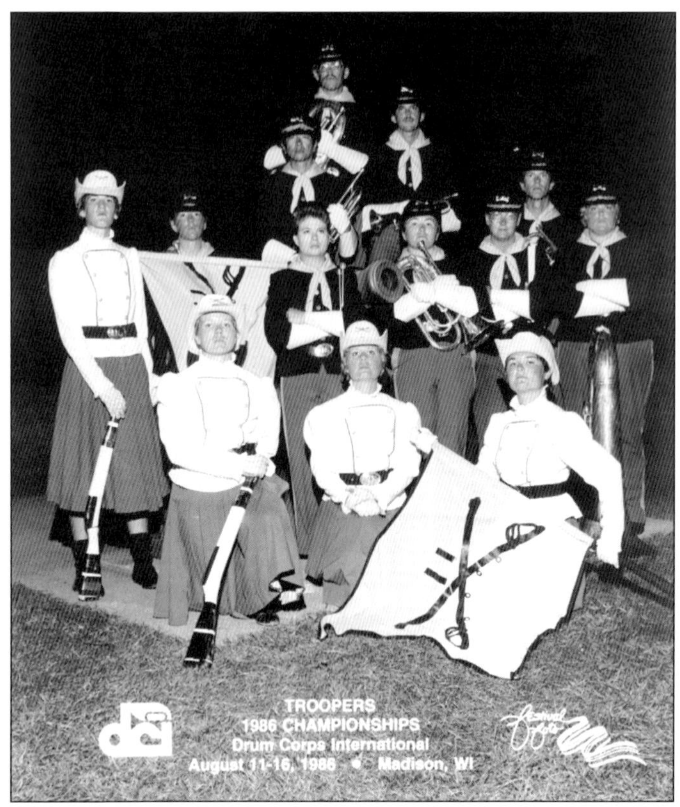

The Troopers "age outs" pose at the DCI Championships in Madison, Wisconsin, on August 11–16, 1986. Corps members have to be between the ages of 13 and 21. From left to right are (first row) Eileen Sturm, Billi Jo Krum, and Jane Starkweather; (second row) Lyn Mears, Mary Purser, Cassandra Schults, unidentified, Becky Blink, and Tami Herne; (third row) Stephen Takata, unidentified, and Kurt Gilbert; (forth row) Alex Clegg. (© Festival Photo, courtesy of Pat Chagnon.)

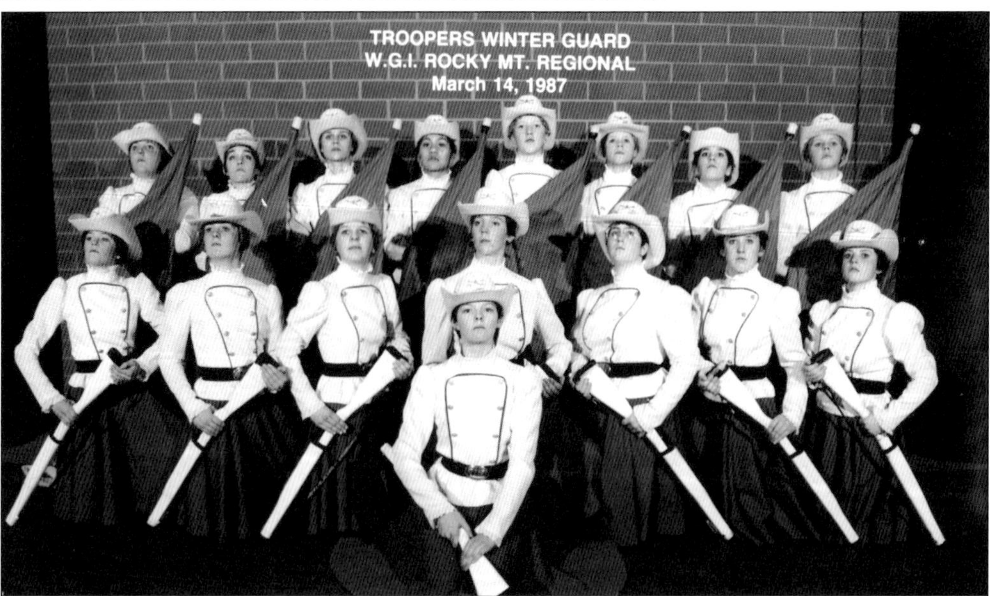

The Troopers winter guard is shown at the Winter Guard International, Rocky Mountain Regional contest on March 14, 1987. From left to right are (first row) Trish Estes; (second row) Teresa Andreen, Julie Mills, Lisa Weatherbee, Kari Gilbert, Kathy Frantz, Gayle Garner, and Jamie Oldham; (third row) Amanda Fawn, Russett Cool, Juli McConanaghy, Jackie Sawyer, Renee ?, Janel Williams, Bobbi Jo Spaine, and Michelle Heiney. (Courtesy of Pat Chagnon.)

Troopers bass drum player Shawn "Zebe" Alsup marches in the Fourth of July parade in Chicago in 1987. Later that day, the Troopers performed in a competition in New Berlin, Wisconsin, where they placed first. The Troopers competed 22 times in eight states that year, including Ohio, Indiana, Wisconsin, South Dakota, Wyoming, Colorado, Alabama, and Arkansas. (Photograph from the Jones family, courtesy of Pat Chagnon.)

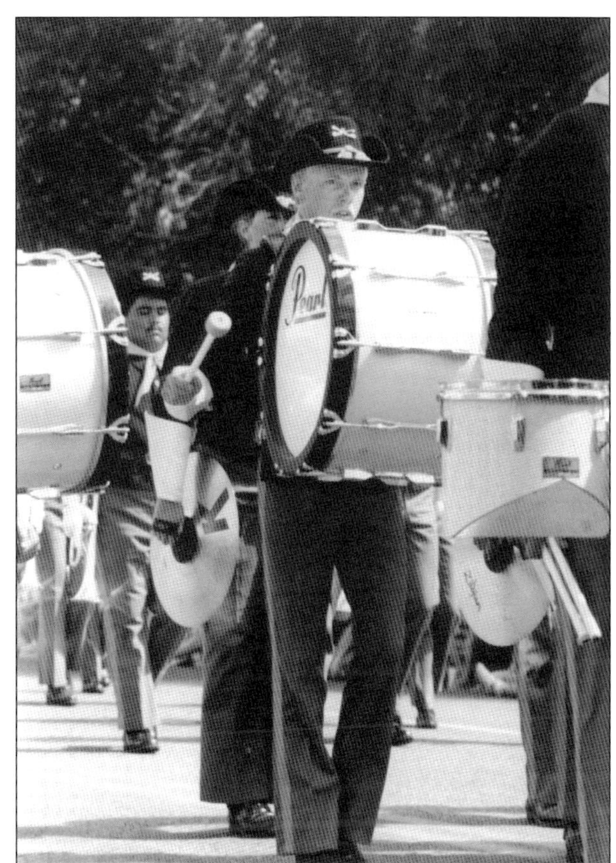

The Troopers' mellophones are on the field at the DCI World Championships Semifinals in Madison on August 14, 1987. Ernie Zimny, the timing judge, walks alongside Mark Monterastelli, Randall Lewis, and Sheron Thomen, taking notes. The Troopers placed 17th that year. (Photograph by Orlin Wagner, courtesy of Drum Corps World Archives.)

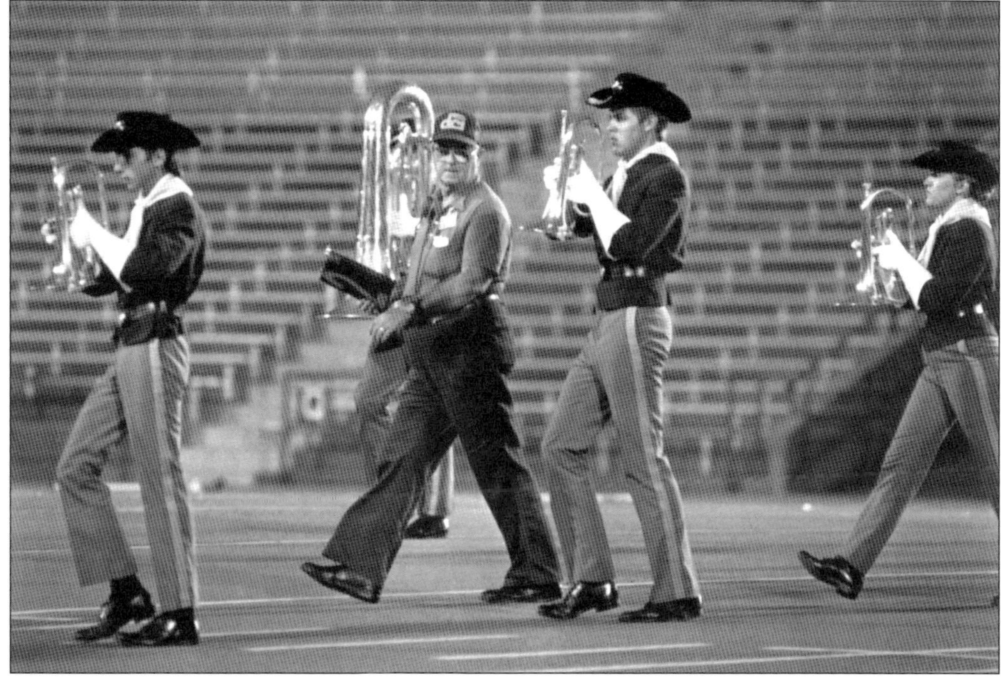

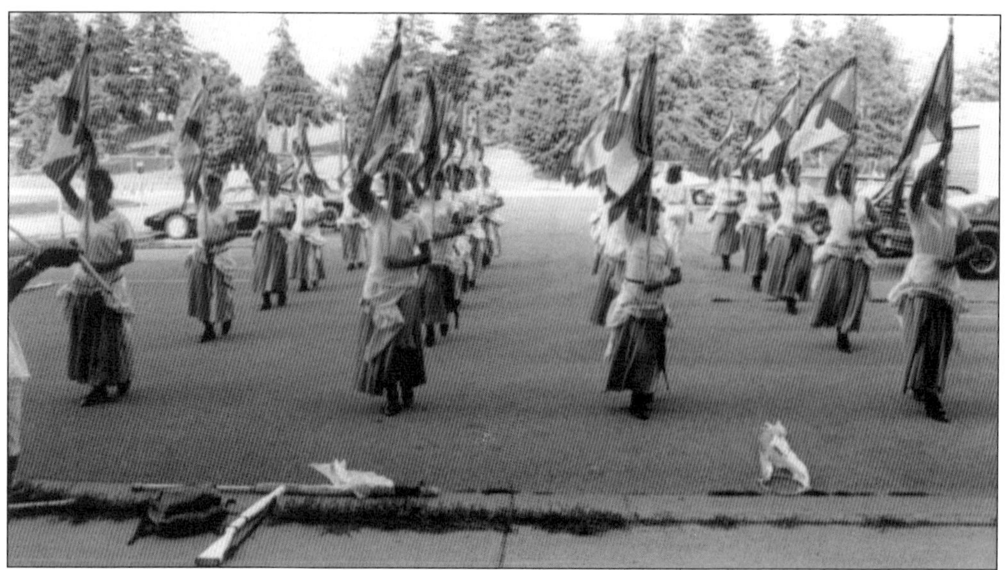

The Troopers color guard practices in 1988. John Masterson became the Troopers' second director that year. Beginning in 1976, he played soprano bugle for three years before becoming the drum major from 1979 to 1981. Masterson served as the director until 1991. Since that time, he has been on the Troopers board and the DCI board. (Courtesy of Drum Corps World Archives.)

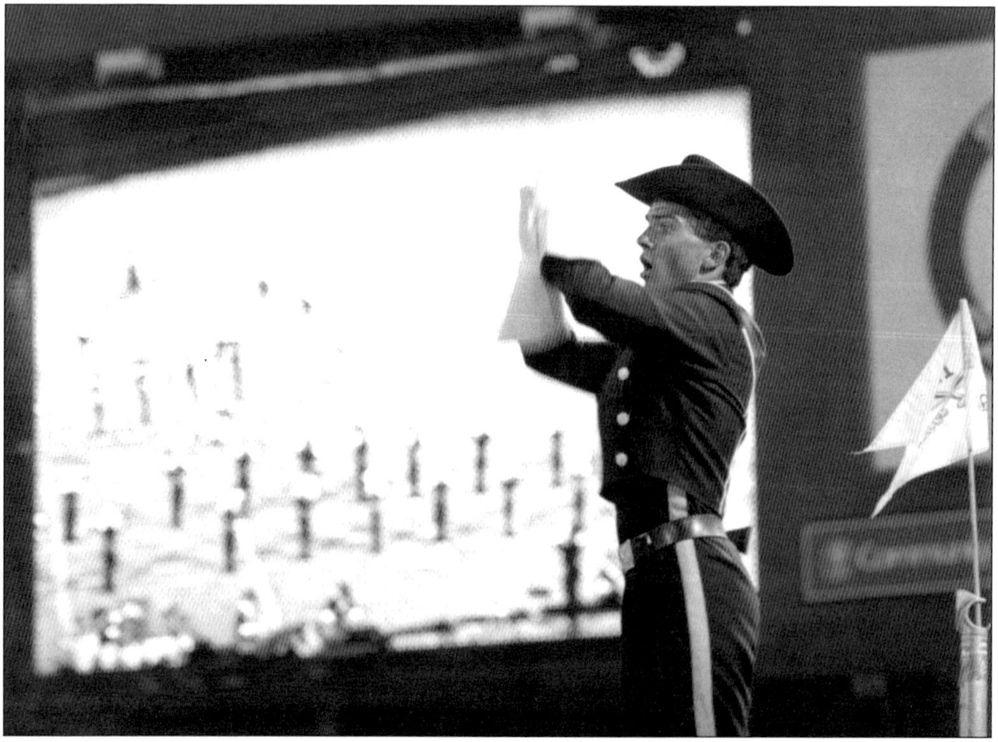

Drum major Tony Monterastelli directs the Troopers Drum & Bugle Corps at a performance at Busch Stadium in St. Louis, Missouri, on August 12, 1988. The corps can be seen on the Jumbotron in the background. It was one of the largest crowds for which Monterastelli and the Troopers had ever performed. (Courtesy of Mike Monterastelli.)

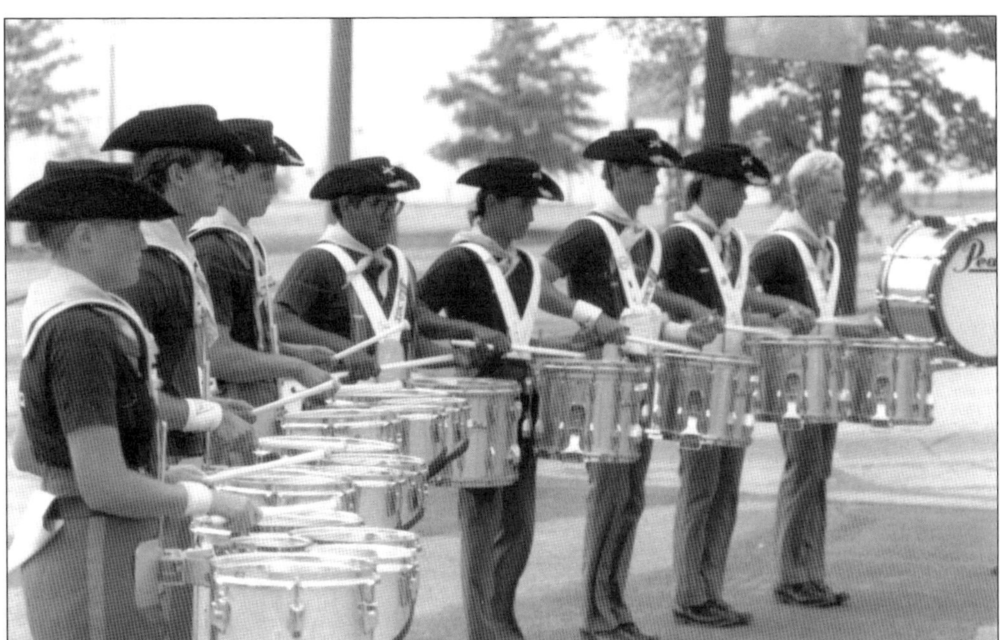

The Troopers snare drummers practice before the DCI Championship Semifinals at Arrowhead Stadium in Kansas City, Missouri, on August 19, 1988. They finished in 19th place that year. (Photograph by Barbara Loeffelholz, courtesy of Drum Corps World Archives.)

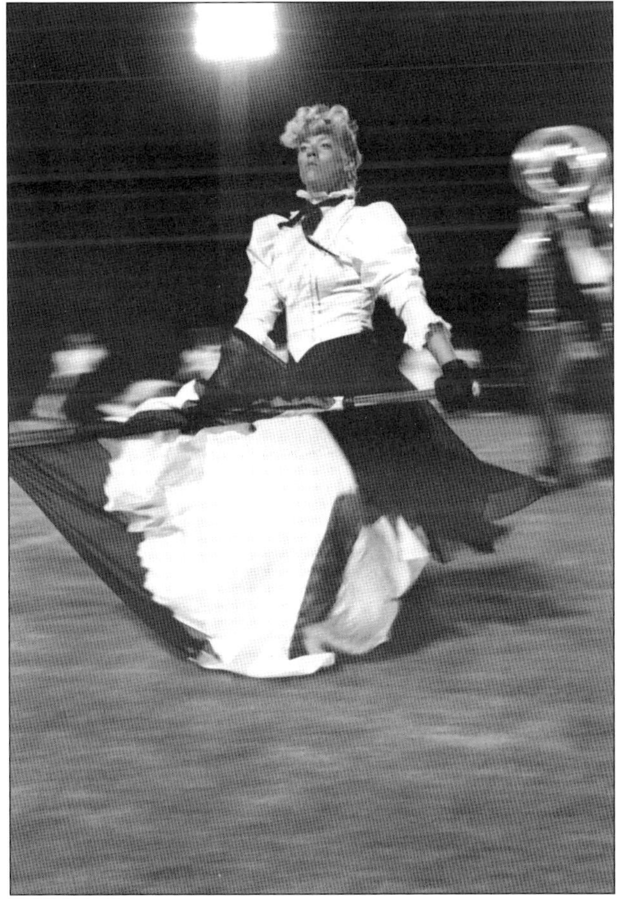

Tanya Florence, a member of the Troopers color guard, performs in 1989. The music selection that year included two tried-and-true Troopers favorites: "How the West Was Won" and "Promised Land." The Troopers had played the two songs for 14 years. They also played two new selections in 1989, "Cheyenne" and "No Goodbyes." (Photograph by Boyd Garey, courtesy of Drum Corps World Archives.)

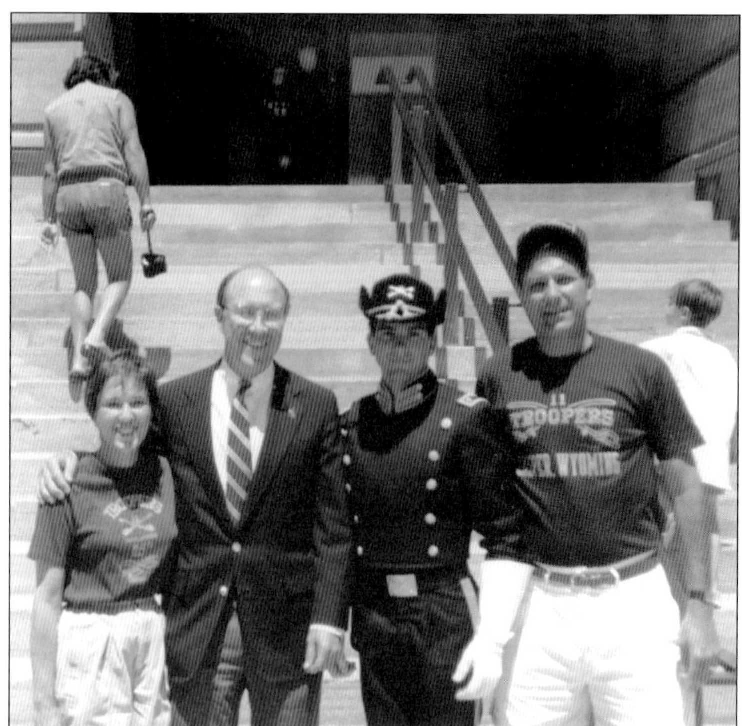

Troopers drum major Tony Monterastelli poses with Wyoming governor Michael Sullivan in Cheyenne on July 20, 1989. Tony's mother, Carol Monterastelli, is on the left, and his father, Mike Monterastelli, the Troopers assistant director, is on the right. The Troopers had held a special performance on the lawn of the Wyoming state capitol building for state employees before the Drums Along the Rockies show that evening in Cheyenne. (Courtesy of Pat Chagnon.)

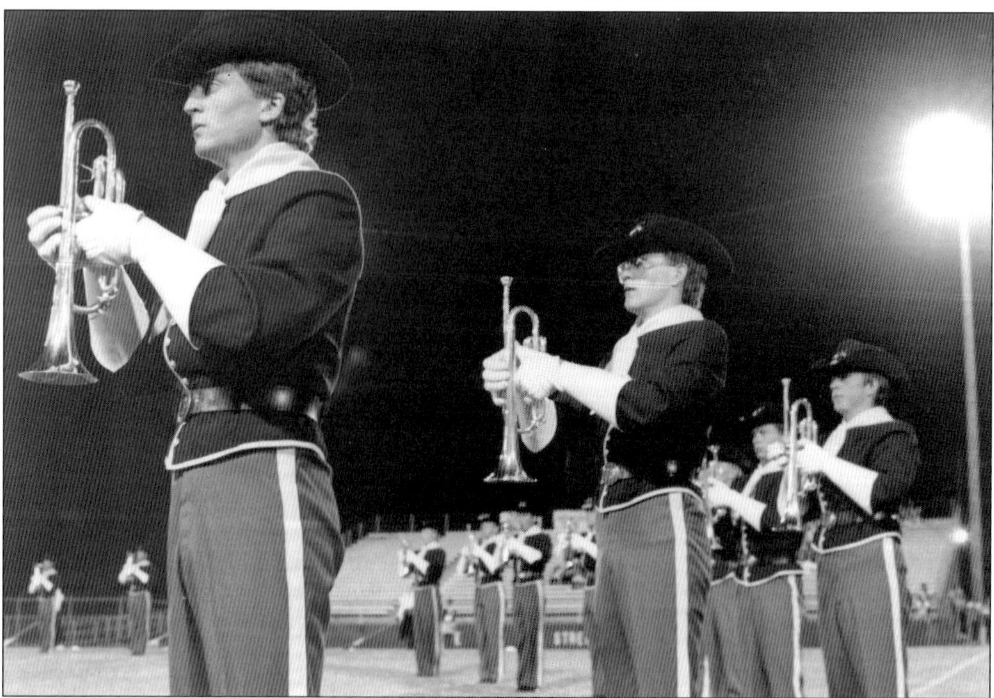

The Troopers horn line is shown in mid-performance in 1989. The Troopers were led by drum major Tony Monterastelli and guard captains Bobbie Jo Spaine and Trish Estes. That year, the corps totaled 133 members, with 56 horns, 29 drummers, and 28 members of the guard. (Photograph by Boyd Garey, courtesy of Drum Corps World Archives.)

Five

1990s

Rolling Along

The Troopers Drum & Bugle Corps, like all drum corps, continued to change, grow, and adapt over time. The formation of DCI in 1972 cut the direct ties with the American Legion and VFW and their strict, military-like regulations. As the 1990s progressed, the Troopers' performances became more of an artistic tapestry, weaving together music, movement, and props. However, drum corps is also a business, and the Troopers seemed to have forgotten that in the mid-1990s. They came close to folding in 1996 due to financial issues.

The Troopers did not manage to make it into the top 12 at all in the 1990s, but they continued to entertain audiences. They spent two weeks touring Wyoming for the Wyoming Centennial in 1990, and performed a special show on the state capitol grounds in Cheyenne on July 20, 1990. Gov. Mike Sullivan and Pres. George H.W. Bush were in attendance at the capitol, and the president spoke before the performance, saying "I want to say a special thanks first to the Casper Troopers. I've heard of them, but never heard them in action before." The Troopers also traveled to Washington, DC, and marched in Pres. Bill Clinton's inaugural parade on January 20, 1993.

The Troopers Cadets were disbanded in 1995. They had been started as a feeder group for the Troopers when all of the members were from Casper. Now, with more members not being from Wyoming, let alone Casper, there was not the demand for the Cadets.

The Troopers have been playing Western and patriotic music since 1958. It is one of the things that sets them apart from other drum and bugle corps—that and their military-inspired uniforms. Through the years, the Troopers have performed "Ghost Riders in the Sky," "Battle Hymn of the Republic," "Tumbling Tumbleweeds," and "How the West was Won." The 1990s added a new twist on the old themes; most years, the songs were blended into an overall theme. Now they are playing "A Western Odyssey" and "Forging a Frontier."

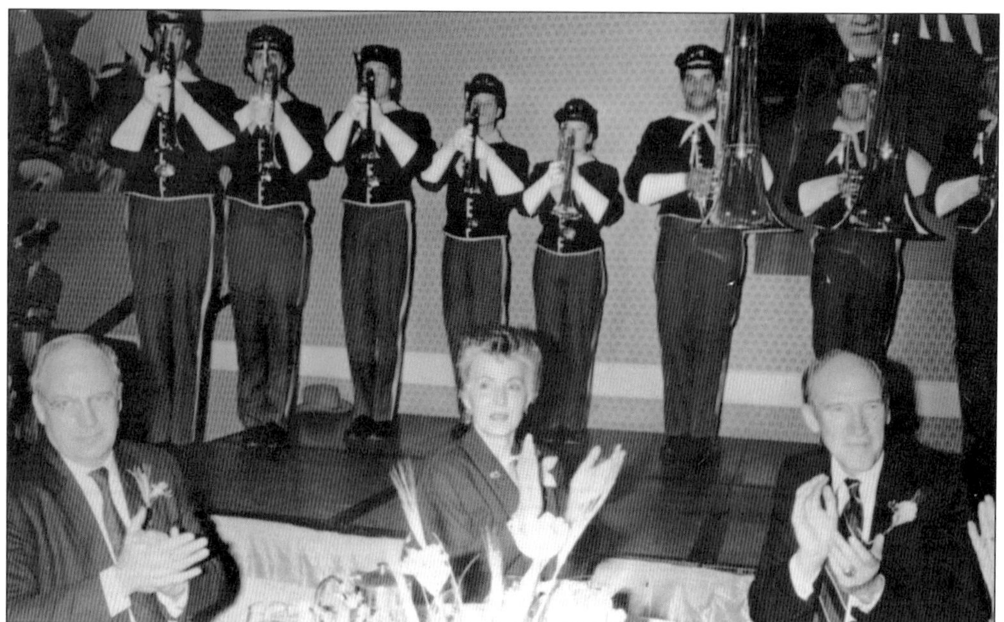

The Troopers provided the musical entertainment the evening Wyoming senator Alan Simpson received the Citizen of the West Award in Denver on January 8, 1990. Then defense secretary Dick Cheney sits with Ann and Alan Simpson at the event. The Troopers, from left to right, are Mike Ottoes, Scott Reinsbach, Robert Schlichting, Cedro Toro, Jennifer Williams, Jim Brown, and Jeff Hoyt. (Courtesy of the Troopers Archives.)

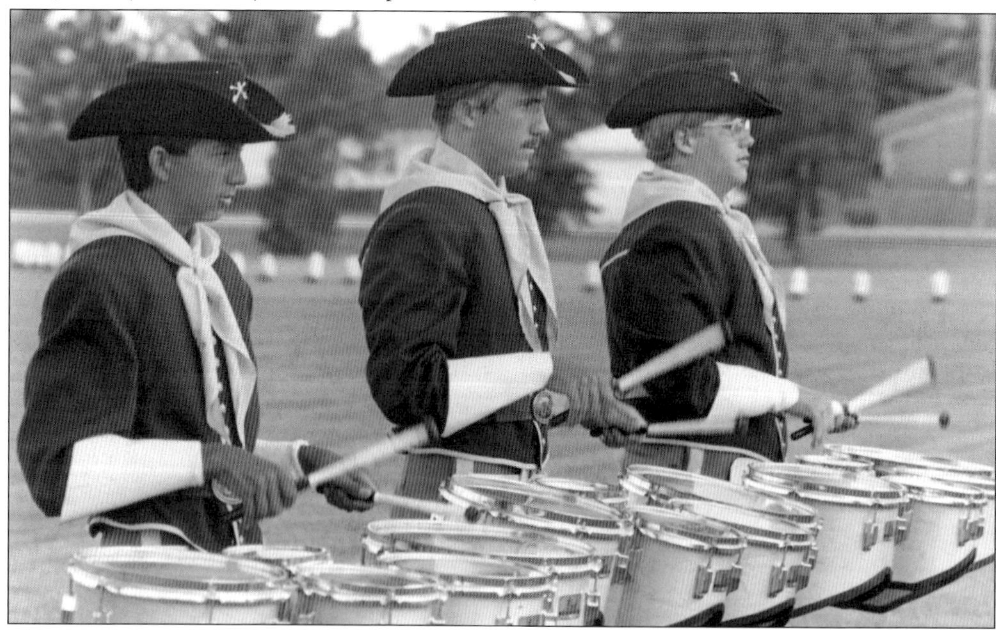

The Troopers multi-tenor drummers perform in 1990. From left to right are Lucas Critchfield, Steve Vaughn, and James Whiddon. The theme for that year's performance was "Music for the Centennial of the State of Wyoming." The musical pieces were "How the West Was Won," "Silverado," "Pop's Hoedown," "Shenandoah," and "America." (Photograph from the Troopers Archives, courtesy of Pat Chagnon.)

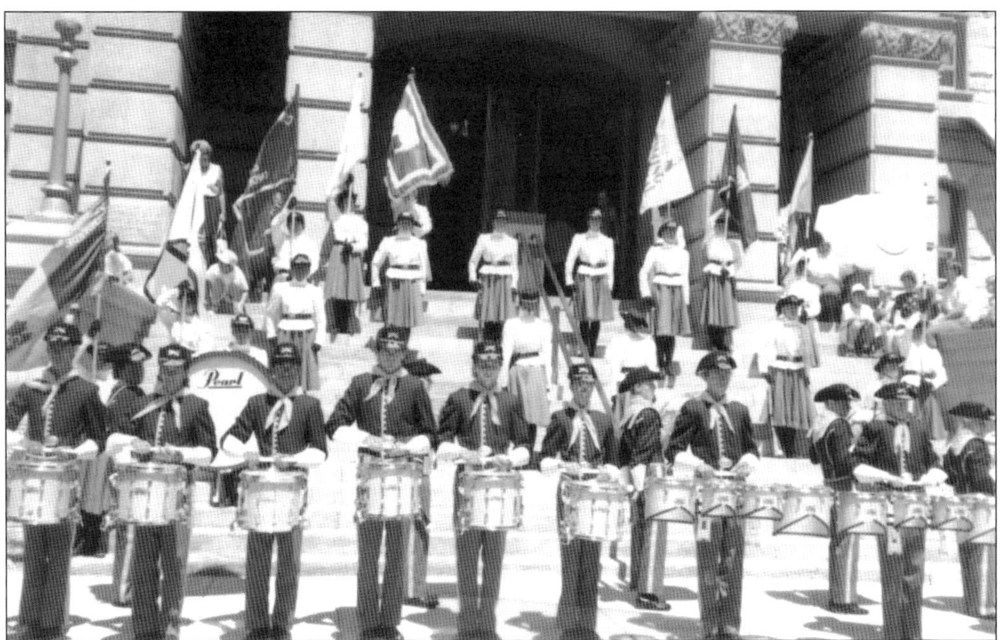

The Troopers perform at the Wyoming state capitol in Cheyenne (above) as part of the Wyoming Centennial Celebration on July 20, 1990. Governor Sullivan and President Bush were part of the audience that gathered on the capitol grounds for the day's festivities. Jennifer Bennett (below) plays the xylophone in the front ensemble while her twin sister, Patricia Bennett, is on the bass drum behind her. The pit included a vibraphone, a marimba, two xylophones, a drum set, timpani drums, suspended cymbals, and bells. The Secret Service stopped drum major Tony Monterastelli and would not let him keep his sidearm—a BB pistol—forcing staff member Rick Ball to return it to the bus. (Both photographs from the Troopers Archives, courtesy of Pat Chagnon.)

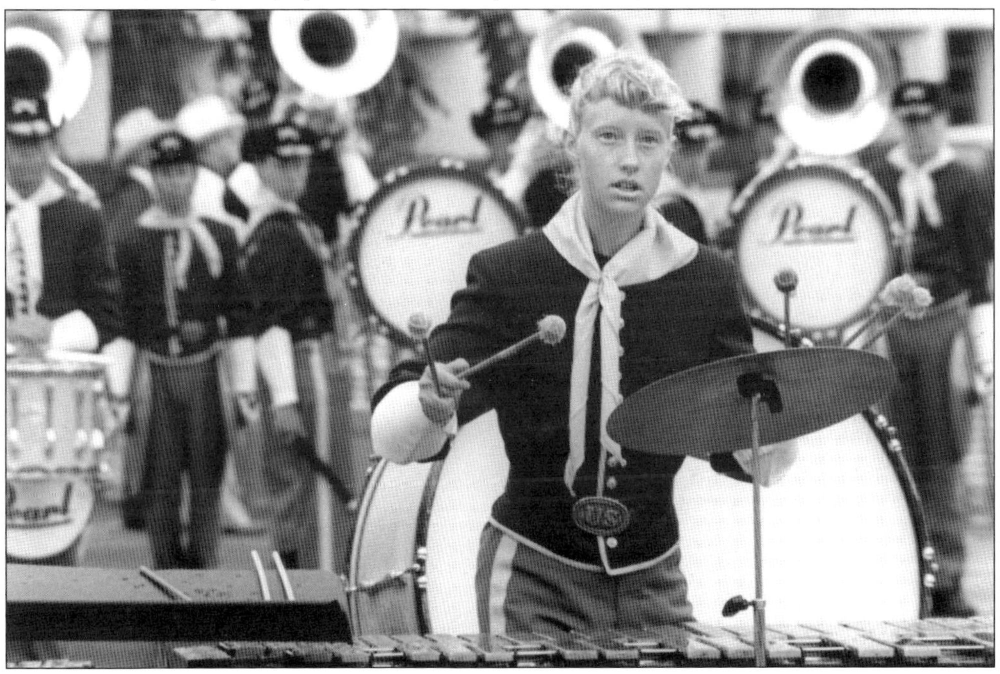

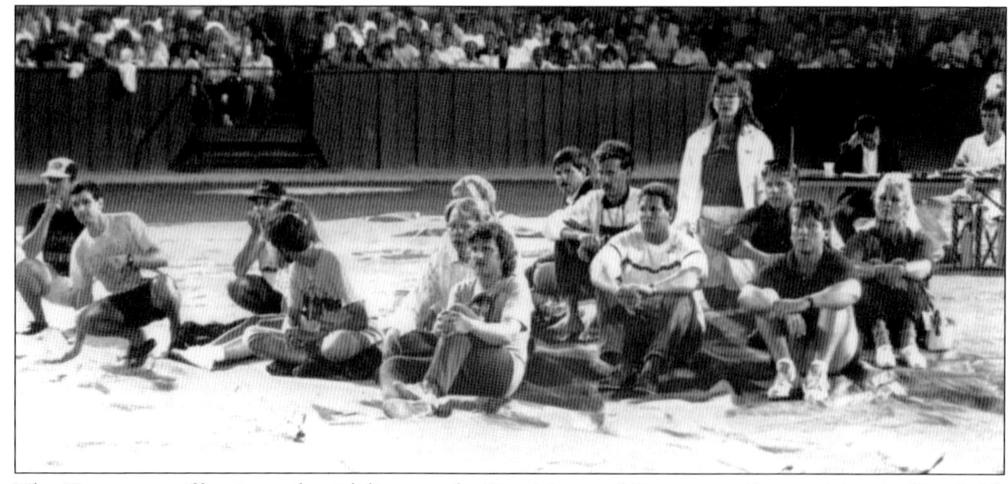

The Troopers staff wait on the sidelines at the Precision and Pageantry Competition in Pittsfield, Massachusetts, on August 8, 1990. From left to right are Jim ?, Doug Smith, Lou Boldrighini, unidentified, Scott Slutter, unidentified, Derek S., Milward Simpson, Larry Davis, David "D.J." Jennison, Bernard Rosenburg, Sue Masterson, Ed Medford, John Fisher, and Lynne D'Angelis. (Photograph by Moe Knox, courtesy of Drum Corps World Archives.)

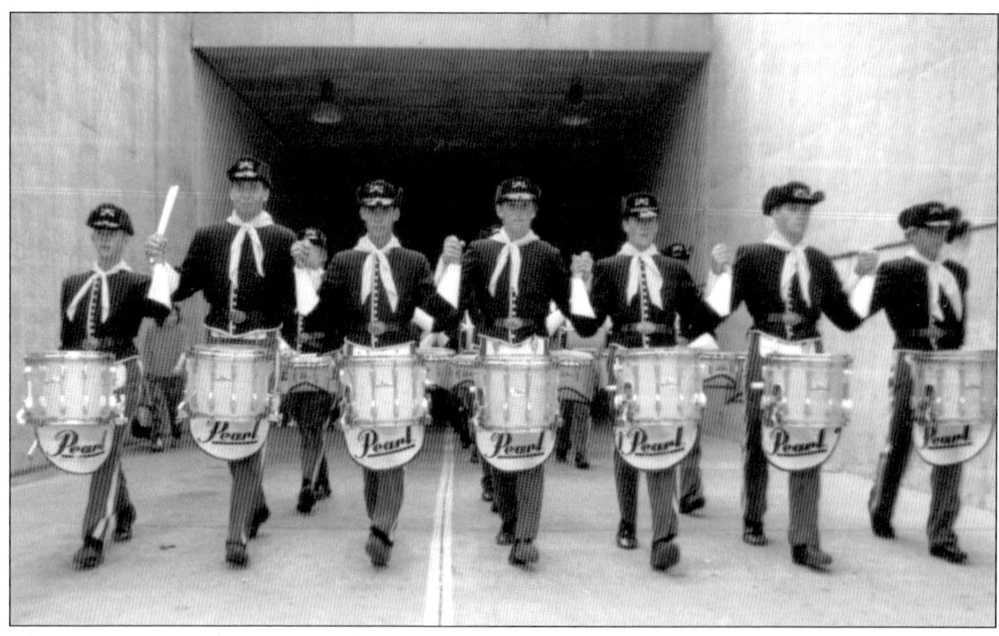

The Troopers snare drummers walk out of the Rich Stadium tunnel at DCI World Championships Semifinals in Buffalo, New York, on August 17, 1990. From left to right are Joe Weaver, Kyle Kallmayer, Frank Favacho, Pete Simpson, Kevin Redmond, Kevin Stevens, and T.J. Simmons. They placed 17th that day. (Photograph by Bill Tietjen, courtesy of Drum Corps World Archives.)

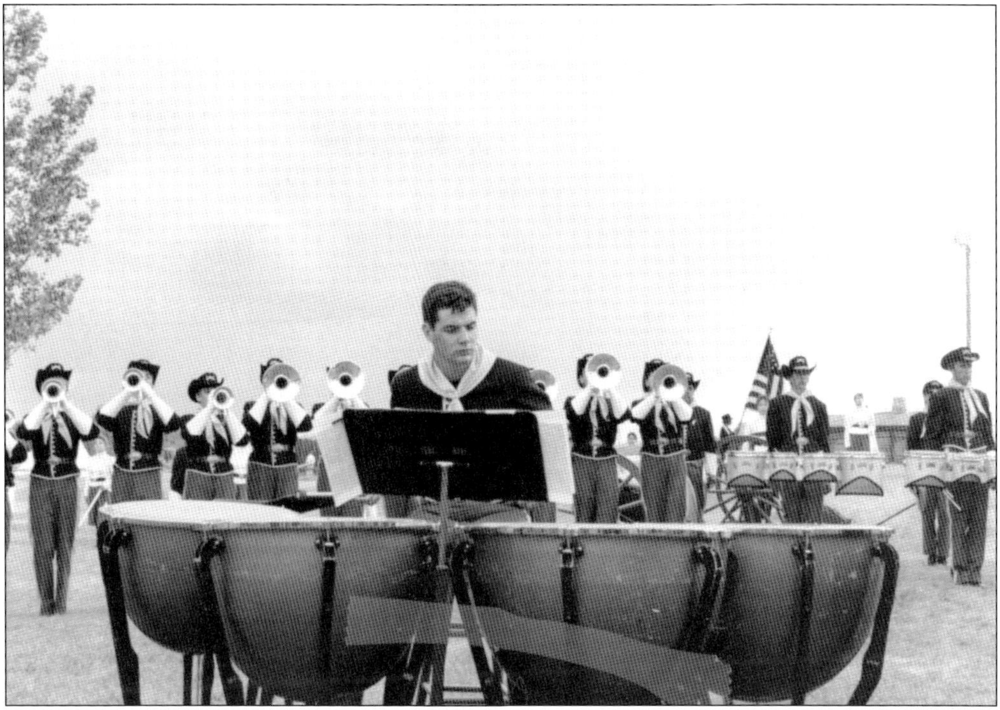

Troopers drummer Darrin Duff plays the timpani drums on the grounds of Fort Caspar Museum in 1991. The Troopers often have a stand-alone performance at the museum and use the fort buildings as a backdrop for publicity photographs. (Courtesy of the Troopers Archives.)

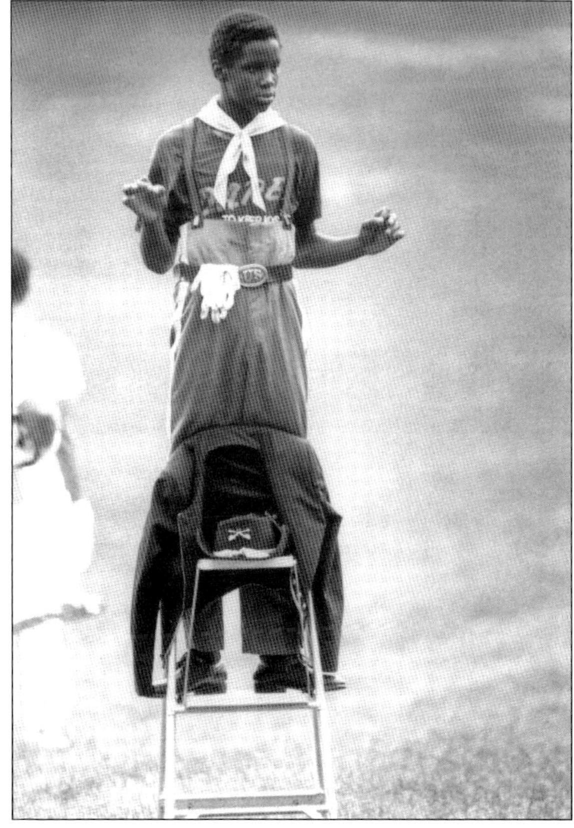

The Troopers back conductor Kazell Wallace is shown during a practice in 1991. Wallace was in the cymbal line and served as back conductor for the performance of the song "Lonesome Dove." His brother Ezra Wallace was in the horn line, and their father, Ivory Wallace, was one of the bus drivers. (Photograph by Orlin Wagner, courtesy of Drum Corps World Archives.)

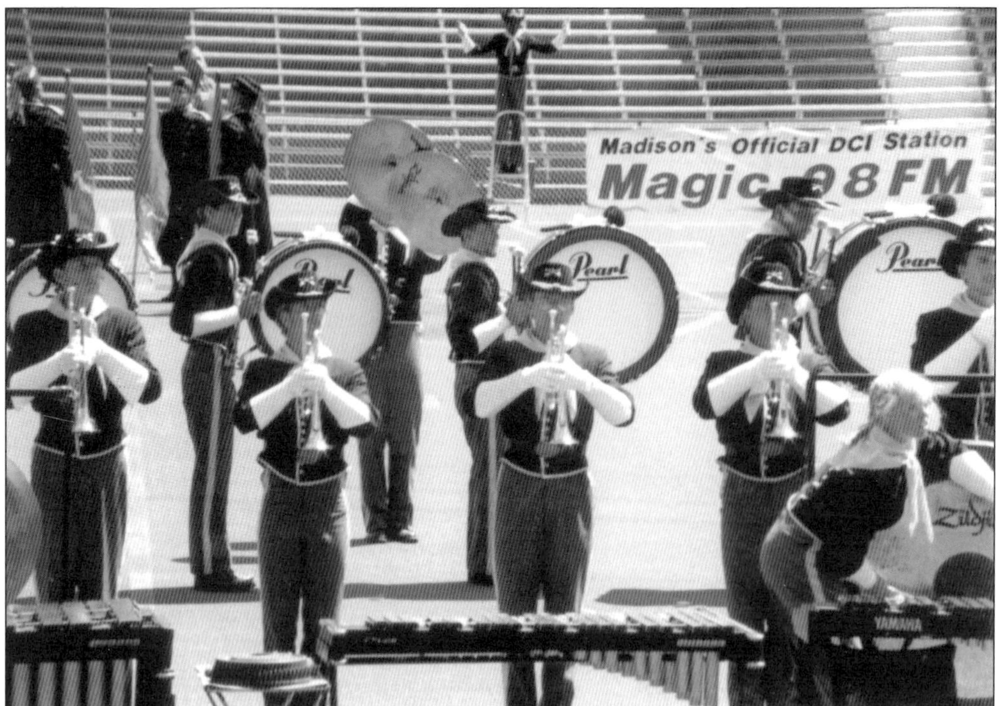

The Troopers perform at the Preview of Champions Preliminaries in Madison on July 27, 1991. They finished 20th that day. The music selections for the 1991 season were all pure Hollywood magic: "The Cowboys" from the movie *Sunset* and music from the miniseries *Lonesome Dove* and the movies *Oklahoma Crude* and *Dances with Wolves.* (Photograph by Mike Bunton, courtesy of Drum Corps World Archives.)

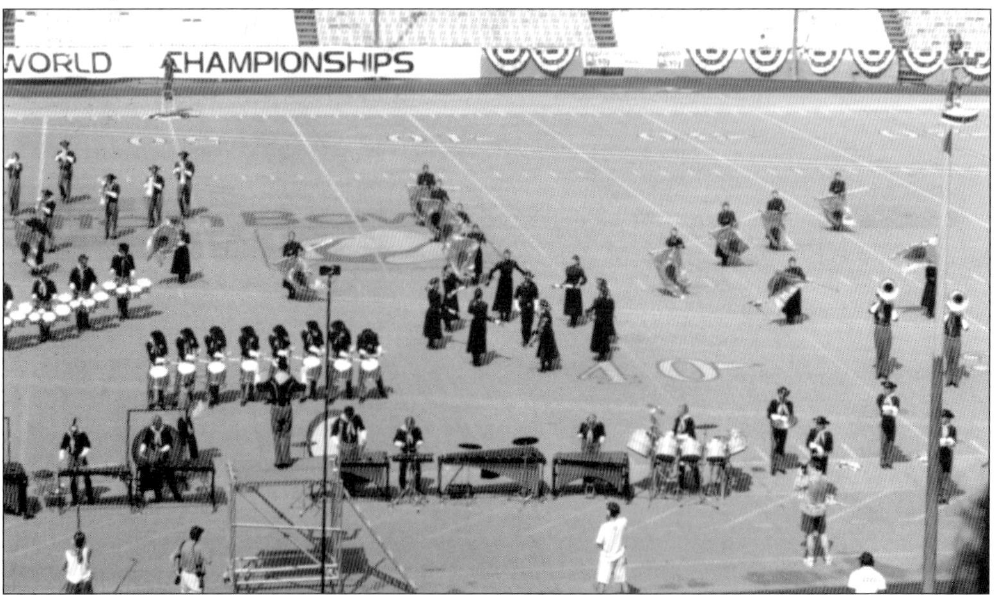

The Troopers perform at the DCI World Championships Quarterfinals at the Cotton Bowl in Dallas on August 15, 1991. They placed 21st that year in the final standings for DCI. The Troopers performed in 15 states from Arizona to New York in 1991. (Courtesy of the Troopers Archives.)

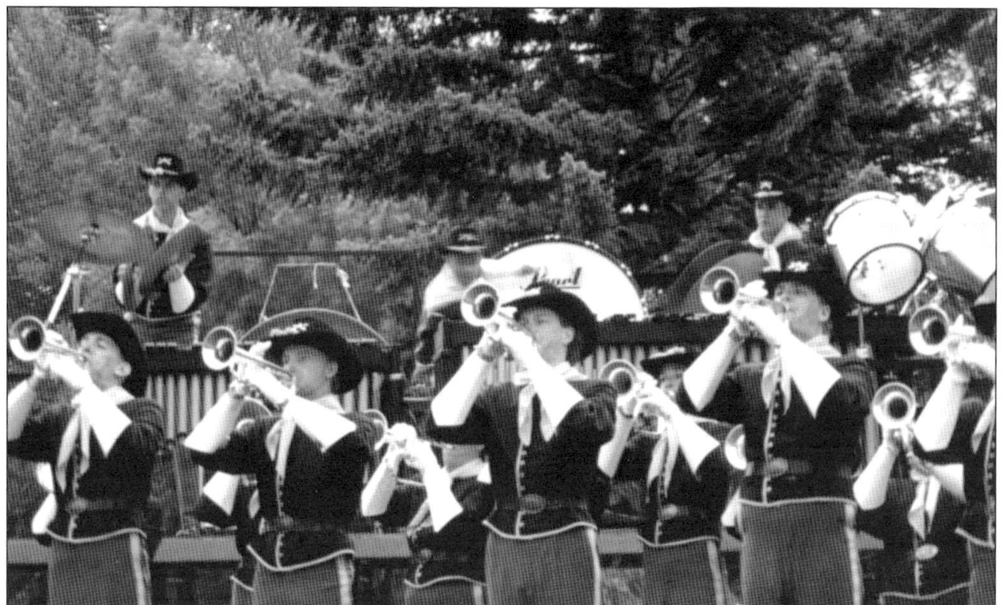

The Troopers play in a park in 1992. The sopranos in front, from left to right, are Josh Burnham, Nathan Claiborn, Robert Schlichting, and Scott Reinsbach. In the pit in back on the right, Matt Canepa plays the cymbals. (Photograph from the Troopers Archives, courtesy of Pat Chagnon.)

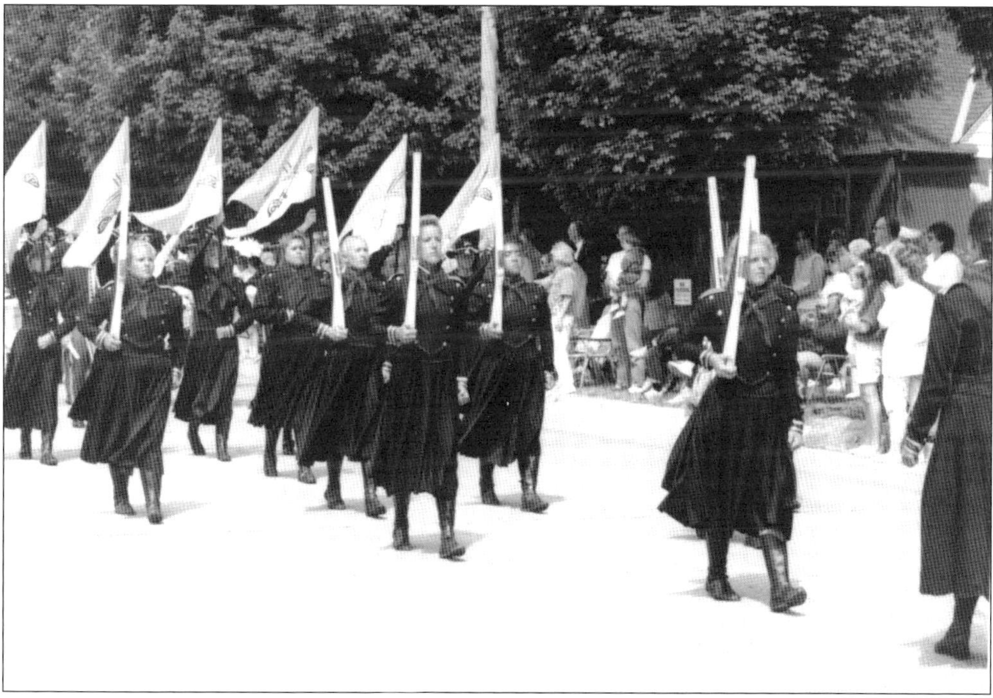

The Troopers color guard marches in a parade in 1992. They are Kari Gilbert (back to the camera); Kellie Smith (facing Gilbert); and, from left to right (first row), Rachel Holdren and unidentified; (second row) Lisa Crimm, unidentified, and Ayumi Hattori; (third row) Kristen Claiborn, Tammie Leslie-Burch, Charity Carstens, Cindy Moline, and drum major Mathew Krum. (Photograph by Hermann Alsup, courtesy of Drum Corps World Archives.)

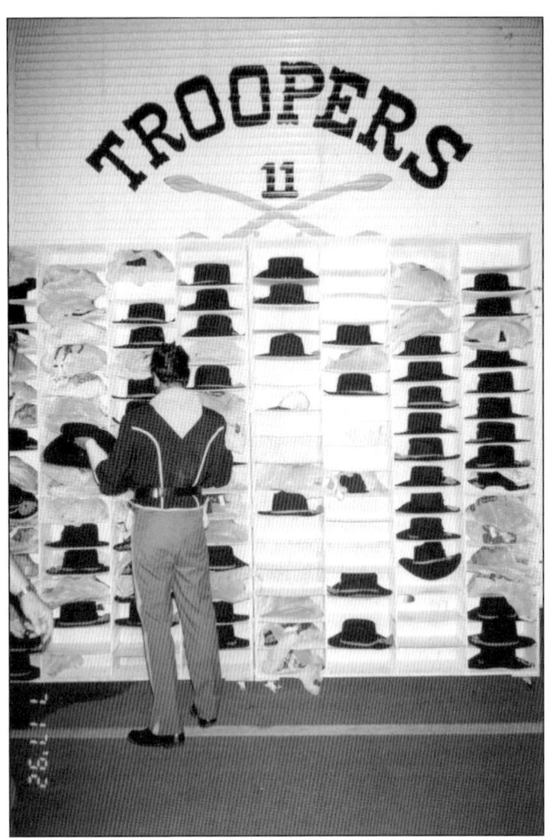

Troopers contra player Junior Martinez stands in front of the hat storage and either retrieves or puts away his hat on July 17, 1992. The Troopers have specialized storage for their uniforms and hats to protect them throughout the season. They travel with a semi-truck that stores all of their gear. (Photograph by Colby Springer, courtesy of Drum Corps World Archives.)

The Troopers perform at DCI World Championships Quarterfinals in Madison on August 13, 1992. A quote from the 1992 DCI Championship Program states: "Long before it became fashionable to publicly declare oneself as patriotic, the Troopers were openly proud to be known as 'America's Corps.' Throughout the history of DCI, the corps' image and unswerving commitment to performing patriotic and western music have made it a perennial favorite." (Courtesy of the Troopers Archives.)

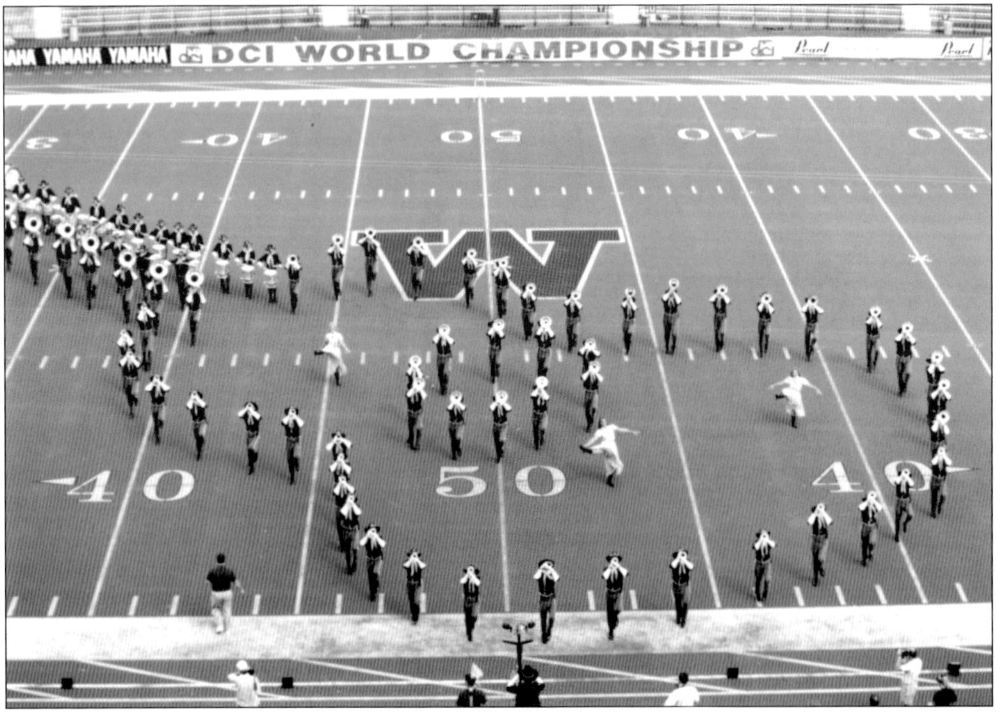

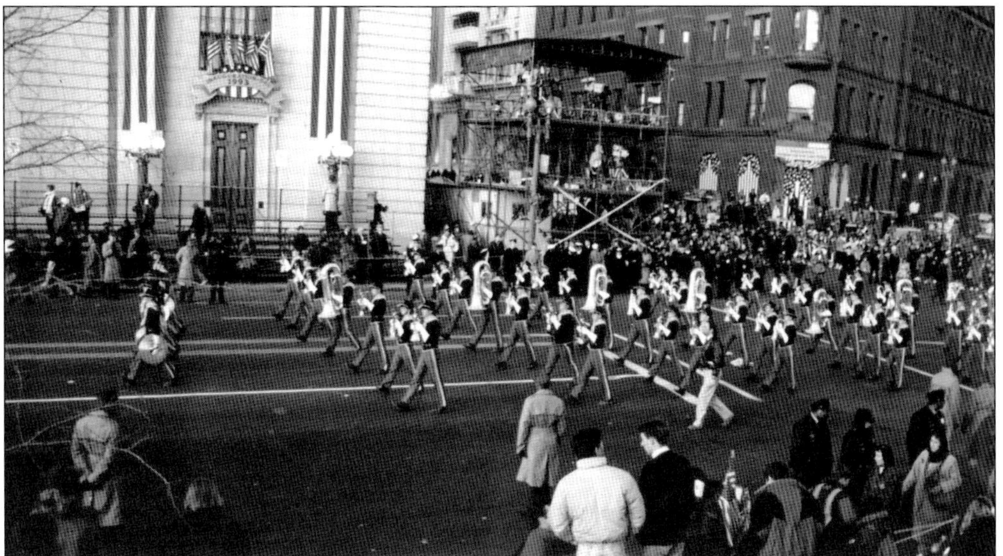

The Troopers march in the inaugural parade for President Clinton in Washington, DC, on January 30, 1993. The Troopers performed in 15 competitions that summer, opening the season in Ogden, Utah, and finishing the summer in Jackson, Mississippi. (Photograph from the Troopers Archives, courtesy of Pat Chagnon.)

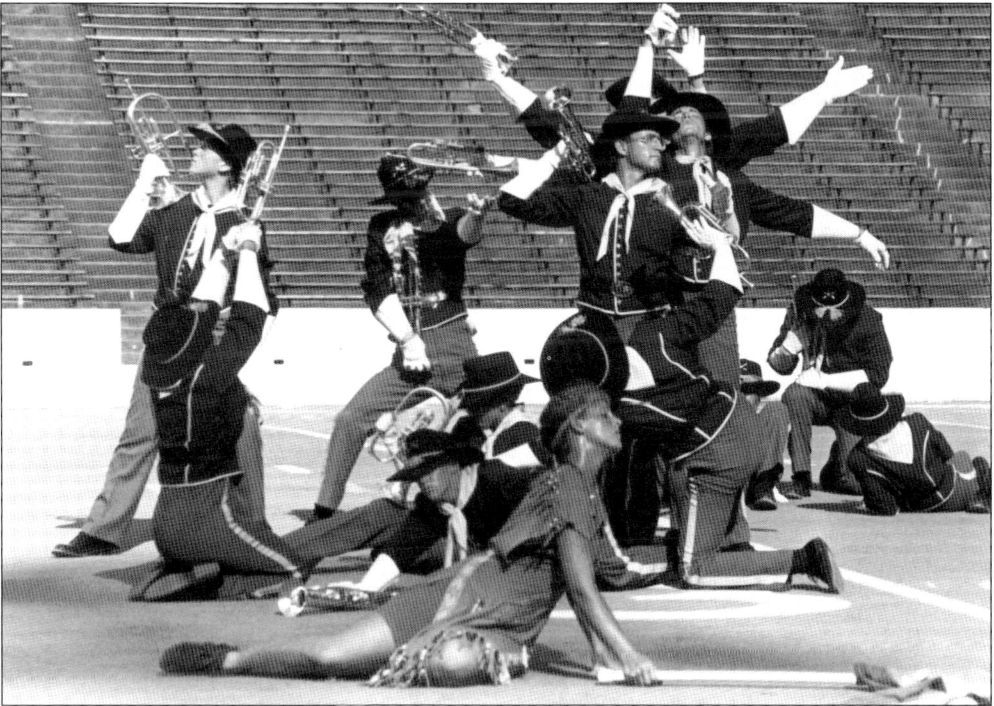

The Troopers strike a pose during the "Charles Country Overture" by Joseph Wilcox Jenkins in 1993. Following the overture, they closed the show with a performance of the "Battle Hymn of the Republic" that featured an updated look to some of their classic drill moves highlighted by several of the corps' sponsor and victory flags and banners from years past. (Photograph by Alan Winslow, courtesy of Drum Corps World Archives.)

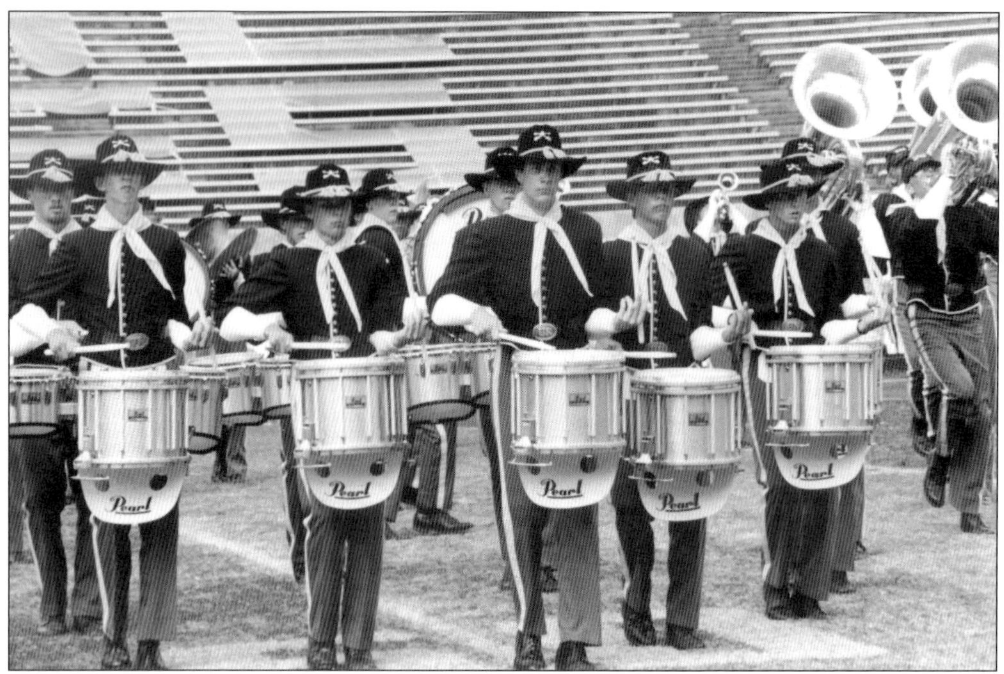

The Troopers drummers perform at the DCI World Championships Quarterfinals in Jackson on August 19, 1993. The snare drummers are, from left to right, Todd Brotze, Larry Carson, Ryan Collins, Brian Chavez, Kenny Bailey, and William Gunn. Behind the snares are the multi-tenors; from left to right are Matt Foldenauer, Mike Farrar, and T.J. Simmons. (Photograph by Dan Scafaldi, courtesy of Drum Corps World Archives.)

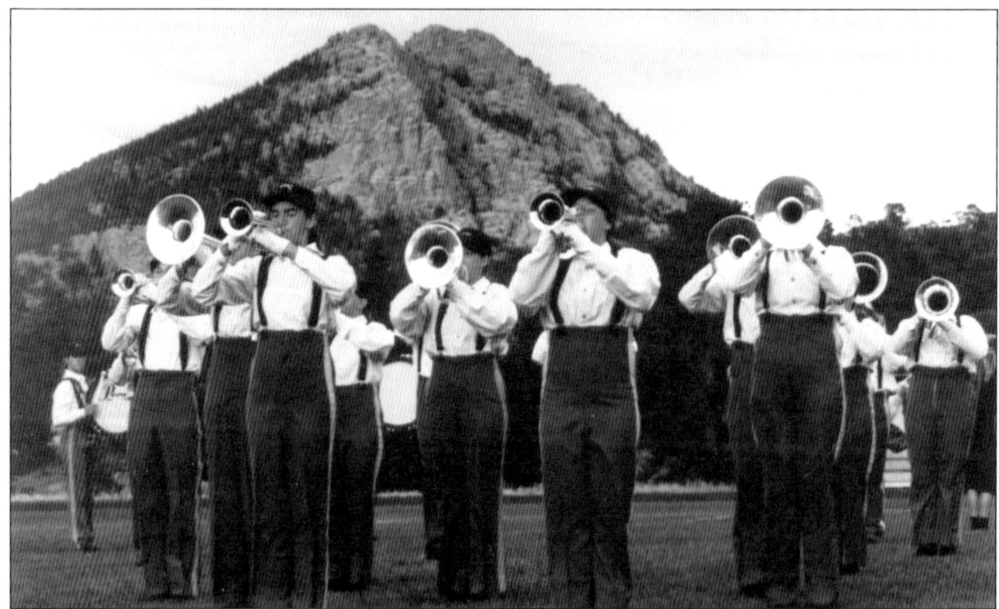

The Troopers Cadets play in a park in Glenwood Springs, Colorado, in June 1994. They were on their way back from a West Coast tour where they performed at competitions in Arizona, California, and Utah. The next year was the final year of the Cadets. (Photograph by Ron Walloch, courtesy of Drum Corps World Archives.)

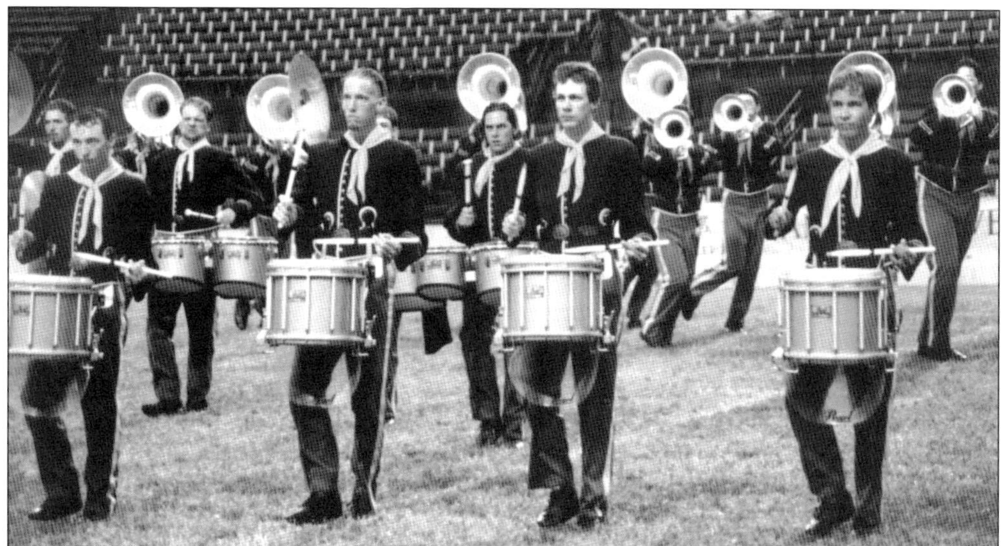

The Troopers snare line plays in the rain in Erie, Pennsylvania, on August 4, 1994. From left to right are Kenny Bailey, Shane Garoutte, Ryan Collins, and Brian Chavez. The black stripes on the drum sticks were in honor of Jim Jones. He had passed away on June 11, 1994. The corps delayed the start of their first tour to perform at his funeral in Casper. (Photograph by Dan Scafaldi, courtesy of Drum Corps World Archives.)

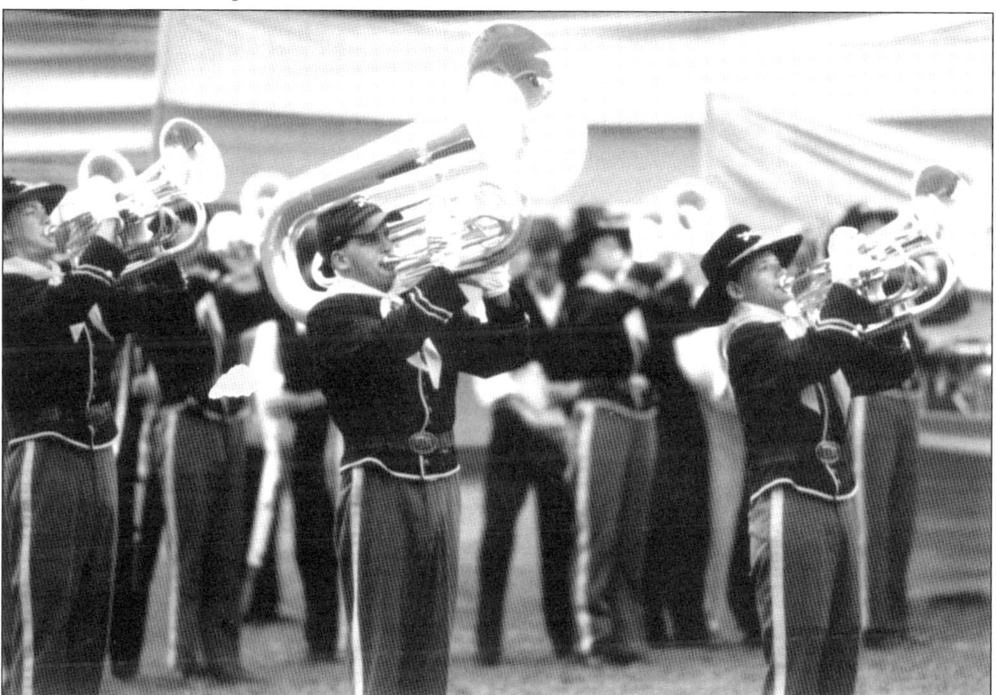

The Troopers horn line plays a show opener in 1994. From left to right are Eric Hankins (baritone), Troy ? (contra), and Melanie Moser (baritone). The show that year was called *Southwestern Sketches* and the opener, "Sunrise," was composed by Casper local Fred Taylor. The rest of the show included "Scherzo," "Santa Fe Saga," and Symphonic Dance No. 3 "Fiesta." (Photograph from the Troopers Archives, courtesy of Pat Chagnon.)

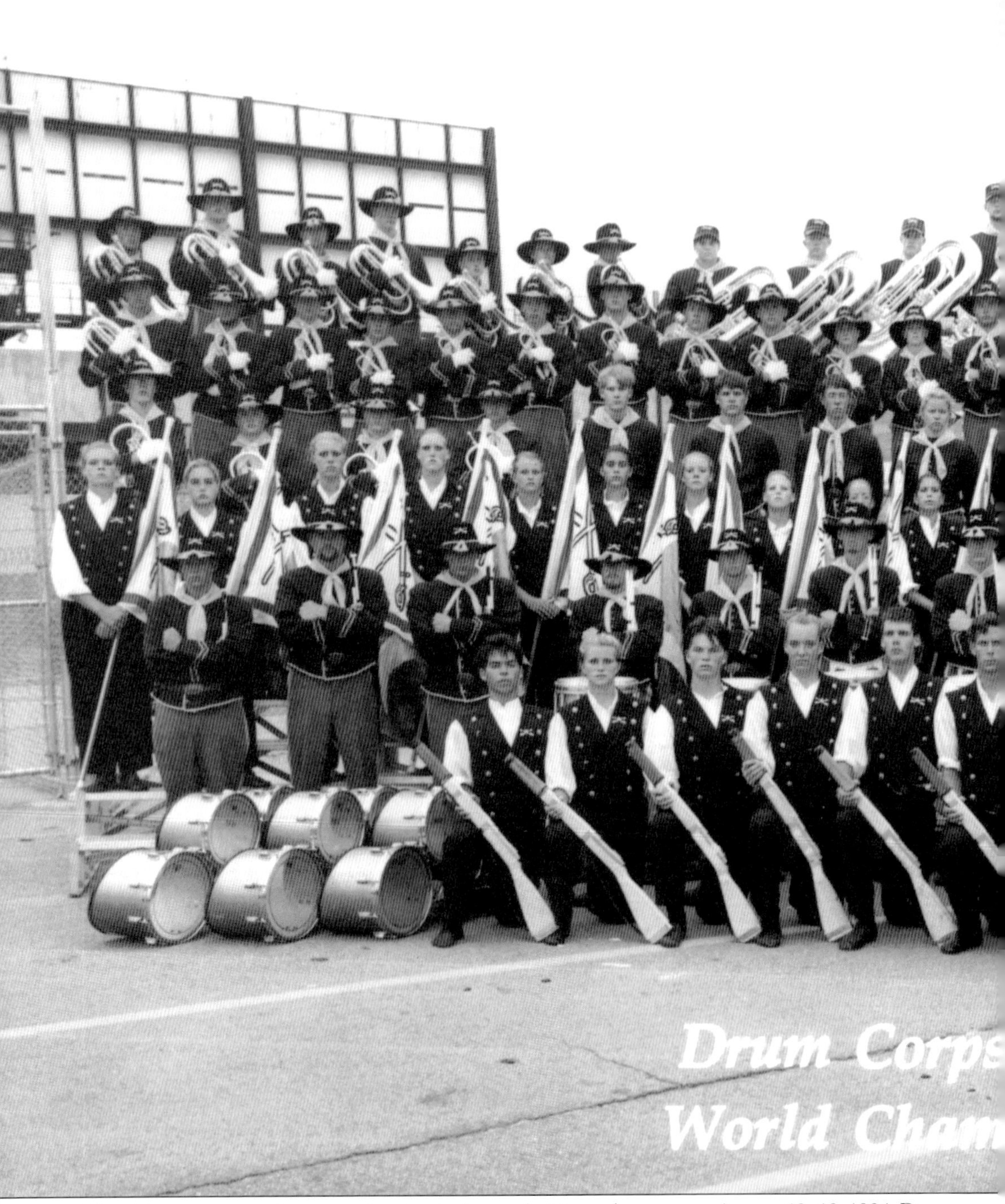

This Troopers group shot was taken in Foxborough, Massachusetts, on August 18–19, 1994. Drum major Rick Brown is kneeling at far right in the front row. The corps had 106 members; 28 were in the guard, 14 played drums, there were 53 horn players, nine members of the front ensemble,

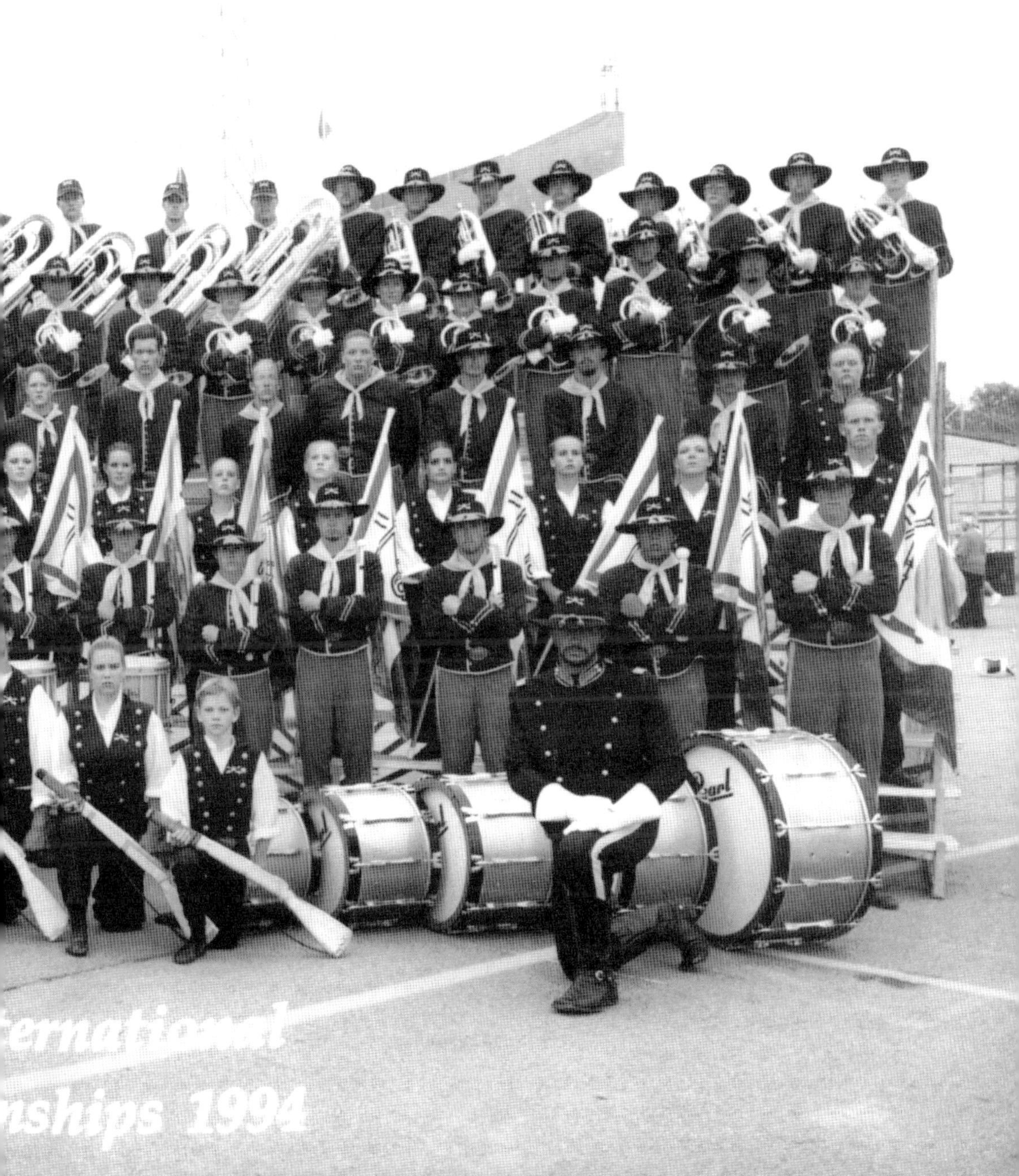

one drum major, and one second conductor. Tanya French was the second conductor, and the guard captains that year were Bobbie Jo Spaine and Roger Saint Vincent. (Photograph from the Troopers Archives, courtesy of Pat Chagnon.)

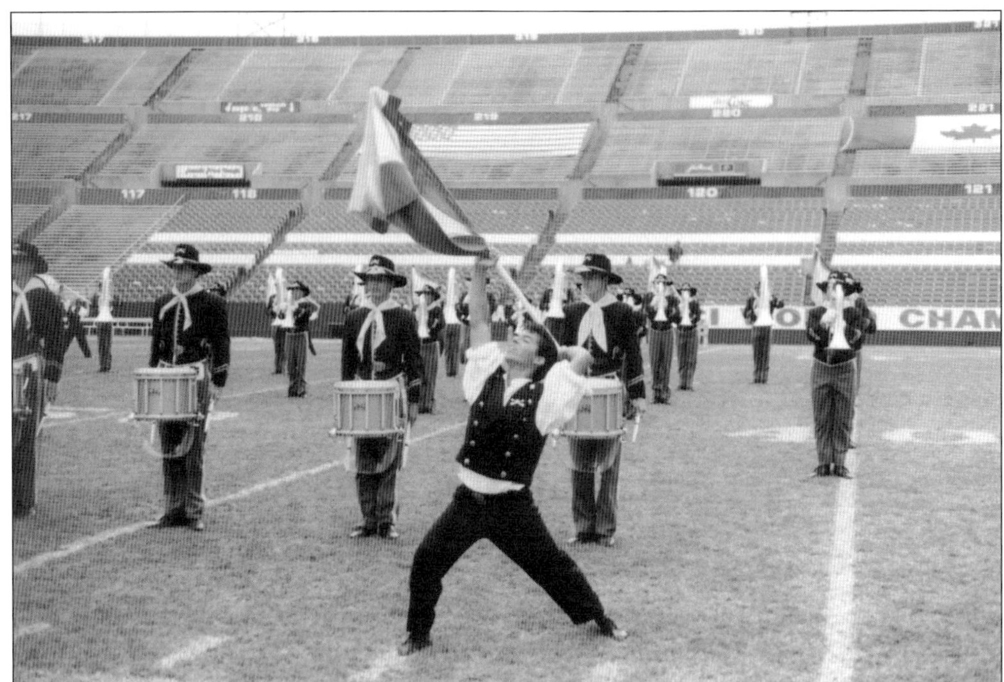
The Troopers perform at the DCI World Championships Quarter- or Semifinals in Foxborough on August 18 or 19, 1994. Guard member Kelly Joseph is in front of the snare drummers, who are, from left to right, Shane Garoutte, Ryan Collins, Brian Chavez, and Jason Mulqueen. The Troopers began coed participation in the guard in 1993. (Courtesy of Drum Corps World Archives.)

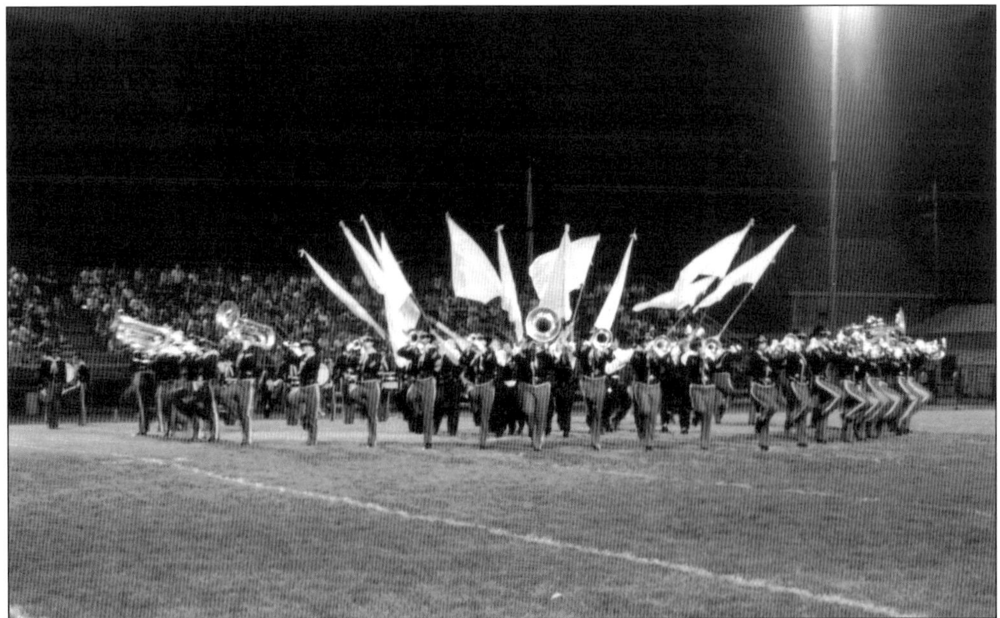
The Troopers perform a revival of the wagon wheel formation at the US Open in Marion, Ohio, on August 7, 1995. They placed fourth that day. The Troopers competed at 25 different competitions in 13 states that summer, from New York to Utah. (Photograph by Marc Tobin, courtesy of Drum Corps World Archives.)

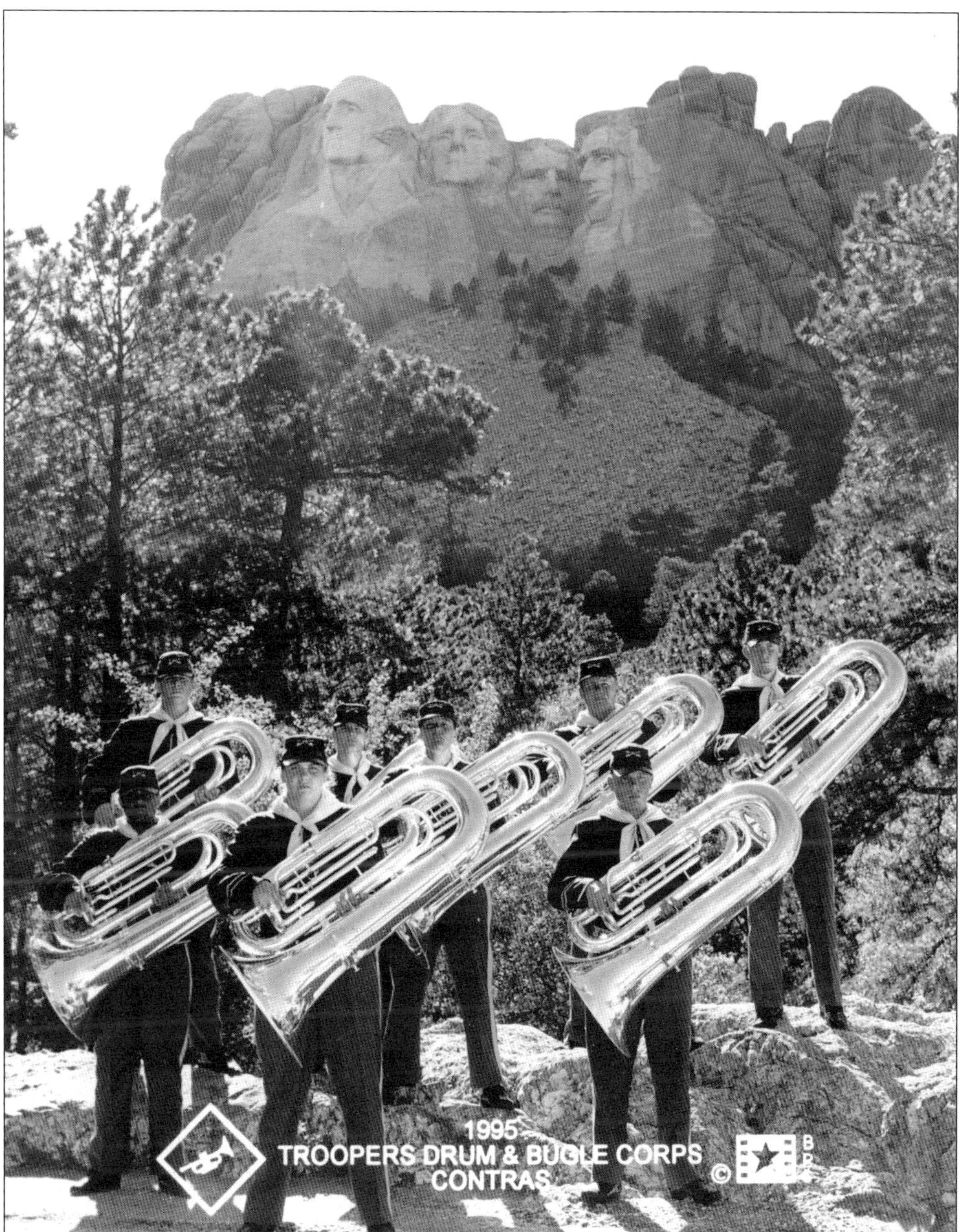

The Troopers contra line poses in front of Mount Rushmore National Memorial in South Dakota in 1995. The contra, or "marching tuba," is the lowest-pitched member of the drum corps' horn line and is the counterpart to the marching band's sousaphone. (Photograph from the Troopers Archives, courtesy of Pat Chagnon.)

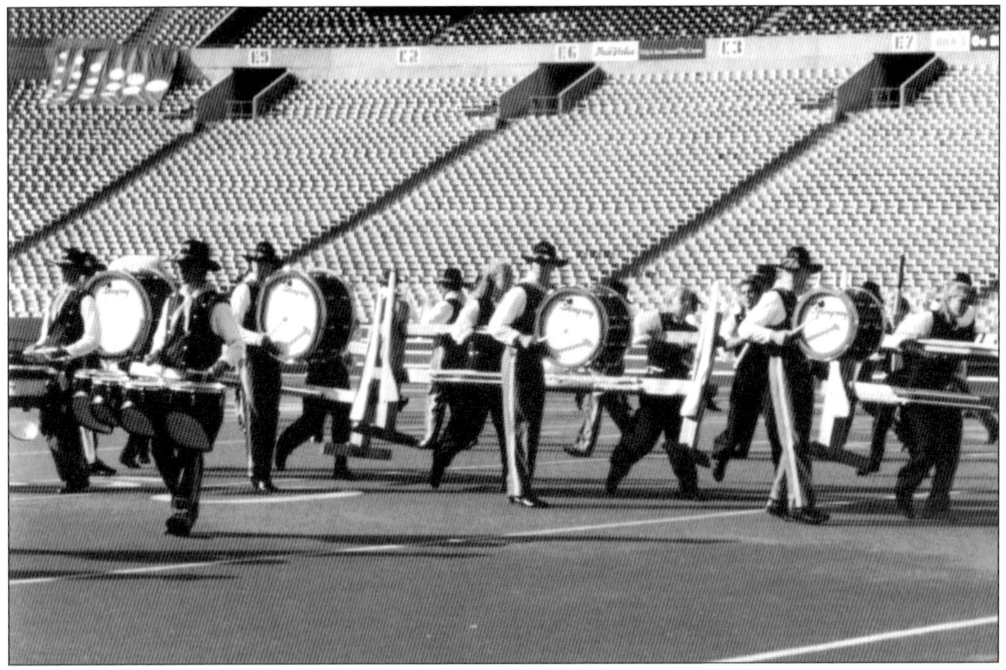

The Troopers perform at the DCI World Championships Quarter or Semifinals in Buffalo on August 16 or 17, 1995. The drum line (above) is shown during the performance. The horn line and color guard (below) march down the field. The show was titled *A Copland Canvas* and featured music from *Fanfare for the Common Man* and *Appalachian Spring*. According to the 1995 DCI Championship program, the "Troopers paint a musical portrait of one of America's most beloved composers." (Above, photograph by Ron Walloch, courtesy of Pat Chagnon; below, courtesy of the Troopers Archives.)

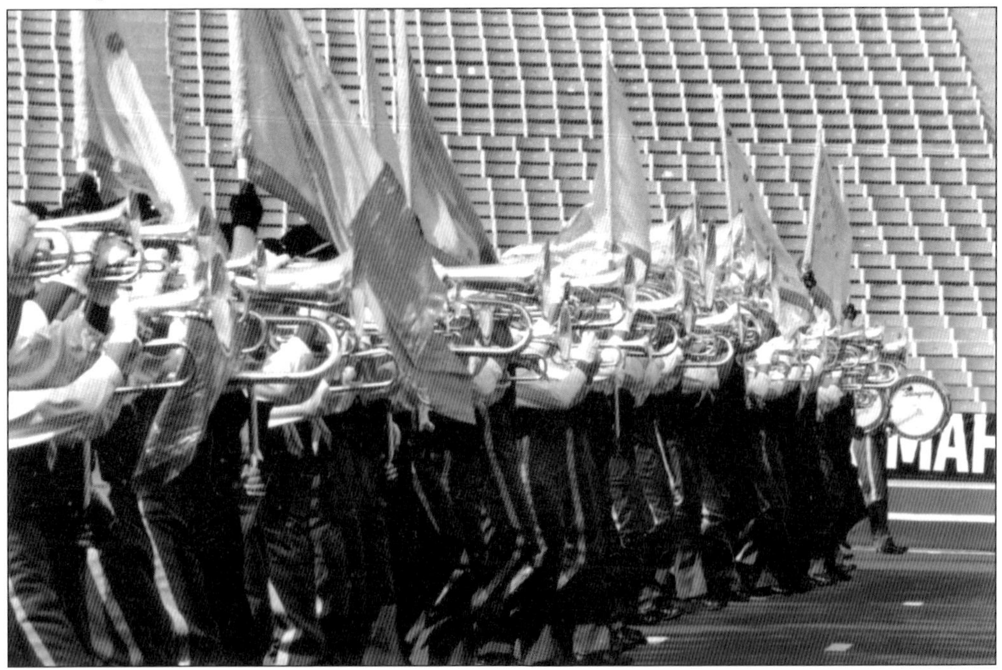

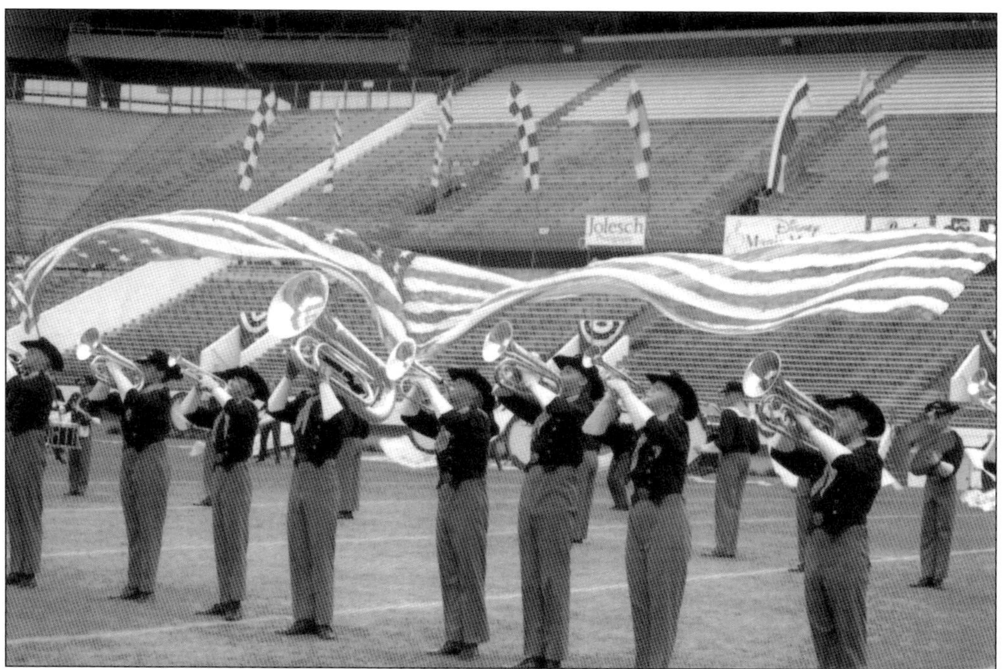

The Troopers perform at the DCI World Championships Quarterfinals in Orlando, Florida, on August 15, 1996. Behind the horn line (above) flies a large US flag. From left to right are Jeff Lane, Sarah Braz, unidentified, Adam Corson, Dennis Kroening, two unidentified, and Orlando Redden. Below, the color guard is, from left to right, (first row) Amy ?, Jennifer Henderson, and unidentified; (second row) Michelle Baker, Nicole Larson, and unidentified. The Troopers finished 19th that year in the DCI Championships. (Both photographs by Karen Sunmark, courtesy of Drum Corps World Archives.)

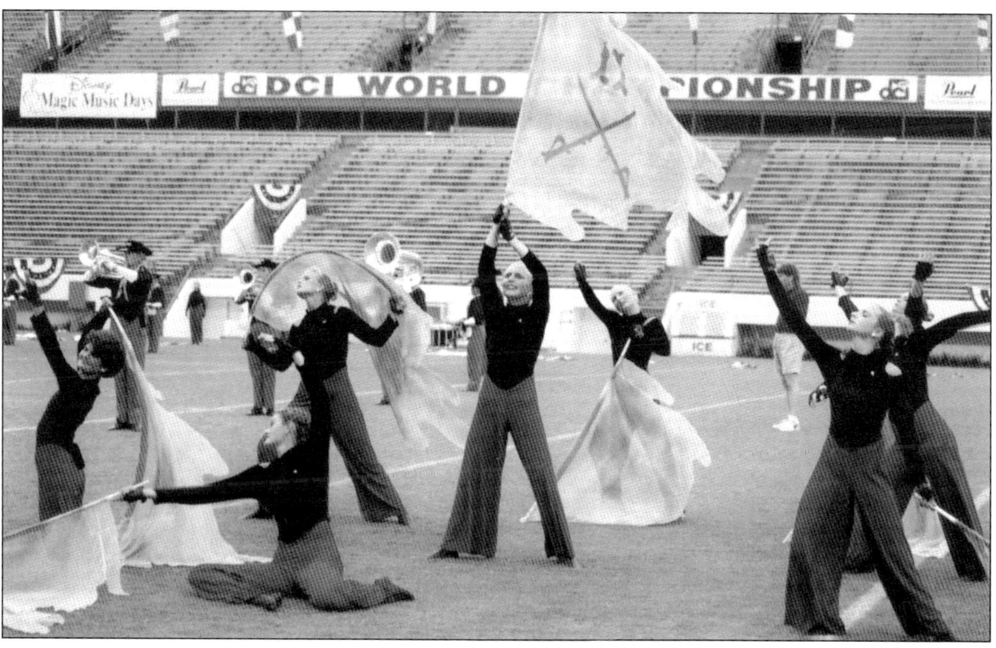

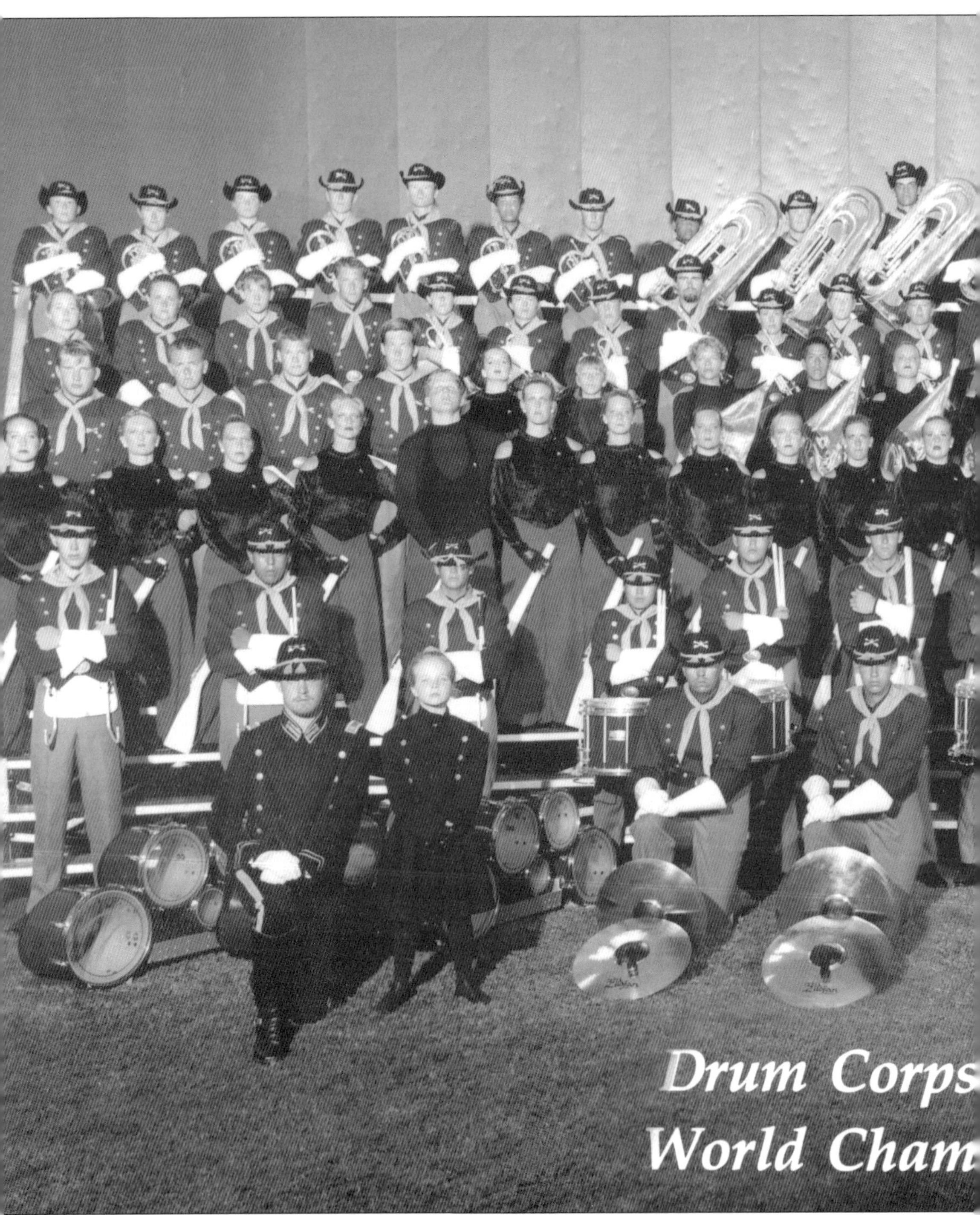

This Troopers group shot was taken at the DCI World Championships in Orlando in 1996. Drum major Joshua White is kneeling at far left in the first row, and standing next to him is Amber Evald,

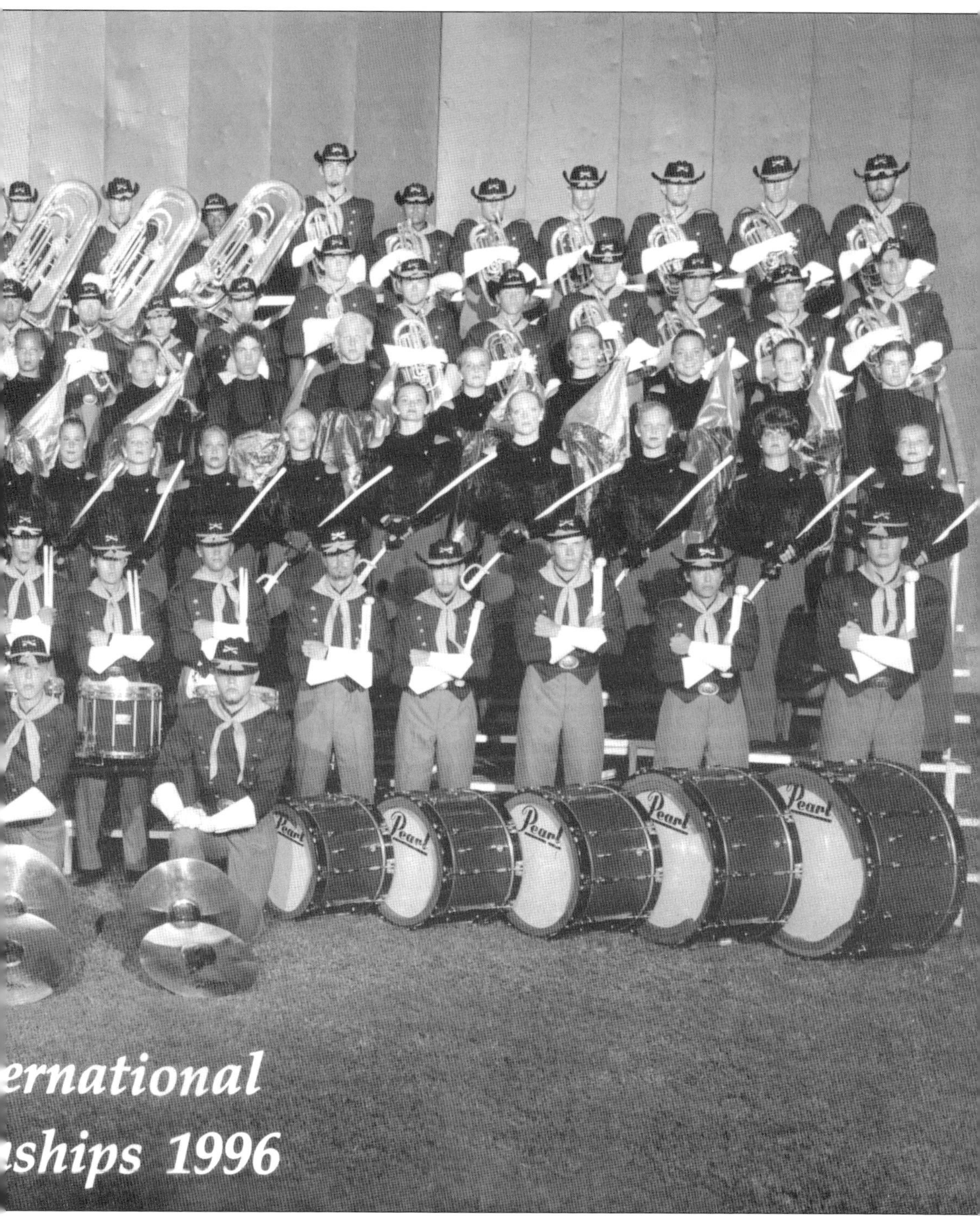

an honorary Trooper. Her mother, Sheri Evald, was tour director in 1995 and 1996. (Photograph from the Troopers Archives, courtesy of Pat Chagnon.)

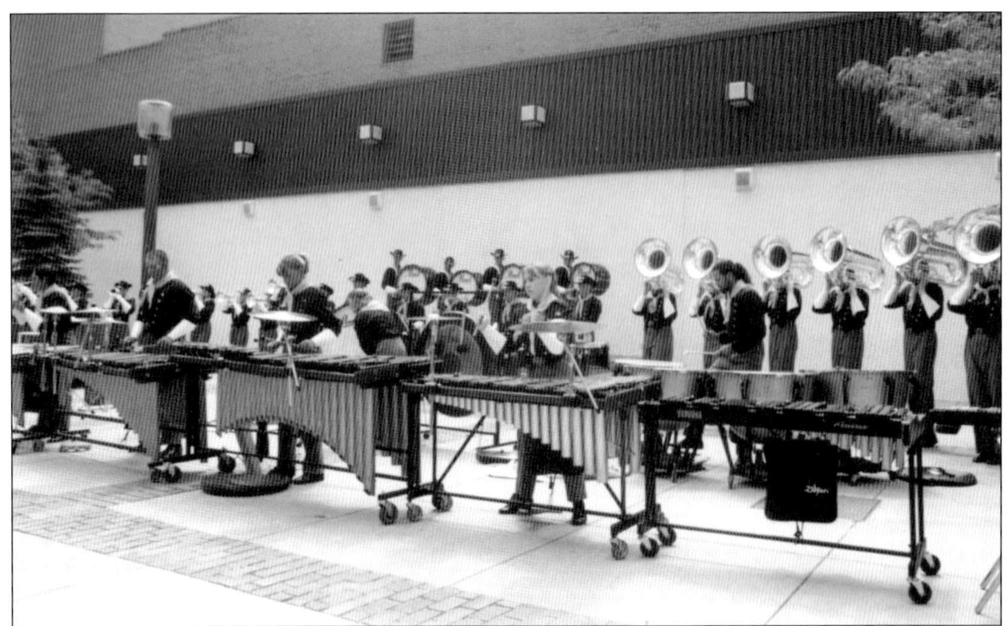

The Troopers play in the First Interstate Bank Plaza, located at the corner of First and Center Streets in downtown Casper, in July 1997. A quote from the 1997 DCI yearbook states: "There is no corps that 'says' America with as much pride, nor is any other corps more associated with the American flag, music of the American west and unabashed patriotism." (Courtesy of the Troopers Archives.)

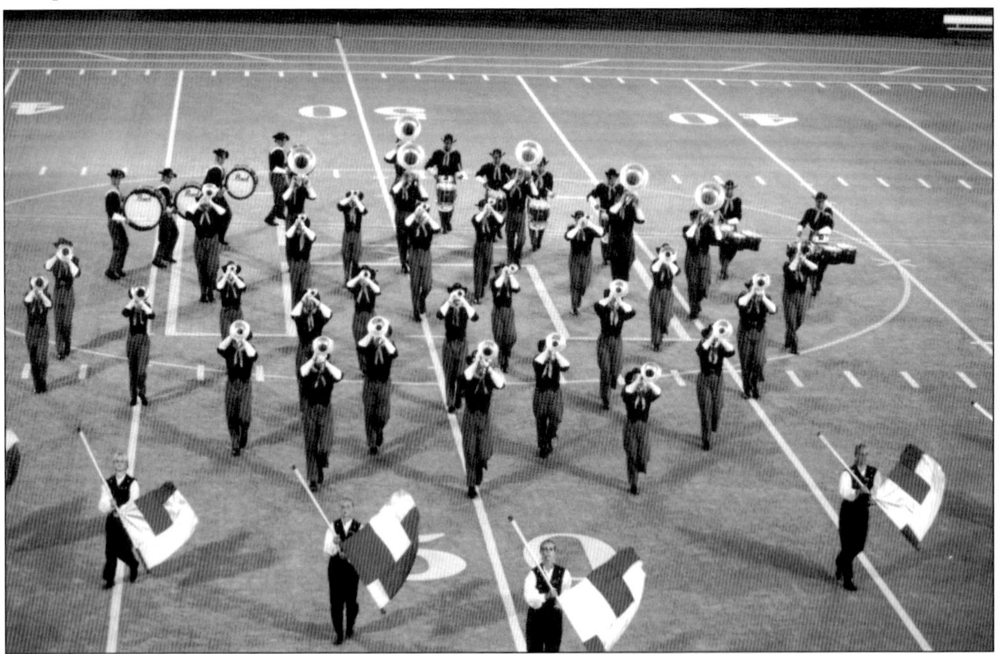

The Troopers perform at a contest in Hornell, New York, on July 30, 1997. They finished in seventh place that day. The musical performance was titled *New Beginnings* and included the songs "American Salute," "The Way West," "Magnificent Seven," and "America the Beautiful." (Photograph by David Rice, courtesy of Pat Chagnon.)

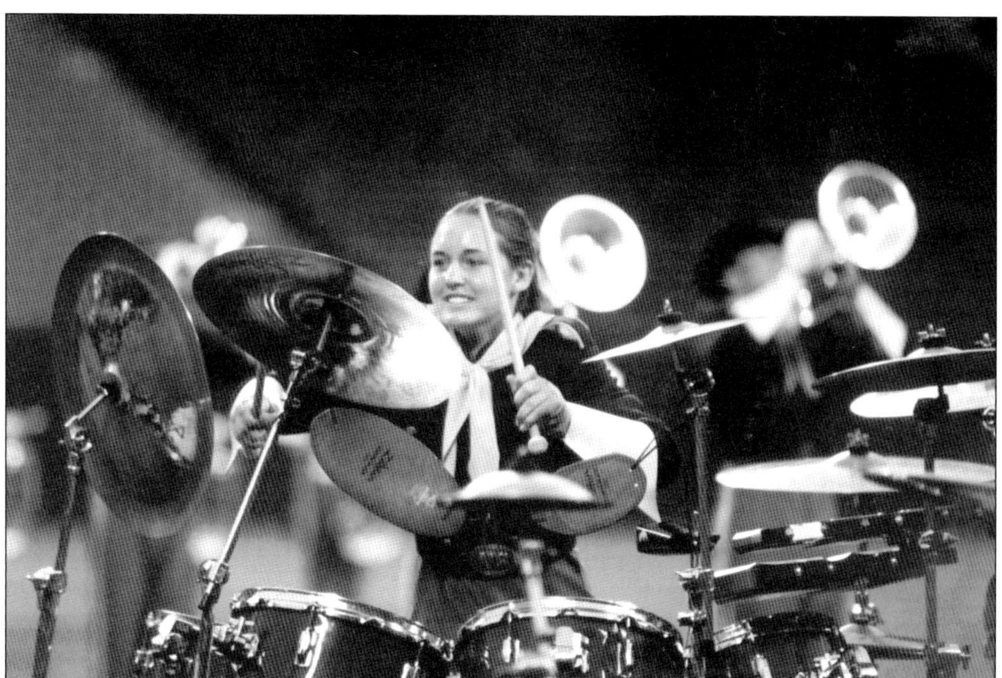

Drummer Amelia Young performs with the Troopers at Drums Along the Rockies at Mile High Stadium in Denver on July 18, 1998. Young is part of the front ensemble, or pit. The Troopers finished eighth that day. (Photograph by David Rice, courtesy of Pat Chagnon.)

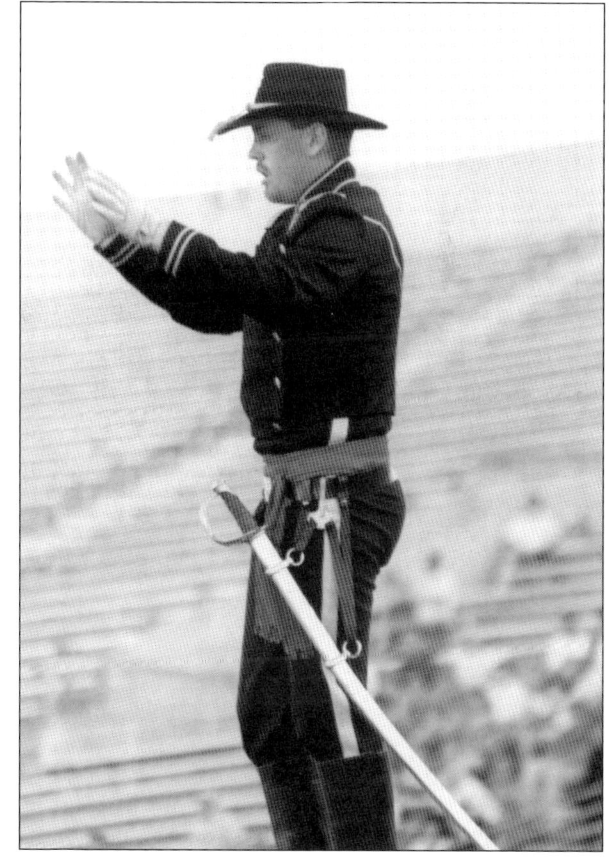

Troopers drum major Joshua White is pictured on top of the scaffolding at the DCI Mid-America Competition in Ypsilanti, Michigan, on August 1, 1998. White was in his last year as drum major, a position he had held since 1995. The Troopers drum major is the only one in DCI who is armed with a revolver. (Photograph by Dan Scafaldi, courtesy of Drum Corps World Archives.)

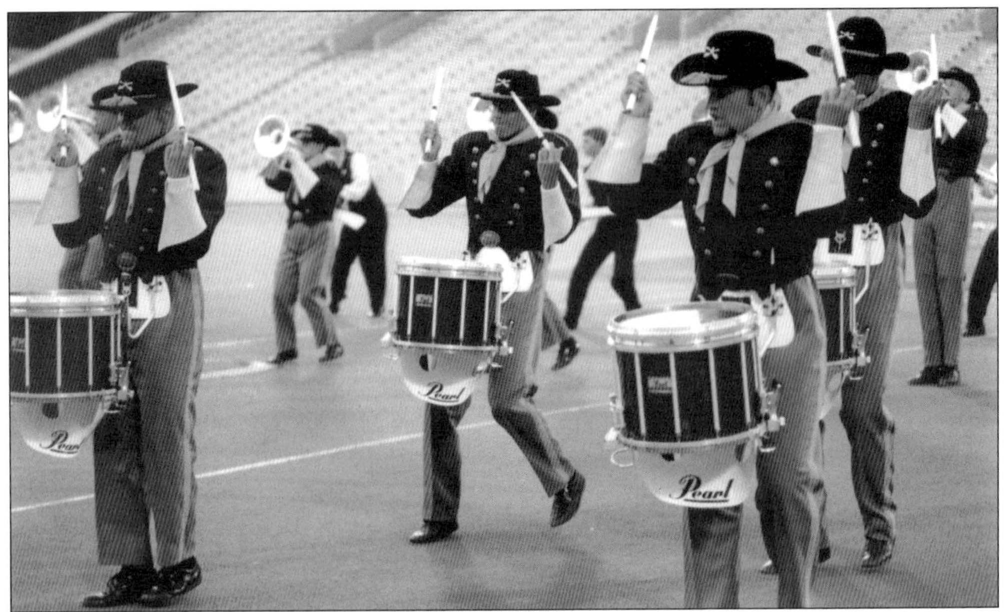

The Troopers snare drummers are shown at a performance in 1998. From left to right are (first row) Marc Cook and Greg Duchscher; (second row) Tanner Franks and Joe Foldenauer. The theme that year was *Forging a Frontier*, and the music selections were "Silverado," "Tombstone," "Ghost Riders in the Sky," and "How the West Was Won." (Photograph by Ron Walloch, courtesy of Drum Corps World Archives.)

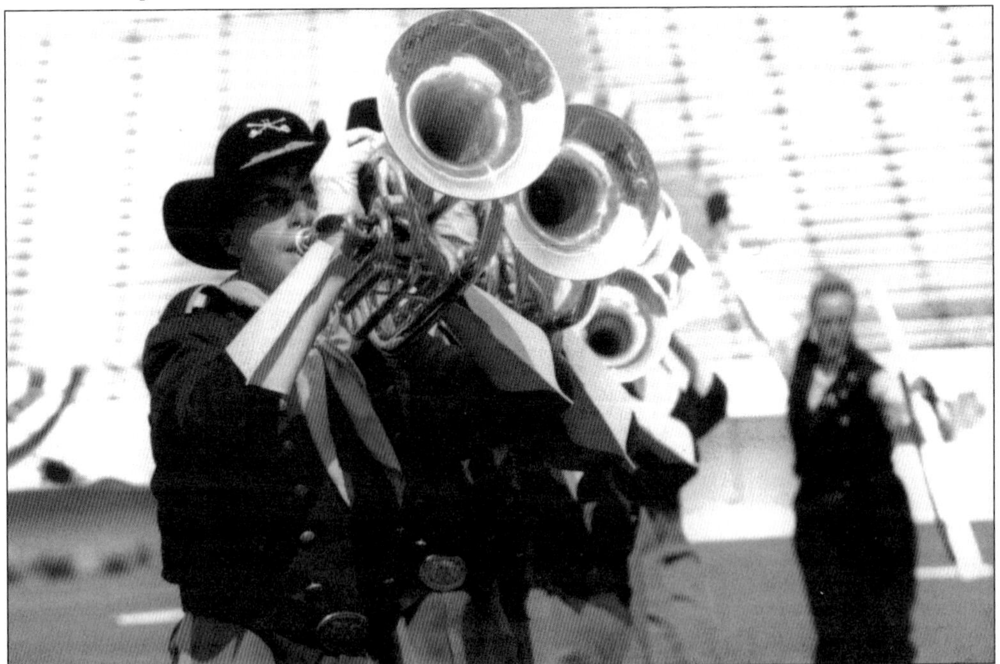

The Troopers baritones play at the DCI World Championships Quarterfinals in Orlando on August 13, 1998. Scott Bradford is the lead baritone in the line. This was his rookie year, and he went on to march with the Troopers for four years. They finished in 14th place at the DCI Championships. (Photograph from the Troopers Archives, courtesy of Pat Chagnon.)

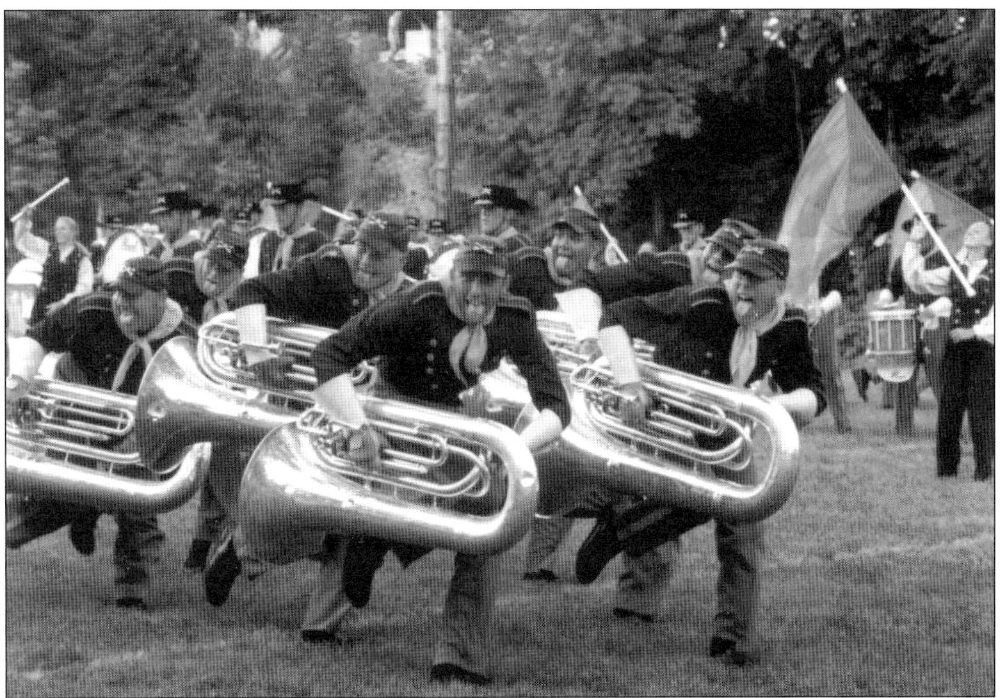
The Troopers contra players are caught mid-performance in 1999. From left to right are (first row) Jake McIntosh; (second row) Mark Quintero, Shane Condie, and Matthew Murphy; (third row) Matt Loup, Warren "Wes" Eagle, and Michael Rossolo. During the fifth movement of *Billy the Kid*, most of the corps did something silly. For their part, the contras stuck out their tongues. (Photograph by Ron Walloch, courtesy of Drum Corps World Archives.)

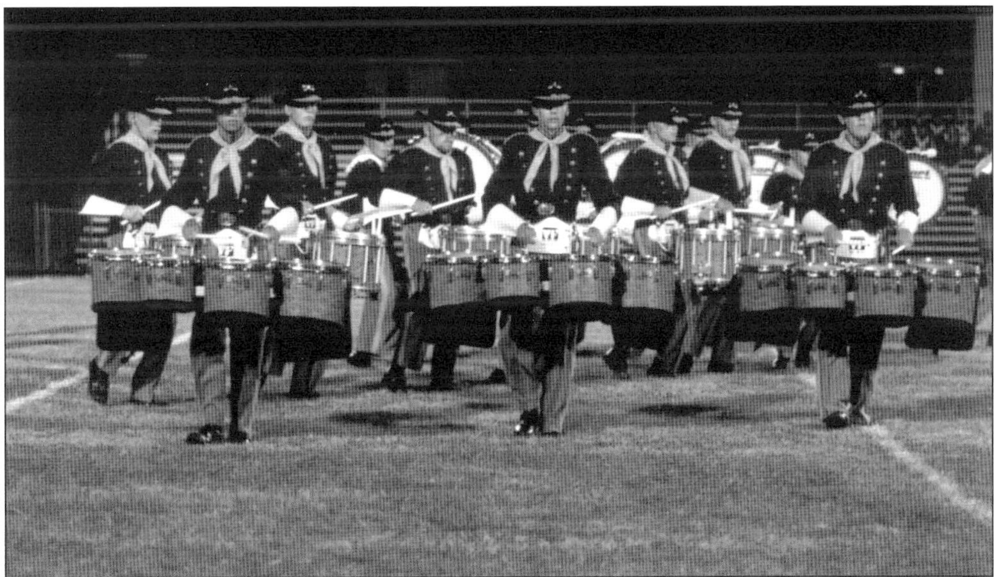
The Troopers drum line performs in 1999. From left to right are (first row) Dan Perkins, Morgan Nowlen, and Jonathan Brownley; (second row) Matt Lippincott, Tyler Bushman, Marc Cook, Tanner Franks, Sam Campbell, and Tyson Fuller; (third row) Juan Soria, Brian Collier, Josiah Halverson, and Danny Vasquer. (Photograph by David Rice, courtesy of Drum Corps World Archives.)

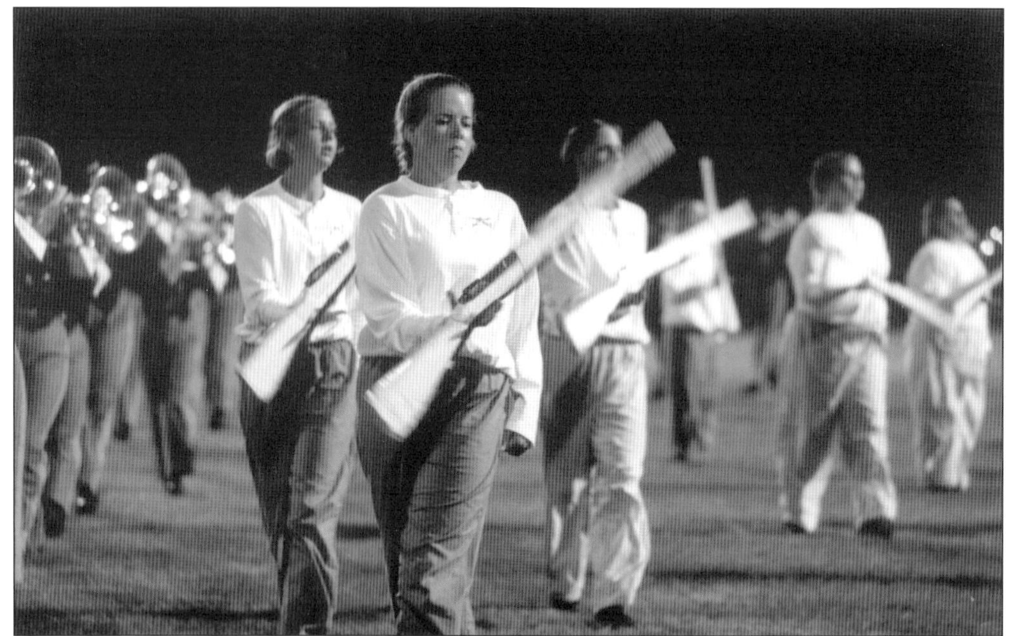

The Troopers color guard twirls rifles in a performance in Wyoming in 1999. From left to right are (first row) Alicia Martin; (second row) Sarah McCormick, Jake Campbell, Brooke Swanson, and Teresa ?. The causal look of the color guard uniforms did not go over well with the judges, so they were quickly changed to a more colorful style (see below). (Photograph by Ron Walloch, courtesy of Drum Corps World Archives.)

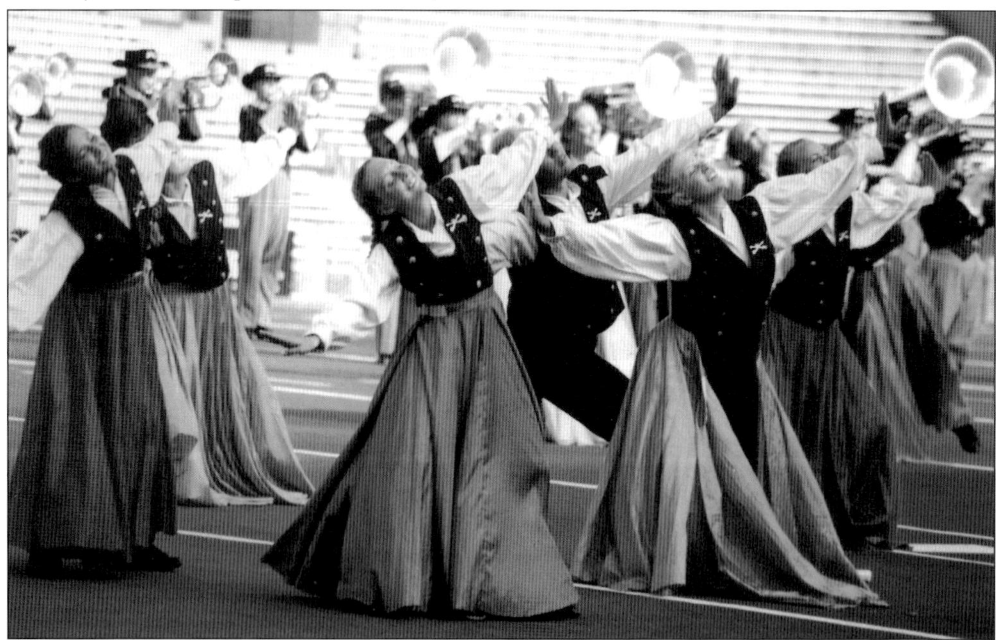

The Troopers color guard performs at the DCI World Championships Quarterfinals in Madison on August 12, 1999. From left to right are (first row) Sara Querhn and Amanda Stephenson; (second row) Lisette Martinez, Warren O'Dell, and Katy Ferguson; (third row) Amber Louton. They finished 21st that year. (Photograph by David Rice, courtesy of Drum Corps World Archives.)

Six

2000s
Turmoil and Reformation

There were several high points for the Troopers Drum & Bugle Corps in the 2000s. Wyoming's governor, Jim Geringer, proclaimed July 13, 2001, to be Casper Trooper Day in Wyoming. His reasoning was that "in the past 44 years, the Troopers have won 11 international championships and have consistently been among the top 20 drum corps in the world. The Troopers are the only drum and bugle corps in the state of Wyoming, and therefore offer a rare opportunity for some of our most talented young people to participate in this unique learning experience." Also in 2001, they were invited to participate in George W. Bush's presidential inaugural parade in January.

Competitively, the Troopers started slipping even more, and 2004 saw them place 23rd at the DCI Finals. Things did not get better from there. They were having financial issues, and in addition, the DCI board of directors suspended the Troopers from competition in late 2005 for noncompliance with membership rules. They remained inactive for the 2006 season while they reorganized. The Troopers board of directors were determined that they would march again. To start this process, Fred Morris was appointed corps director in late spring of 2006, and the Troopers were reinstated as a DCI Division I corps on October 3 of that year.

The Troopers finished out the decade with things looking better. They placed 20th at DCI Finals in 2007, 16th in 2008, and cracked the top 12 in 2009 with a 12th-place finish. The Troopers celebrated their 50th anniversary in 2008, and in 2009, Fred Morris was named Director of the Year by DCI.

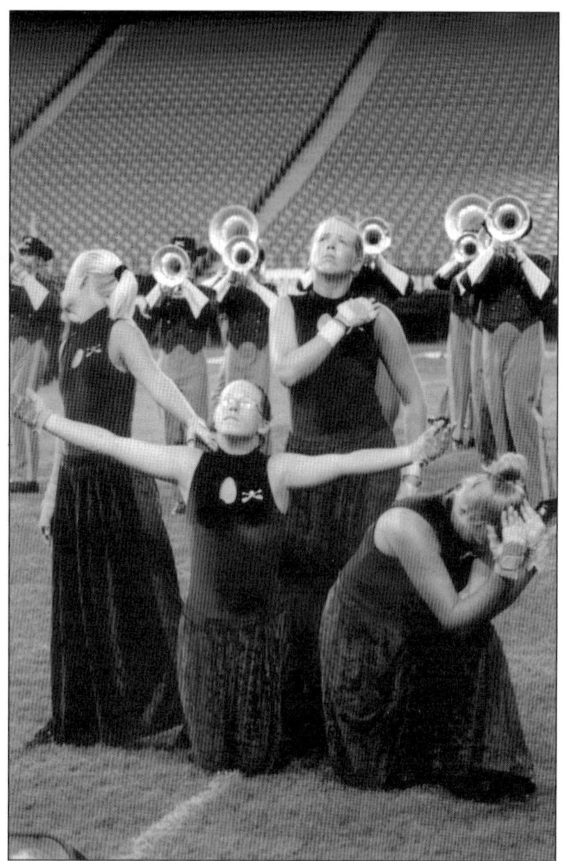

The Troopers color guard performs at Drums Along the Rockies in Denver on July 15, 2000. The 2000 DCI Championship program stated: "This is a show more of the entire nation than its western region—as many past offerings were—as the corps embraces the values that made this country great from sea to shining sea." (Photograph by Karen Sunmark, courtesy of Drum Corps World Archives.)

Drum major Adam Corson walks onto the field in front of the drum line in 2000. The snare drummers, from left to right, are Jon Thornhill, Tanner Franks, Greg Duchscher, Marc Cook, and Nick Waters. Corson was the Troopers' drum major in 1999 and 2000. (Photograph by Richard Wersinger, courtesy of Drum Corps World Archives.)

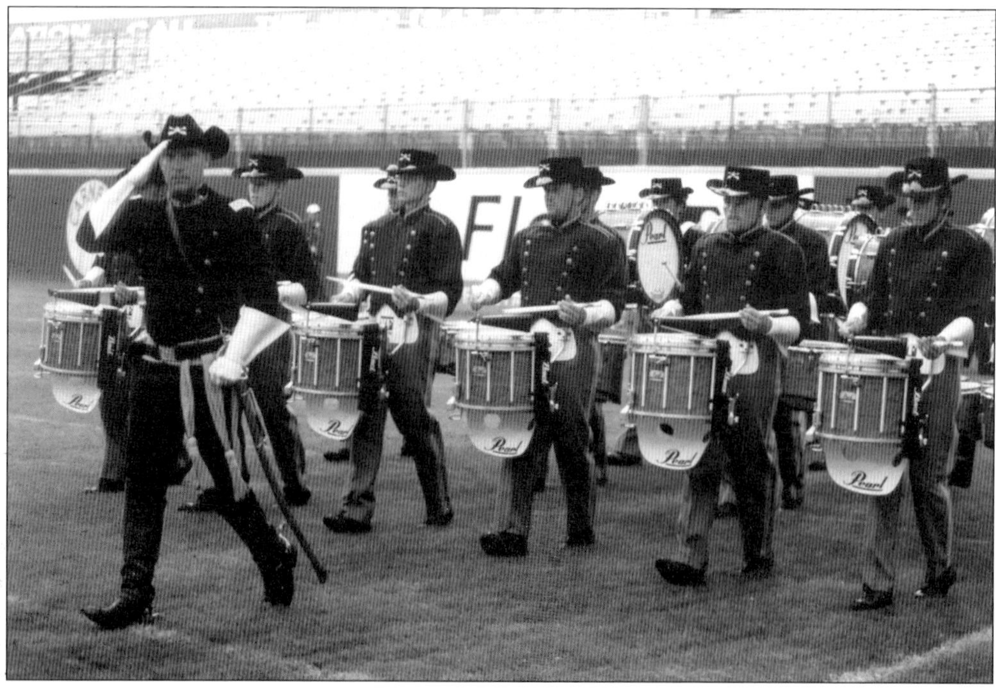

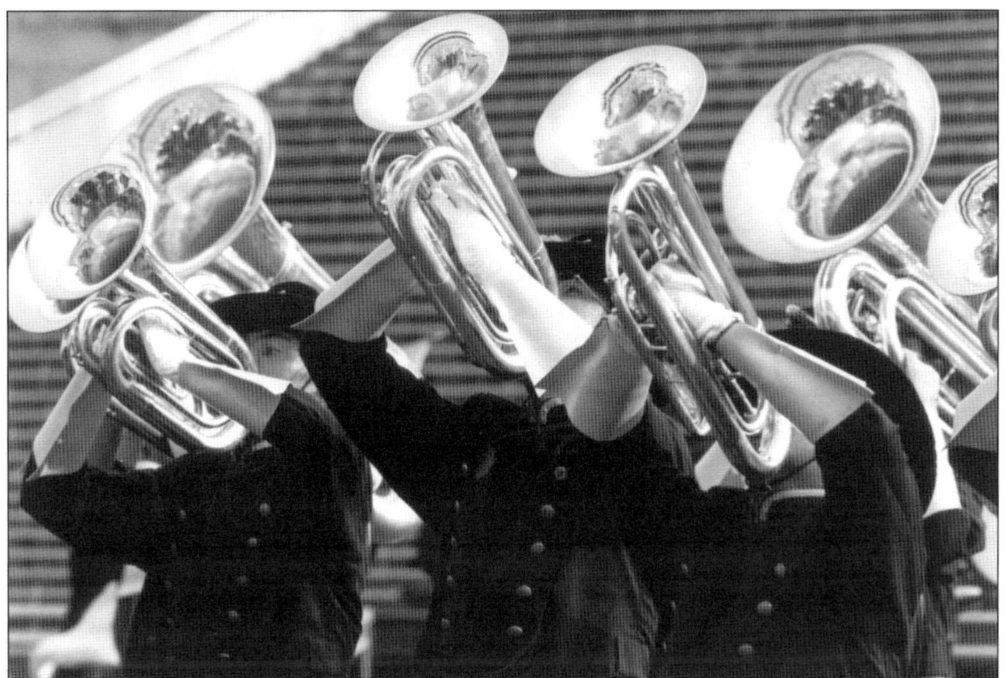

The Troopers baritone line performs at the DCI World Championships Quarterfinals in College Park, Maryland, on August 10, 2000. They placed 19th that year at the DCI Championships. The Troopers participated in 25 competitions in 17 states, from California to New York. (Photograph by Ron Walloch, courtesy of Drum Corps World Archives.)

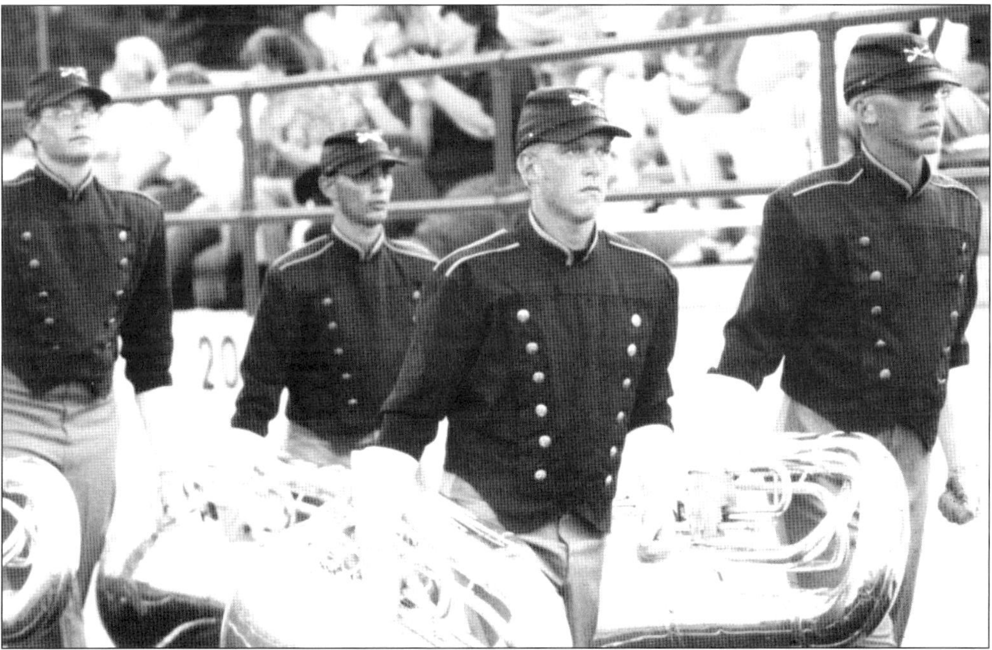

Four Troopers contra players carry their horns past the stands in 2001. From left to right are (first row) Kenny Nelson and Matthew Murphy; (second row) Matt Loup and unidentified. (Photograph by Dan Scafaldi, courtesy of Drum Corps World Archives.)

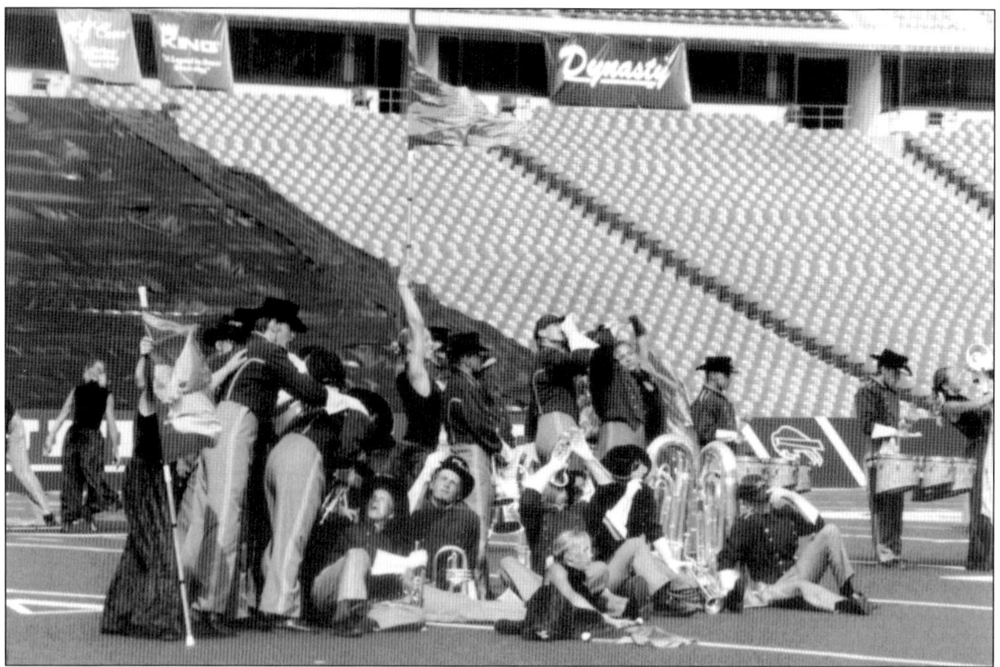

Above, the Troopers strike a pose during their performance at the DCI Championships Division I Quarterfinals in Buffalo on August 9, 2001. The multi-tenor drummers (below) walk in step with each other. They finished 19th that day. The 2001 DCI Championship program stated: "Troopers started the year representing Wyoming in the 54th Presidential Inaugural Parade, an uncommon tribute for a unit that typically performs only during the summer. But 'uncommon' and 'tribute' are words that best describe the entire year experienced by 'America's Corps,' which has chosen to honor Aaron Copland, 'America's Composer,' on the 100th Anniversary of his birth." (Both photographs by Harry Heidelmark, courtesy of Drum Corps World Archives.)

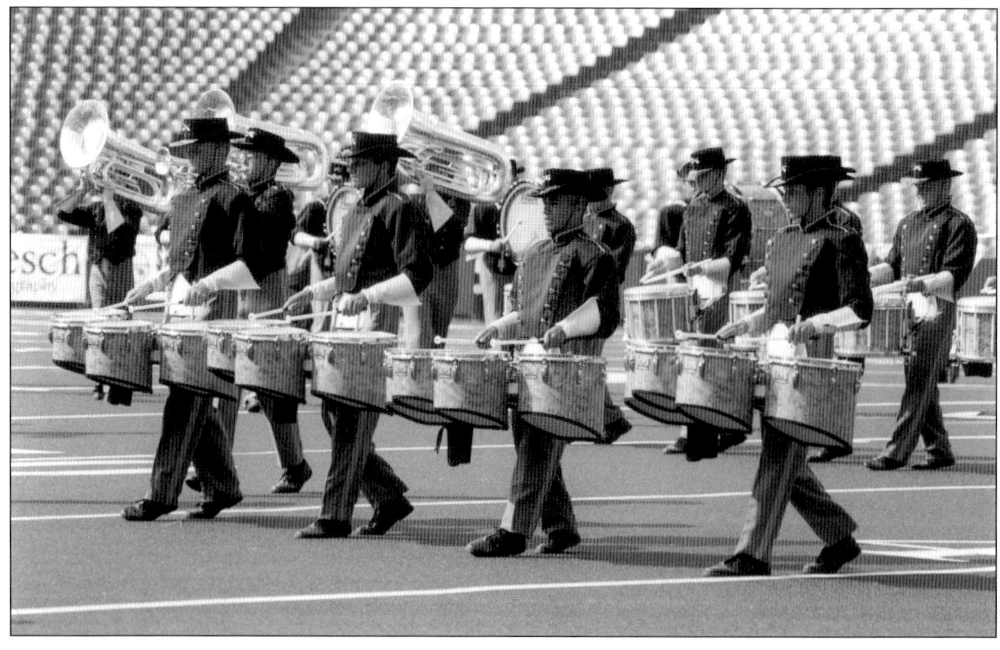

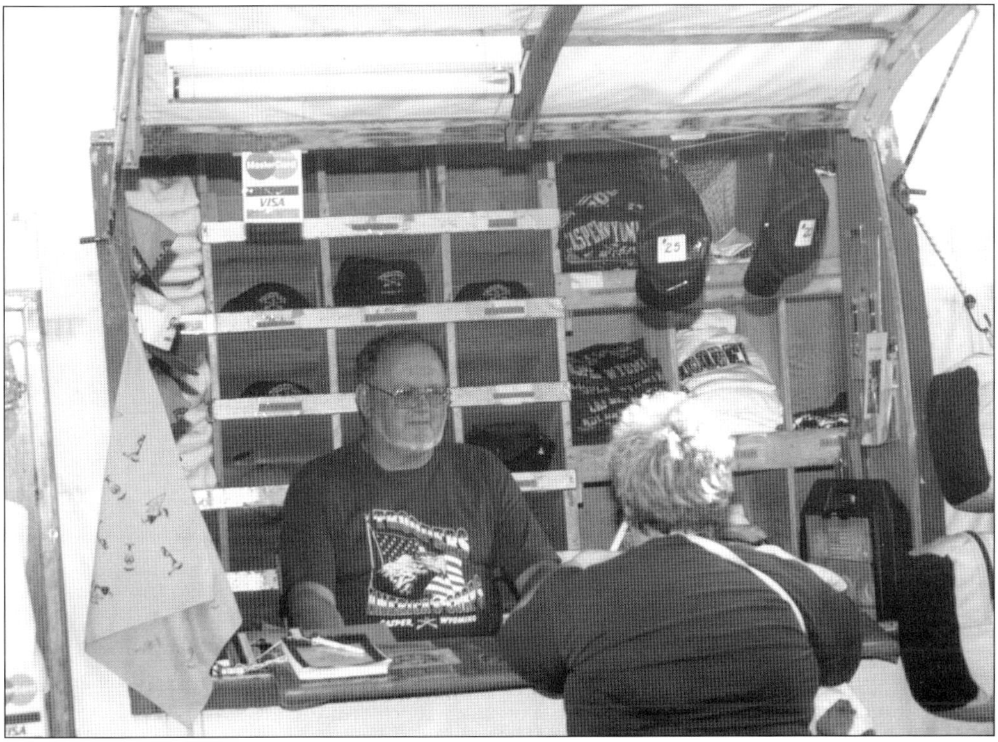

Ted "Dad" Gilbert is shown in the Troopers' sheep wagon selling souvenirs in 2001 or 2002. Gilbert is the father of Karl, Kurt, Kent, Kyle, and Kari Gilbert, who all marched in the Troopers. He and his wife, Traute Gilbert, have also been "Dad" and "Mom" to many other members of the corps. The t-shirt he is wearing was available after the 2001 inaugural parade. (Courtesy of Drum Corps World Archives.)

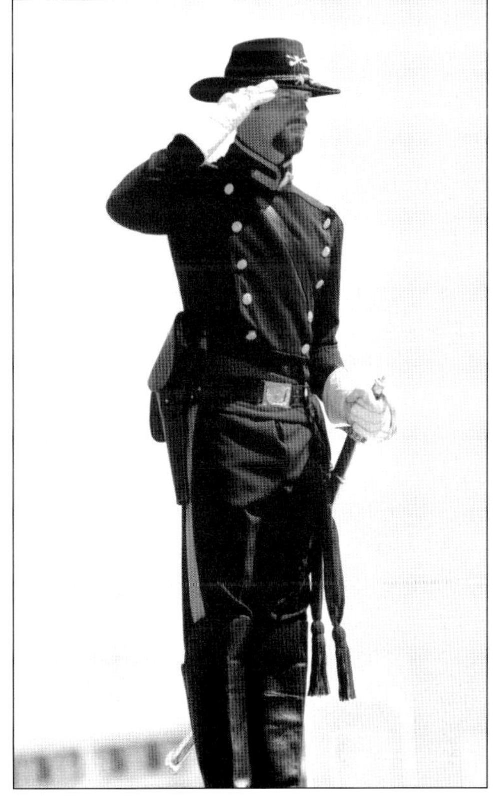

Drum major Daniel Perkins salutes in 2002. Perkins served as the Troopers' drum major in 2001 and 2002. The theme for the show in 2002 was *Red, White, Blue*, and the music was decidedly not Western. The song selections were "Javelin," "An American Elegy," and "Into the Storm." (Photograph by David Rice, courtesy of Drum Corps World Archives.)

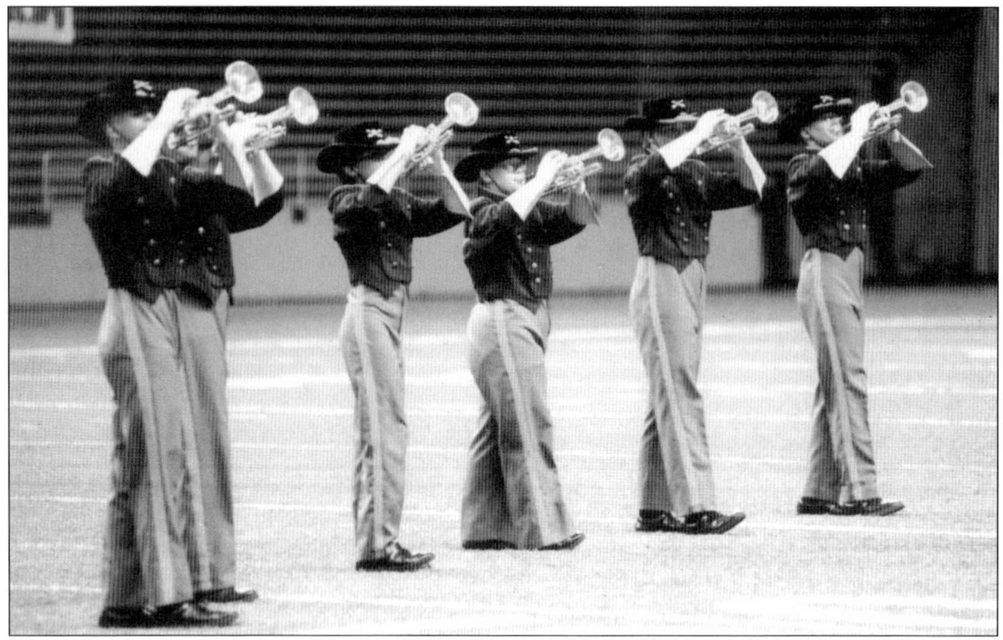

The Troopers trumpet players perform in the Southwestern Championships in San Antonio, Texas, on July 20, 2002. They finished 11th in the afternoon show. The Troopers performed throughout the South and Southwest in the latter half of July 2002. They competed in Arizona, New Mexico, Texas, Louisiana, Mississippi, and Georgia. (Photograph by David Rice, courtesy of Drum Corps World Archives.)

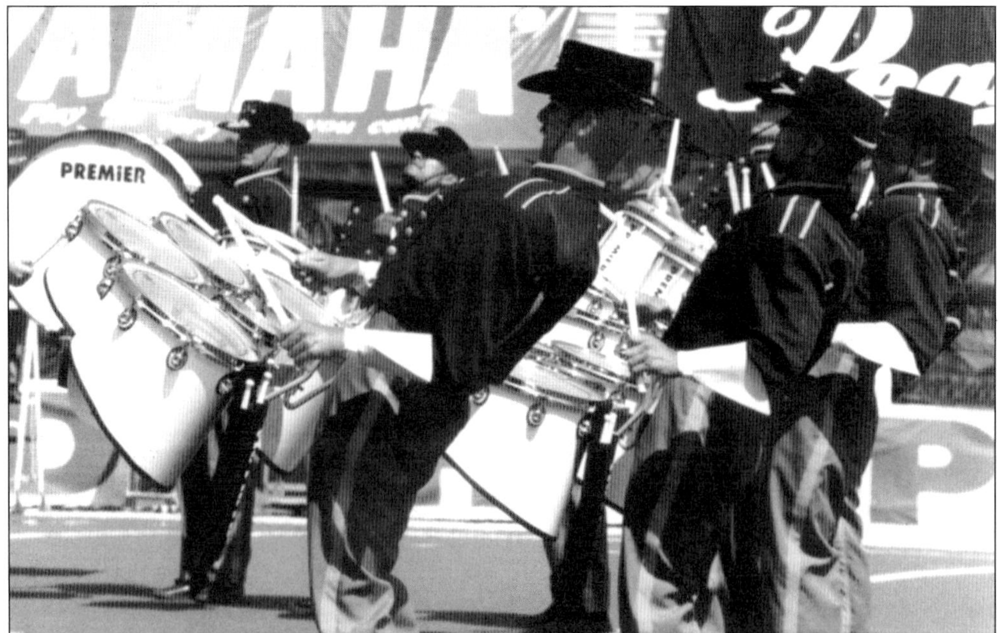

The Troopers drum line is pictured at the DCI World Championships Quarterfinals in Madison on August 8, 2002. They placed 21st in that competition. The Troopers played in 24 competitions in 17 states in 2002, including three in both Wisconsin and Minnesota and two each in Ohio, Illinois, and Texas. (Photograph by David Rice, courtesy of Drum Corps World Archives.)

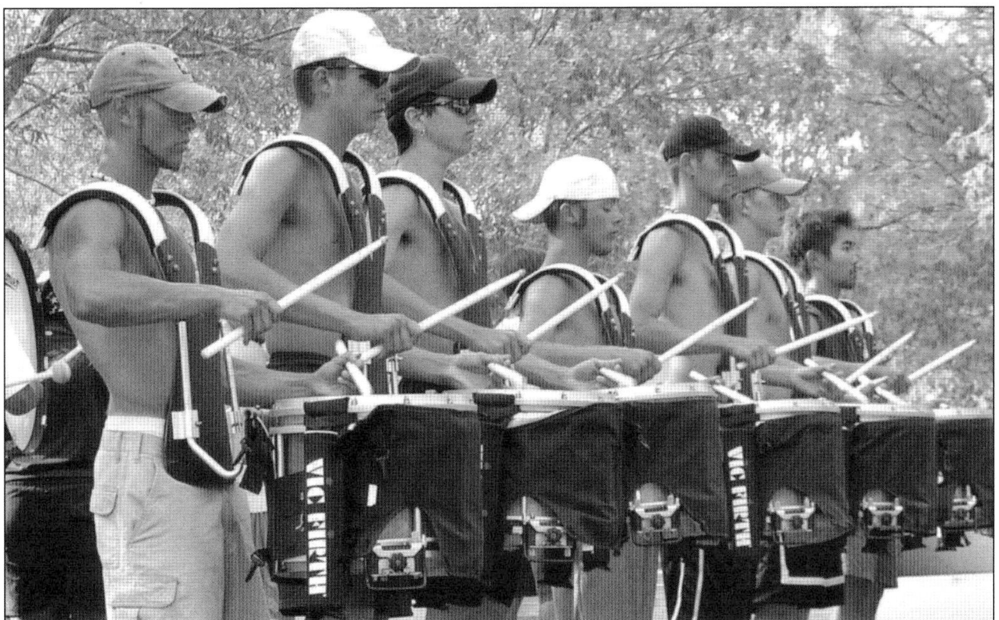

The Troopers snare drummers practice in Albuquerque, New Mexico, before a competition on July 14, 2003. From left to right are Tyson Fuller, two unidentified, Shane Nickels, Adam Poppenhagen, possibly Micah Westblade, and unidentified. They placed sixth in the competition that day. (Photograph by J. McLean, courtesy of Pat Chagnon.)

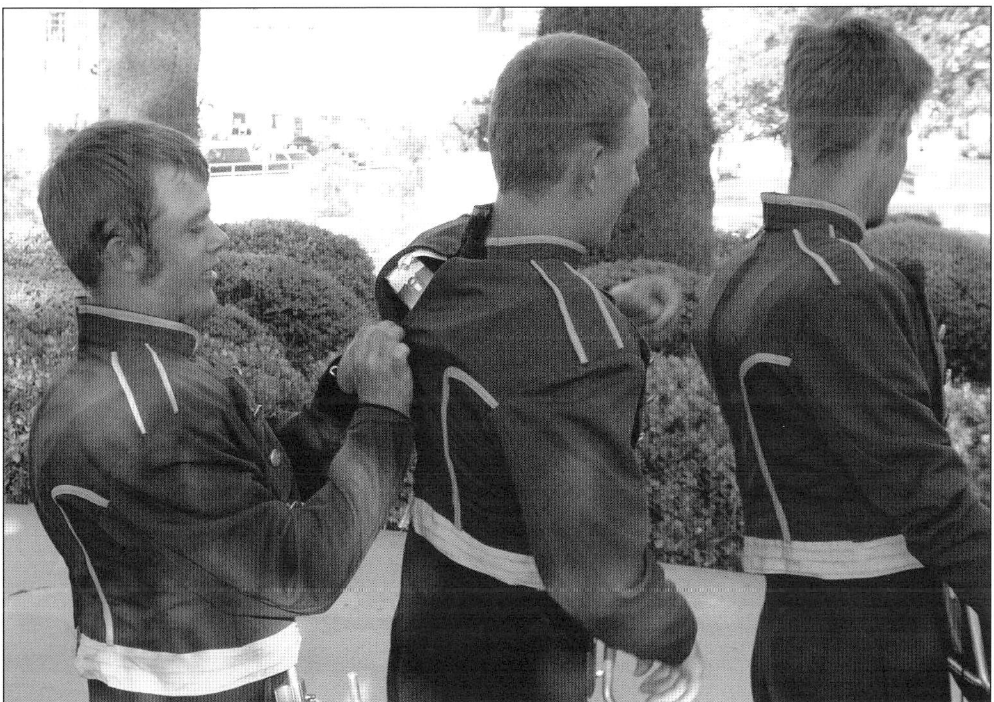

The Troopers get ready for a competition in El Paso on July 15, 2003. The uniforms are designed to accommodate the harnesses and apparatus that the members wear to support their instruments. The Troopers finished in sixth place that day. (Photograph by J. McLean, courtesy of Pat Chagnon.)

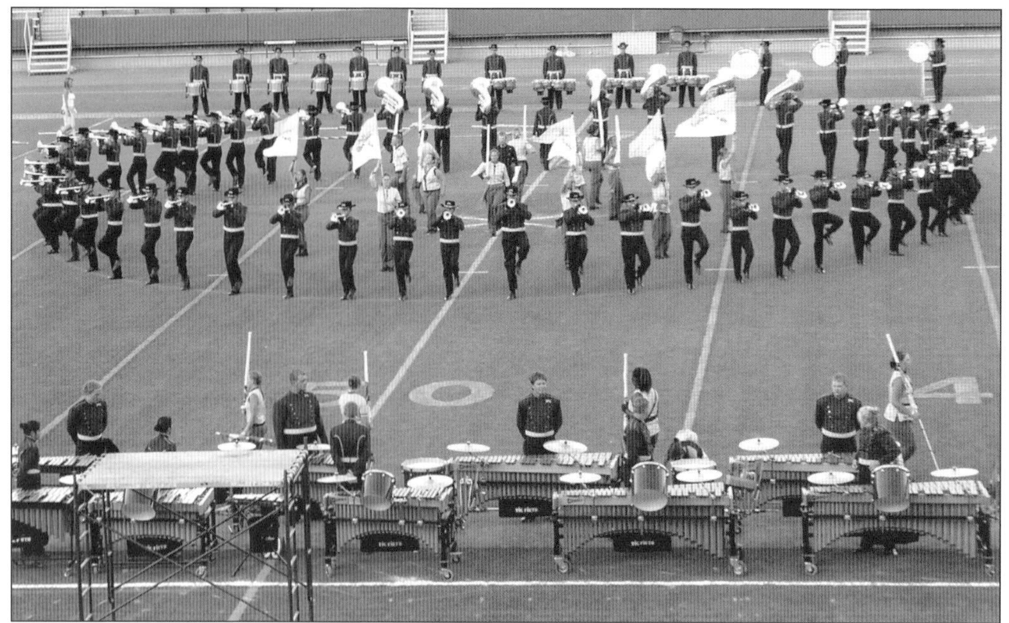

The Troopers perform the sunburst at the Sun Bowl Stadium at the University of Texas in El Paso on July 15, 2003. Drum major Michael Gough is in the center of the circle. The theme that year, *Reflections of the Blue & the Gray*, harkened back to the Civil War and the 11th Ohio Volunteer Cavalry, from whom the Troopers take their name. (Photograph by J. McLean, courtesy of Pat Chagnon.)

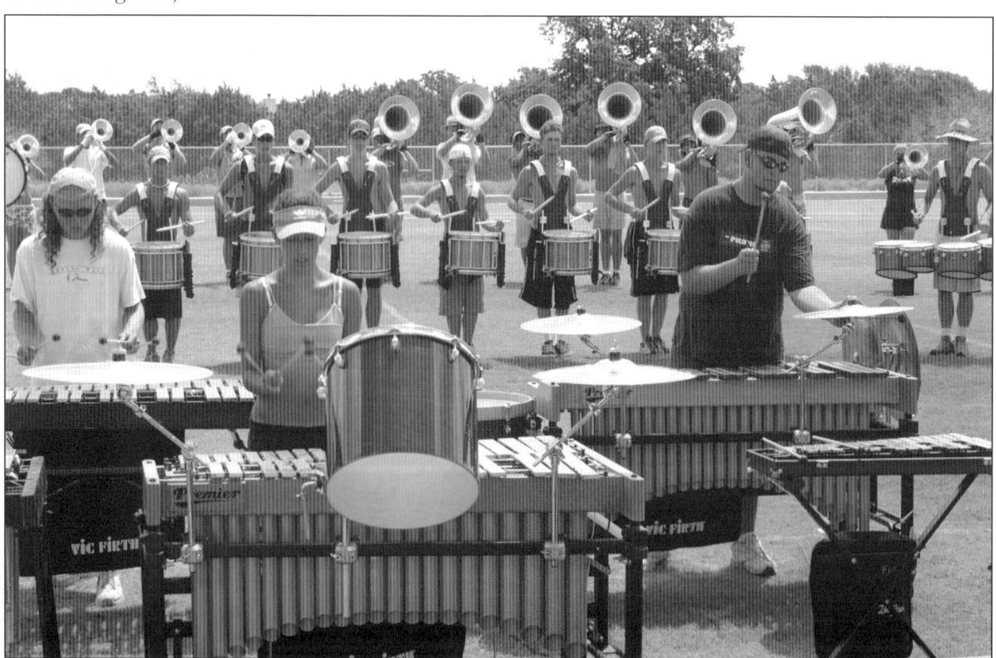

The Troopers practice in a park in Cedar Park, Texas, on July 17, 2003. Members of the front ensemble are, from left to right, unidentified, Ruby Jimenez, and William Watkins. The Troopers had five performances in seven days in Texas. They competed in El Paso, Midland, Leander, San Antonio, and Wichita Falls between July 15 and 21. (Photograph by Lanclos, courtesy of Pat Chagnon.)

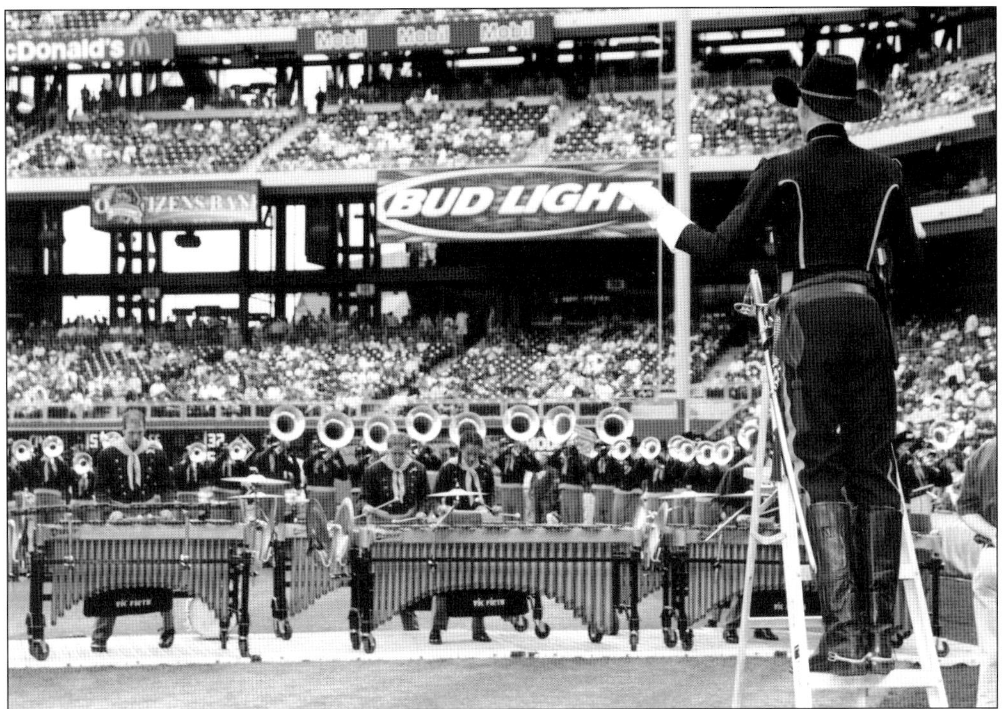

The Troopers play before a Phillies baseball game in Philadelphia, Pennsylvania, on July 22, 2004. Drum major Michael Gough (above) conducts during the performance, and the guard (below) performs with the Phillies mascot the Phillie Phanatic. The Troopers played the day before at the Three Rivers Summer Music Games in Pittsburgh, Pennsylvania, and performed the following day at the DCI Eastern Classic in Allentown. (Both photographs by Heddy Bergsman, courtesy of Pat Chagnon.)

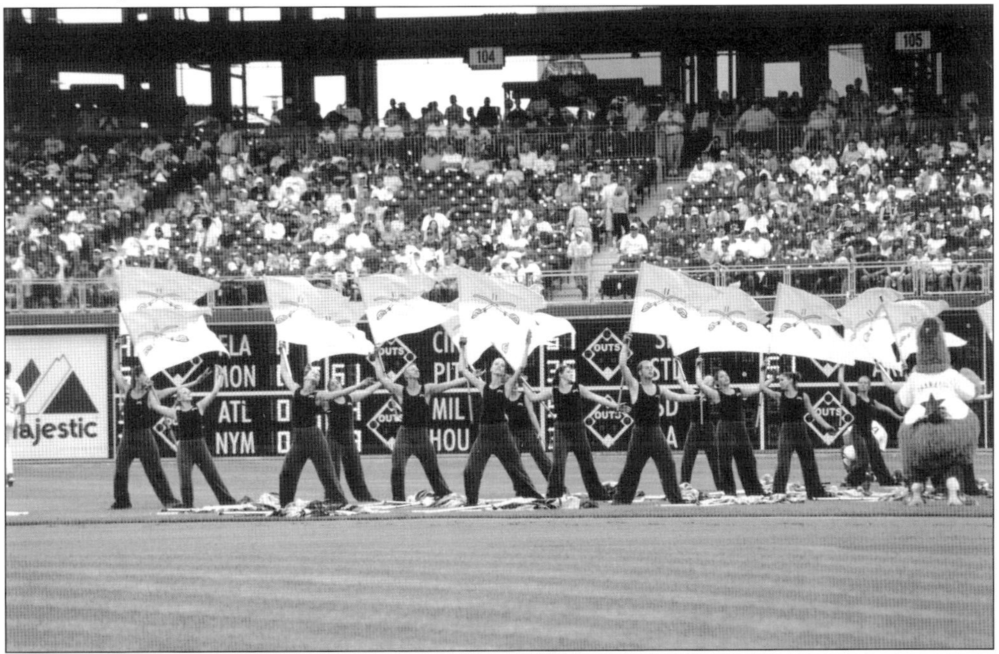

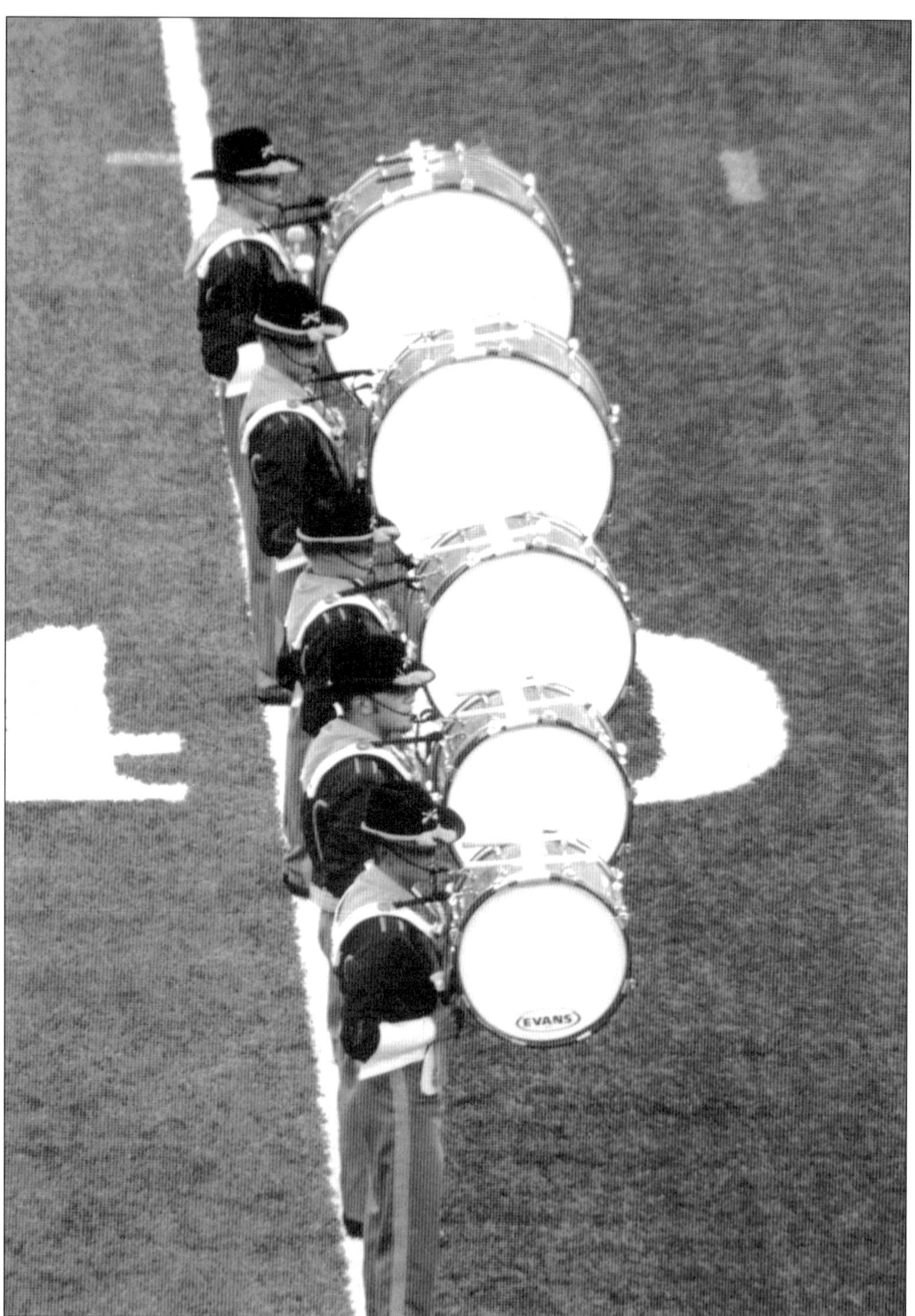

The Troopers bass drummers are pictured on the 40-yard line during the afternoon show at the DCI Midwestern Preliminaries in Indianapolis, Indiana, on July 30, 2005. From top to bottom are Matthew Larson, Jared Floyd, Betsy Sharp, Brian Harris, and Herschel Wilde. The Troopers placed 15th that day. (Photograph by Ron Walloch, courtesy of Drum Corps World Archives.)

The 2007 Troopers tour poster shows a grueling travel schedule. After not competing in 2006, the Troopers came back strong in 2007. They took part in 30 competitions in 19 states, traveling all around the country from as far east as New York to California in the west. (Photograph by Pat Chagnon.)

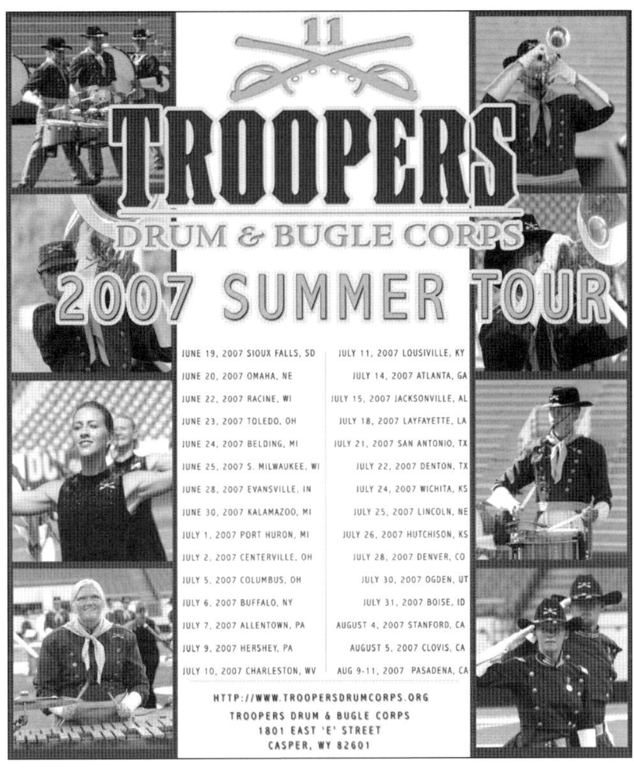

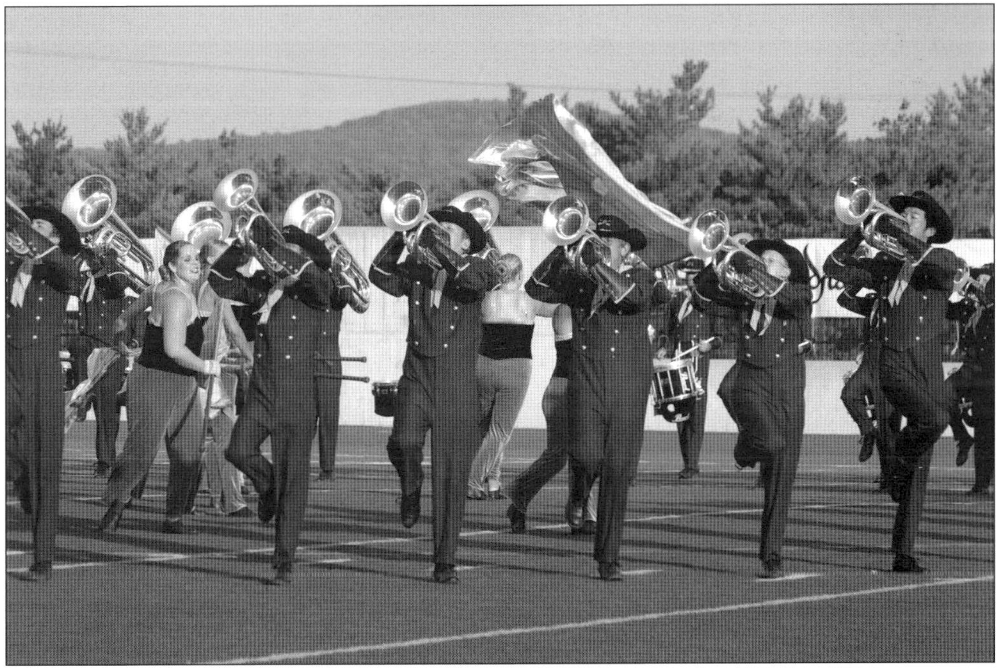

The Troopers perform at the DCI Eastern Classic in Allentown on July 7, 2007. The baritones are, from left to right, Dieter Wiselogel, Brandon Legnion, Jason Weimer, Donnie Godbey, Jenny Hawk, and Tomohide Kodama. Brandi Ball is the color guard member on the left, and Morgan Daisy Jay has her back to the camera. They placed 10th that day. (Photograph by Pat Chagnon.)

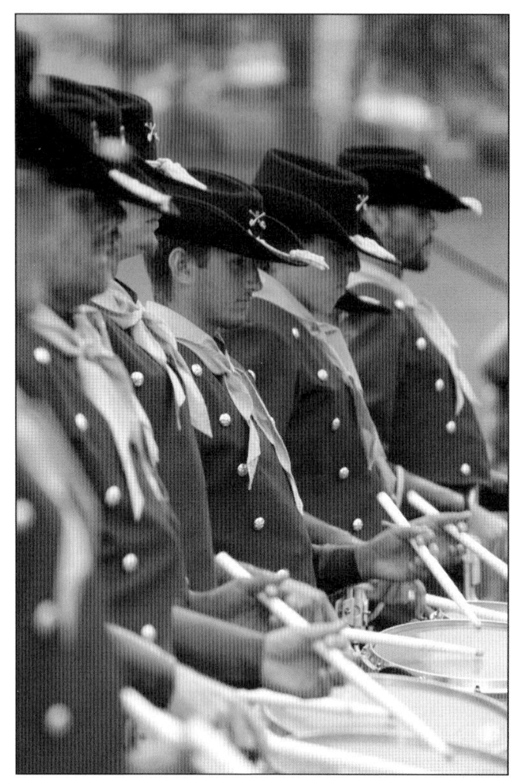

The Troopers drum line (left) performs in Cheyenne on July 27, 2007. From left to right are Mike Craft, Danny Wells, Markus Stratton, Nick Manton, Shawn Hajizadeh, Jonathan Coppinger, and Drew Smith. After the performance, Mike Ottoes (below), with Milward Simpson in the background, spoke about the changes to the Troopers organization over the last year and a half. Ottoes was a horn player in the Troopers between 1988 and 1992. He was part of the administrative team between 1996 and 1998, and was appointed executive director of the Troopers in the fall of 2005. Ottoes was elected to the Troopers Hall of Fame in 2015. (Both photographs by Pat Chagnon.)

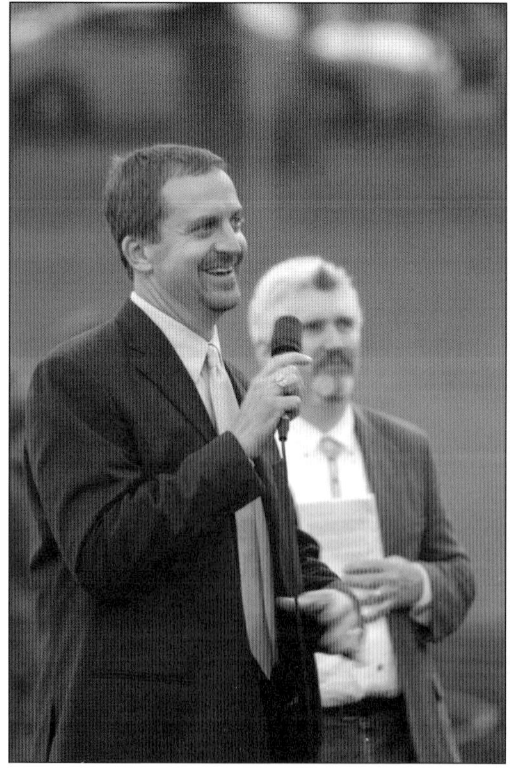

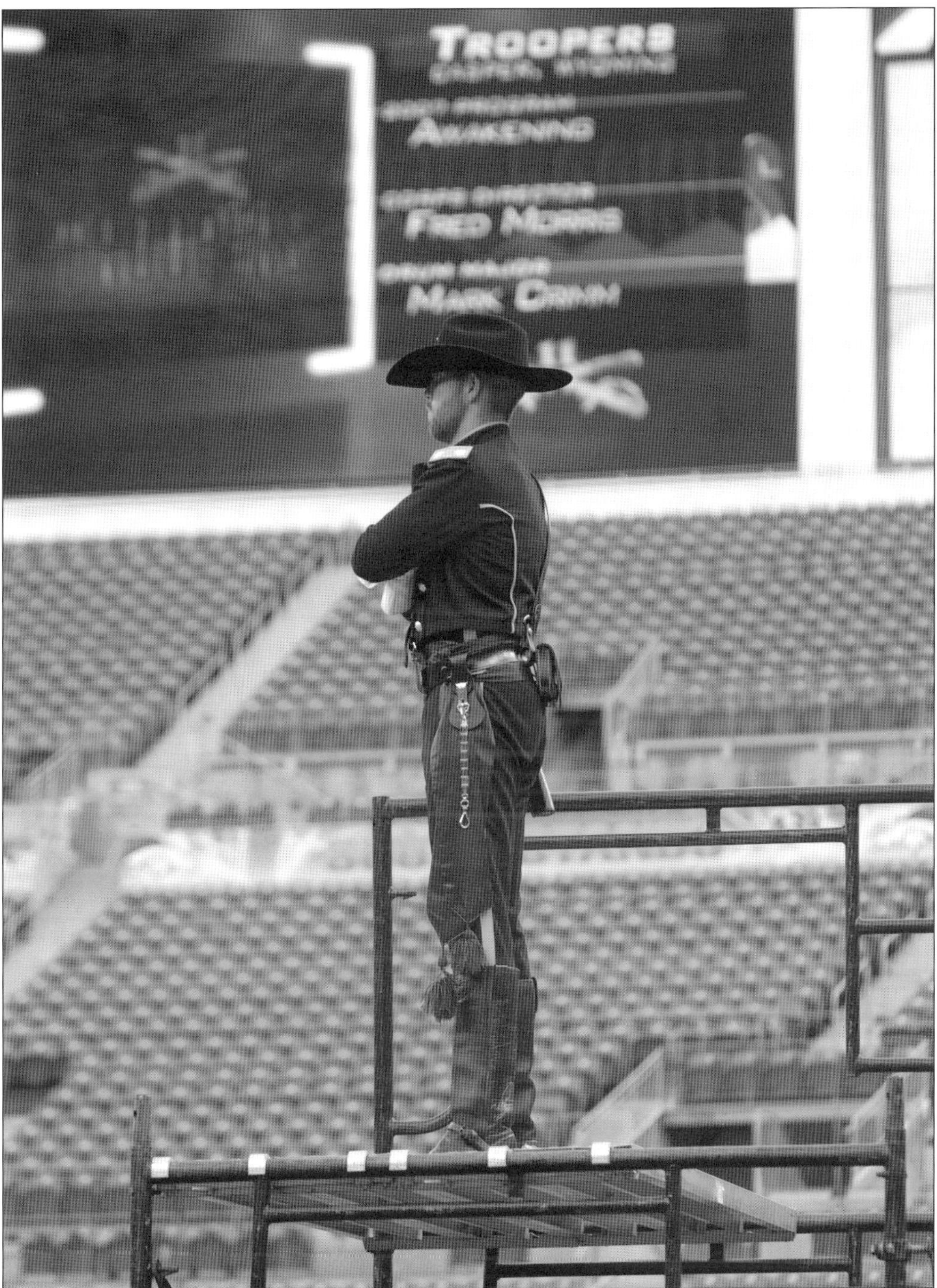

Drum major Mark Crimm waits on the scaffolding before the Troopers' performance at the Drums Along the Rockies in Denver on July 28, 2007. Behind him is an electronic sign with information about the Troopers. Crimm was the drum major in 2005 and 2007. The show was aptly titled *Awakening*, and the musical selections "Joy," "Unsquare Dance," "Ever Braver, Ever Stronger (An American Elegy)," and "American Faces" conveyed the rebirth of the Troopers. (Photograph by Pat Chagnon.)

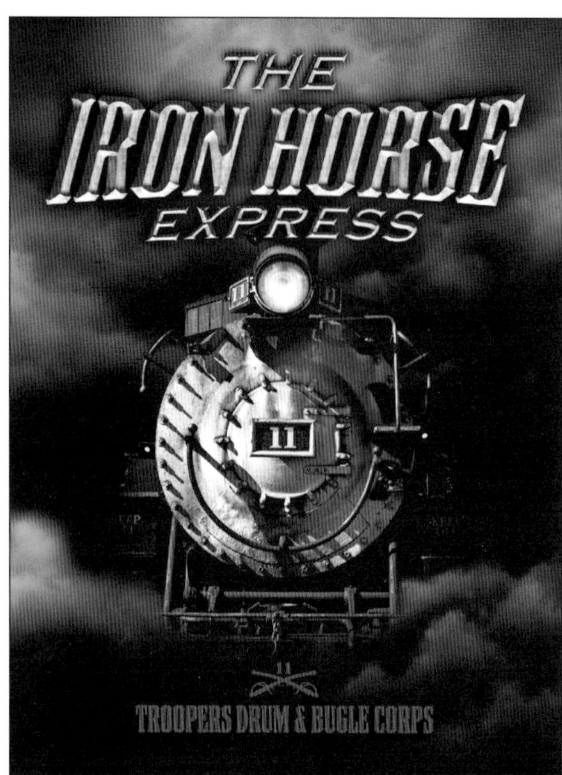

The Troopers' 2008 show poster powerfully displays that year's theme of *The Iron Horse Express*. The program included the songs "Ghost Riders in the Sky," "Canyon of Heroes," "The Ghost Train Triptych," "Sasparilla," "Song of the Gandy Dancers," and "The Great Revival." That year marked the 50th anniversary of the Troopers. (Courtesy of Fort Caspar Museum.)

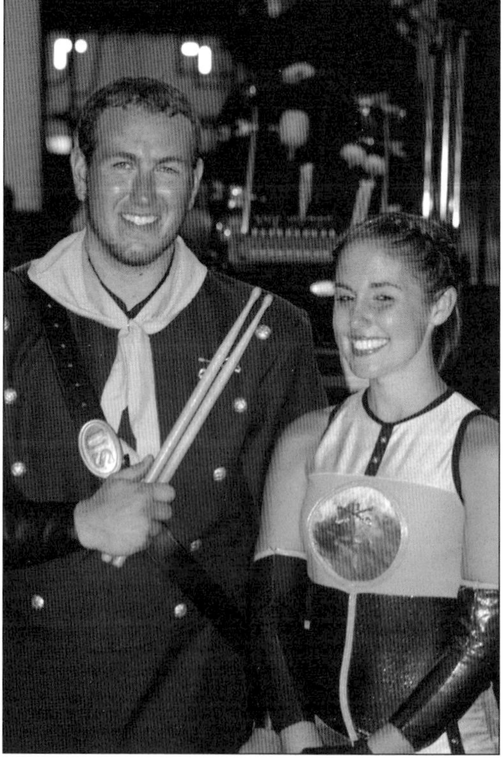

Drummer Casey Knopp (left) and guard Alyson Downs pose for a photograph at the Cornhusker Summer Music Games in Lincoln, Nebraska, on July 14, 2008. The Troopers placed third that day. The drum major that year was Kyle Trader, and the guard commander was Victoria Romero. (Courtesy of the Troopers Archives.)

Seven

2010s

Marching Forward

The Troopers Drum & Bugle Corps started the new decade with a sense of security. The problems of the mid-2000s were behind them, and with Fred Morris as director, the instructional and administrative staffs were getting better each year. The Troopers moved into their current headquarters at 1801 East E Street in Casper in 2006, and local businessman Mick McMurry presented them with the deed to the building in 2011.

The shows were becoming more intricate, both visually and auditorily, while continuing to play Western and patriotic music and incorporating iconic elements from the past. The Troopers used fences, ladders, ribbons, and tarps in their shows in addition to their old standbys of flags, silks, rifles, and swords. In 2011, they performed the "Infinity Chord." The note lasted more than 20 seconds due to the carefully choreographed staggered breathing of the horn players. The Troopers used "Battle Hymn of the Republic" for the 21st time in their show in 2013. That year they also brought back the suicide toss, and the corps formed the number 11 on the field 11 times. Competitively, the Troopers were finishing in the mid-teens and came close to breaking into the top 12 twice. They finished 13th in both 2013 and 2015.

In addition to putting more time and resources into the corps over the last 10 years, the Troopers Drum & Bugle Corps organization has been working with local and regional communities to bring drum corps to more people. In 2011, they added two youth programs: ExSight, a competitive winter guard for teens 14 to 18 in Cheyenne, and Western Wind Marching Band for students 12 to 18 in partnership with the Natrona County School District in Casper. The Troopers also offer a brass master class in Casper with Vibes Fine & Performing Arts, a one-day opportunity to find out what it is like to perform with the Troopers.

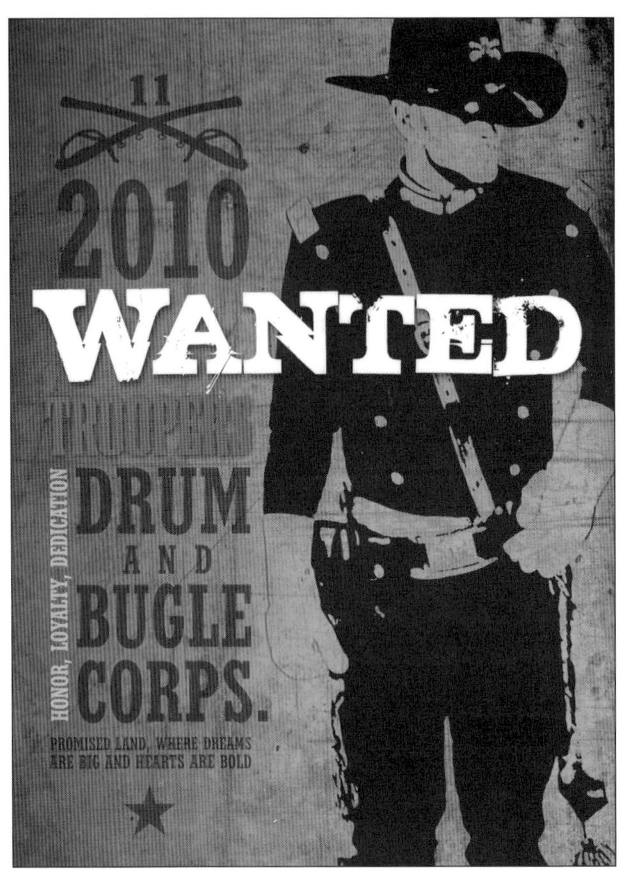

The poster for the Troopers' 2010 program *Wanted* has the look and feel of a Western, but the music selection was varied. For example, the first song in the program, "Wanted Dead or Alive," was by the rock group Bon Jovi, and "Journey to the Center of the Earth" was composed by Peter Graham for the 100th anniversary of the death of science fiction author Jules Verne. (Courtesy Fort Caspar Museum.)

The Troopers' pit gets last-minute instructions from staff member Mike Leitzke before the DCI Eastern Classic in Allentown on August 5, 2011. From left to right are Maria Brandone, Gabriella Vizzutti, Liz Buening, Daniel Sammons, Michael Broyles, Tanner Remick (mostly obscured), and Kelsey Steele. Pit members not pictured are Warren Ertle and David Zamora. They finished sixth at this competition. (Photograph by Pat Chagnon.)

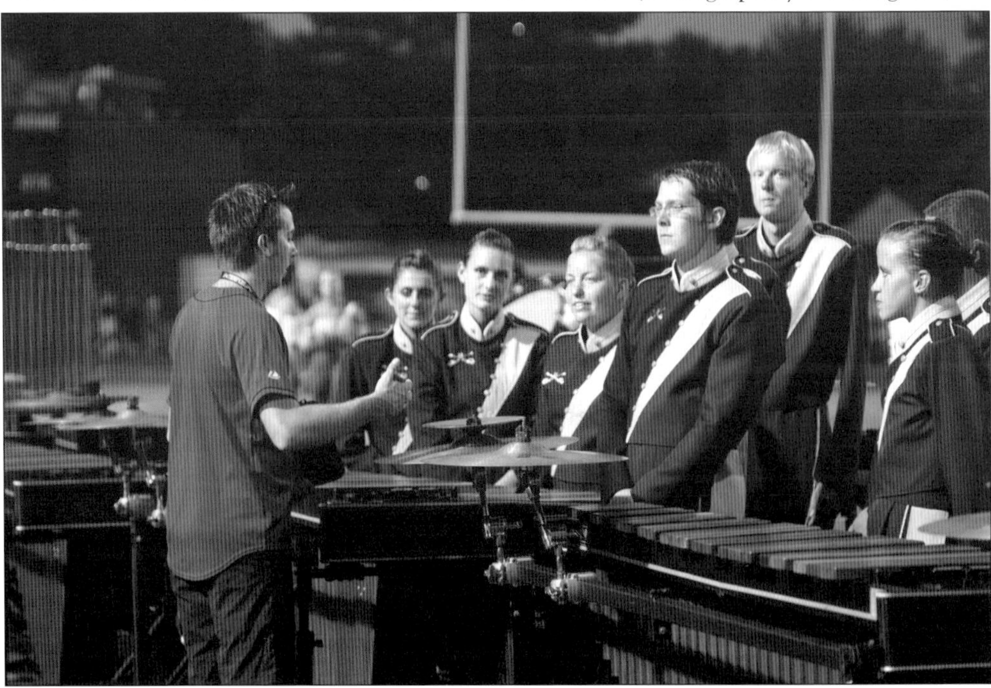

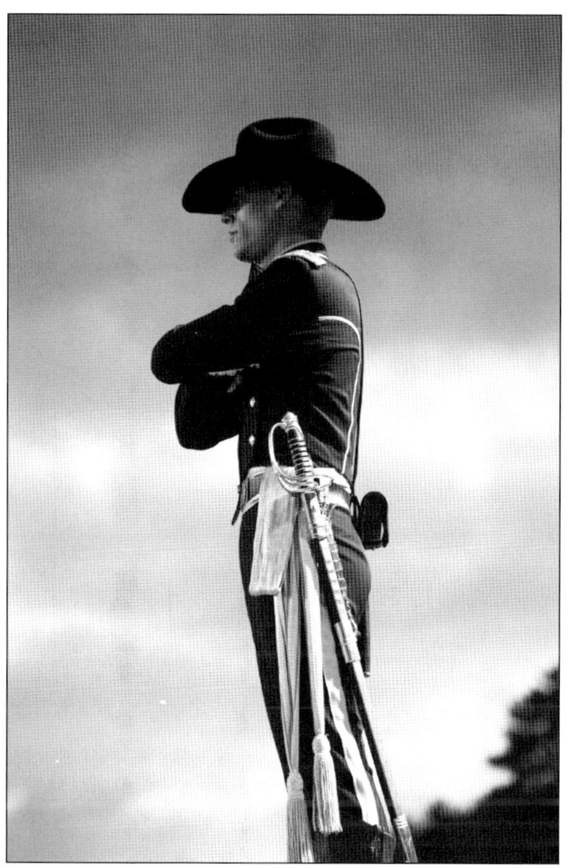

The Troopers competed at the DCI Eastern Classic in Allentown on August 5, 2011. Drum major Josh Jensen (right) stands ready on the scaffolding at the start of their performance. Jenson was drum major for just one year. The Troopers drummers (below) are shown on the field with flags flying around them. They finished in sixth place that day. The Troopers played in 31 competitions in 16 states covering most of the eastern half of the United States that year. They performed four times in both Indiana and Wisconsin and three times in Ohio, Minnesota, and Texas. (Both photographs by Pat Chagnon.)

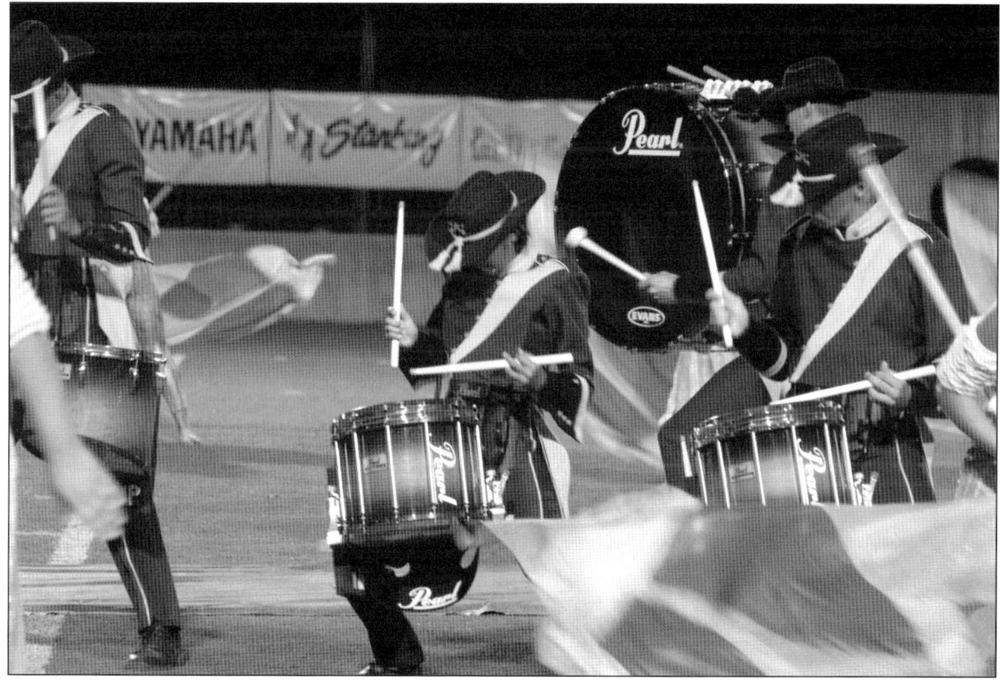

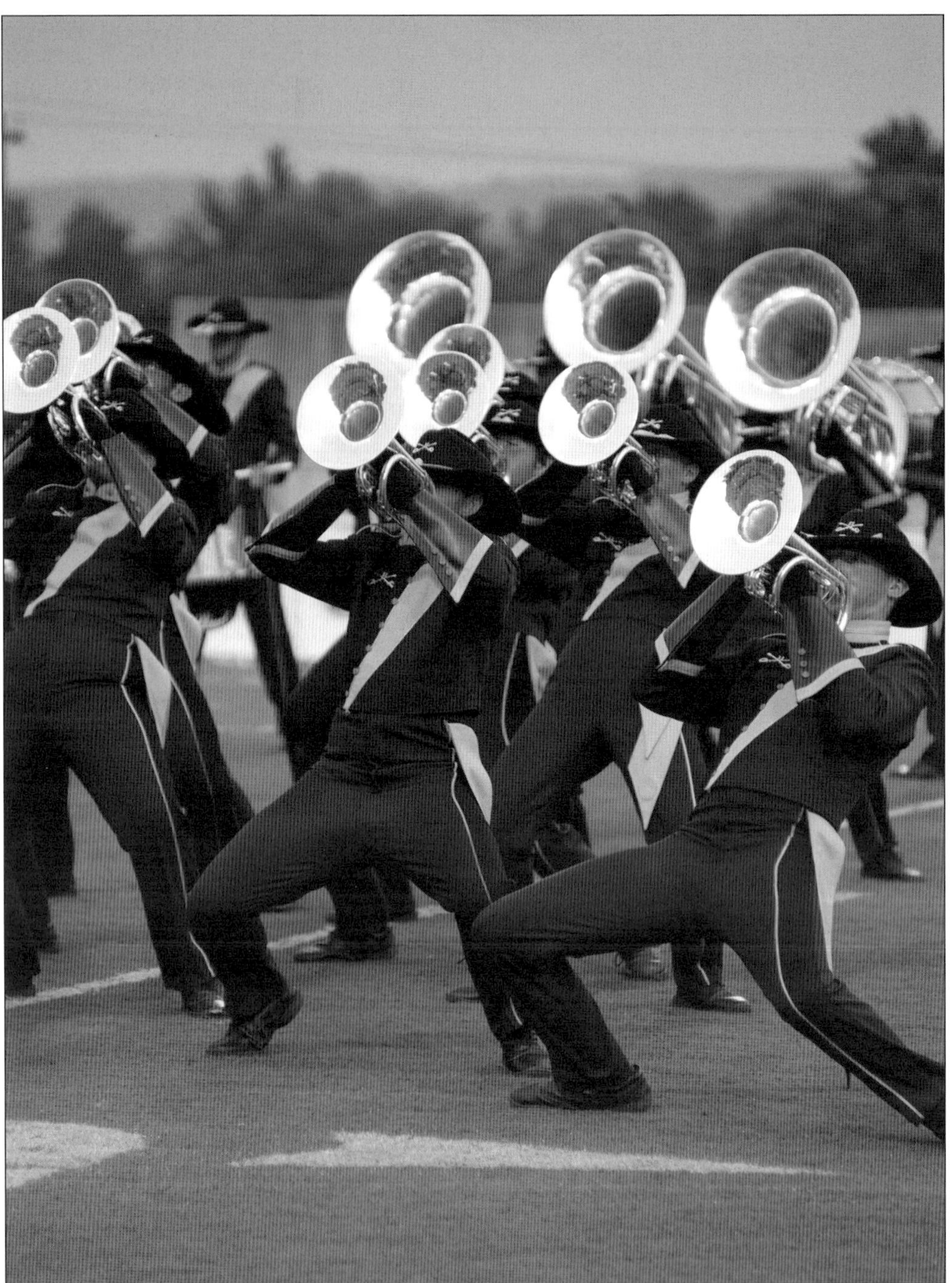

The Troopers horn line gives it their all at the DCI Eastern Classic in Allentown on August 3, 2012. The mellophone players are in front and the contras in back. The Troopers placed seventh that day. The Troopers had an ambitious schedule in 2012: they participated in 28 competitions in 19 states. They started the summer in Battle Creek, Michigan, at the Legends Drum Corps Preview on June 20; they were in Casper for Drums Along the Rockies Casper Edition on July 6; and by August 10, they were in Indianapolis for the DCI World Championship Semifinals. (Photograph by Pat Chagnon.)

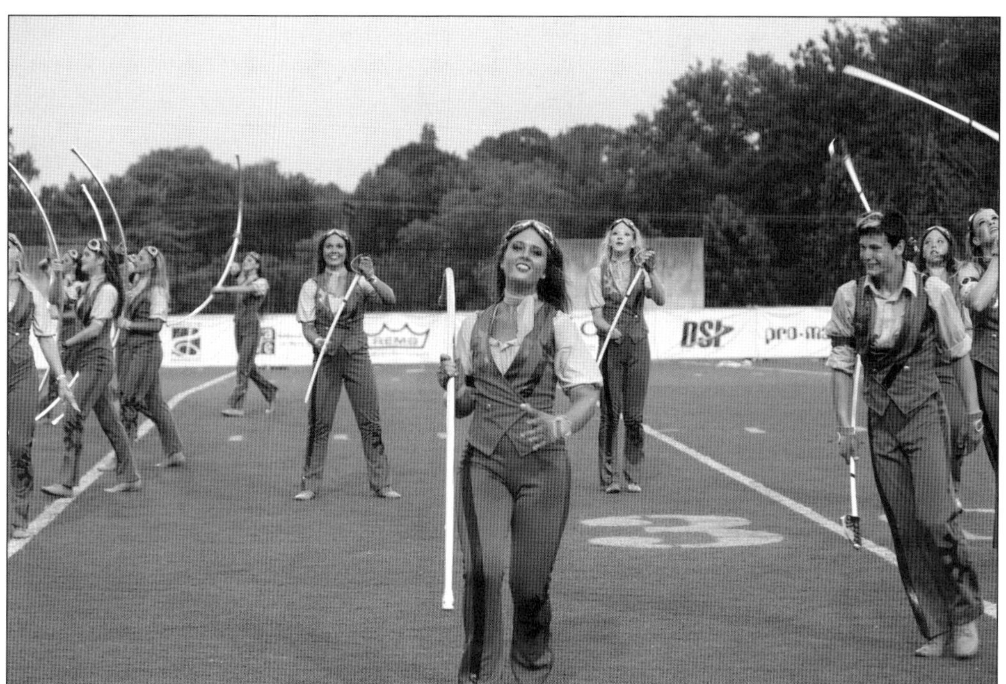

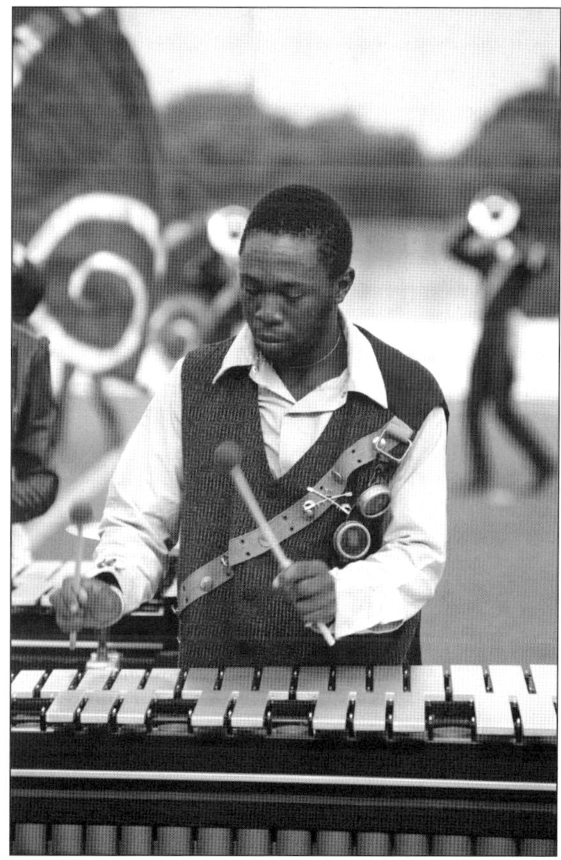

The Troopers perform at the DCI Eastern Classic in Allentown on August 3, 2012. The guard (above) is very enthusiastic during their routine. From left to right are McKenzie Vermillion, Rachel Merchant, Brenda ?, Amber Pitard, Heather Lee DelaTorre, unidentified, Meryl McDonald, McKayla Dolan, Tyler ?, Jessie Barsoum, and Lindsay Greer. Front ensemble member Stephan Clardy (right) plays the xylophone, and both the guard and front ensemble members wore futuristic, steampunk-inspired uniforms. The show theme that year was *This Was the Future*. The musical repertoire included "Galop" from Samuel Barber's *Souvenirs*, Op. 28; *Music for Theatre*; and *The Heiress*. (Both photographs by Pat Chagnon.)

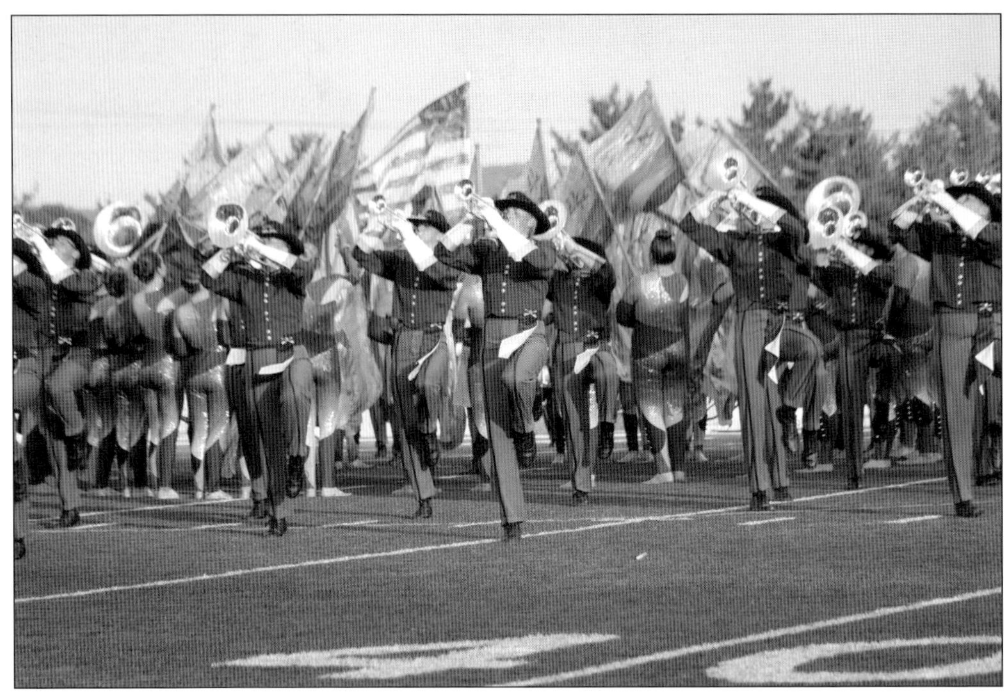

The Troopers march at the DCI Eastern Classic in Allentown on August 2, 2013. Above, the Troopers perform the sunburst maneuver, with the US flag rising from the center. Below, the guard walks onto the field. From left to right are Taylor Thornton, Madison Cairney, Jessie Barsoum, Mandie John, Courtnee Broussard, unidentified, Jocelyn Johnston, and Destinee Dodd. The show theme that year was the *Magnificent 11*. The Troopers described the program this way: "The American West has always represented a sense of beauty, grit and uncompromised passion seen in the wide open spaces that make up the region. The West was a place where battles were fought, towns were created and dreams were fulfilled." (Both photographs by Pat Chagnon.)

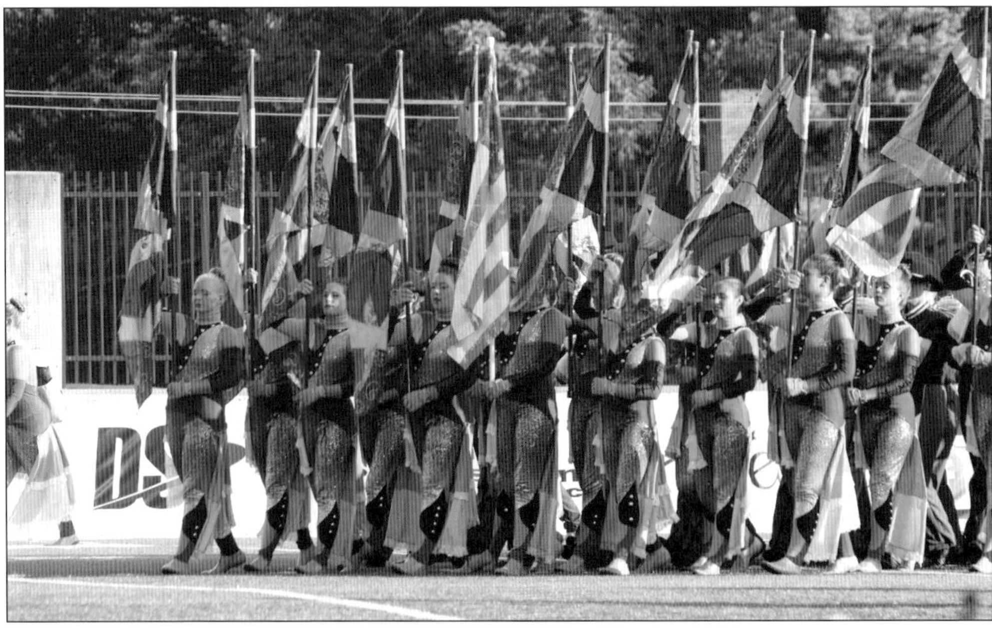

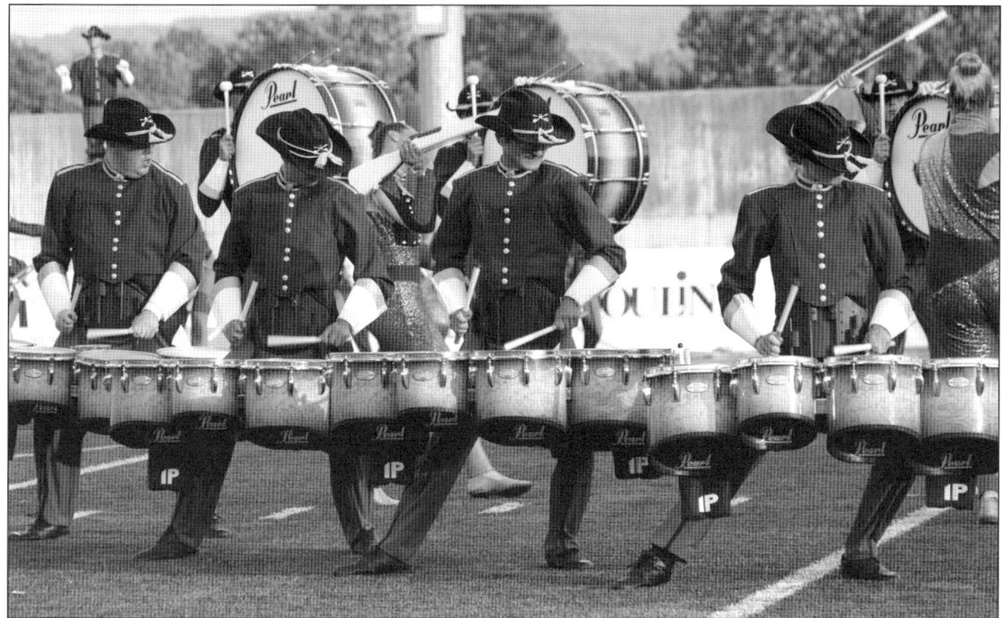

The Troopers multi-tenor drummers perform at the DCI Eastern Classic in Allentown on August 2, 2013. From left to right are Cole Williams, Travis Boren, Dalton Ellis, and Caleb Frankhauser. Back conductor Josh Guttveg is behind Williams. The Troopers finished seventh that day. (Photograph by Pat Chagnon.)

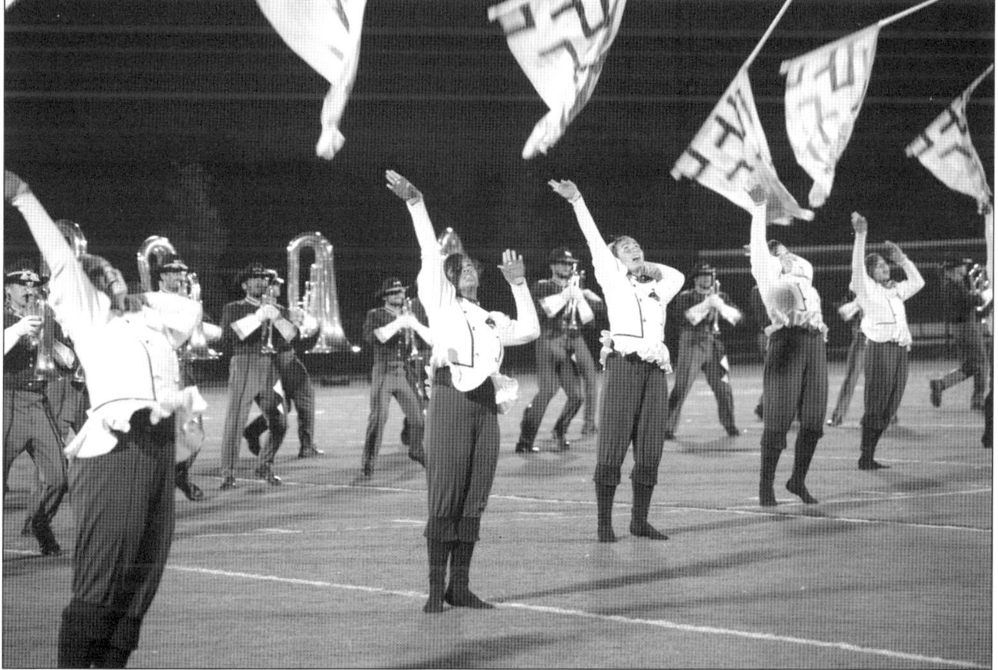

The Troopers guard tosses their flags during the performance at the CYO Nationals Tribute in Quincy, Massachusetts, on July 31, 2014. From left to right are Taylor Thornton, Mikayla Papp, Megan Lemmons, Jessie Barsoum, and Lindsey Nicole. They placed fourth at the event. (Photograph by Pat Chagnon.)

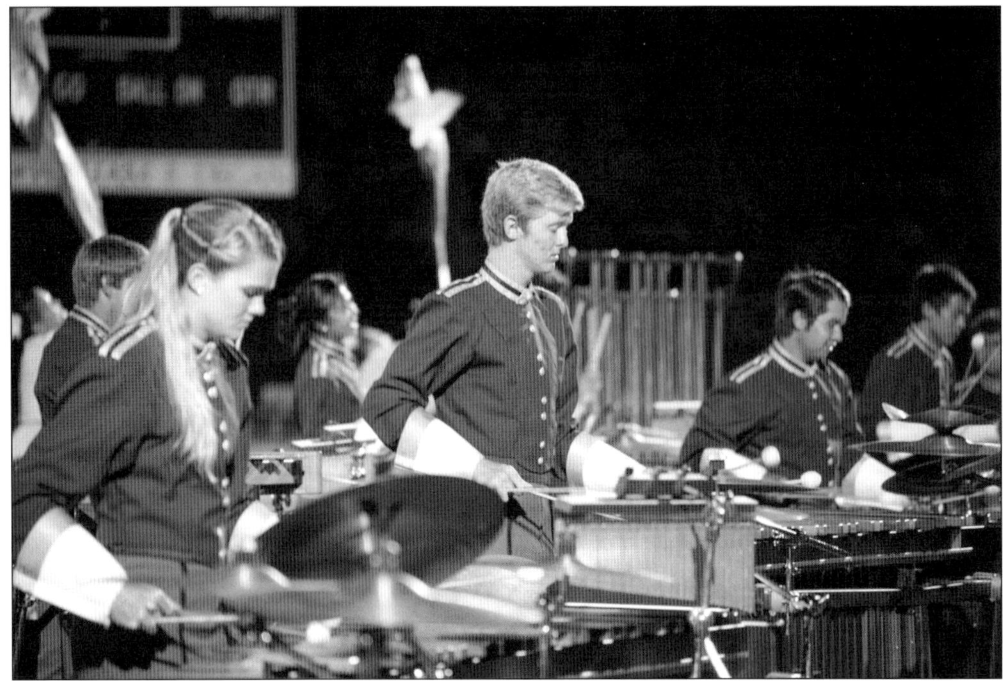

The Troopers perform at the CYO Nationals Tribute in Quincy on the evening of July 31, 2014. The Troopers front ensemble (above) is, from left to right, (first row) Abigail Thomas, Stephen Symank, Christopher Swan, and Ernest Chan; (second row) Graham Deckard and Amelia Baptista. The Troopers multi-tenor drummers (below) are, from left to right, Kurt Doty, Chad Raulston, Salton Ellis, Travis Boren, and Josh Hirner. The show that year, *A People's House*, celebrated Pres. Abraham Lincoln. The musical repertoire included "The Ramparts," "A Distant Image," "Lincoln," "Shenandoah," and "America the Beautiful." (Both photographs by Pat Chagnon.)

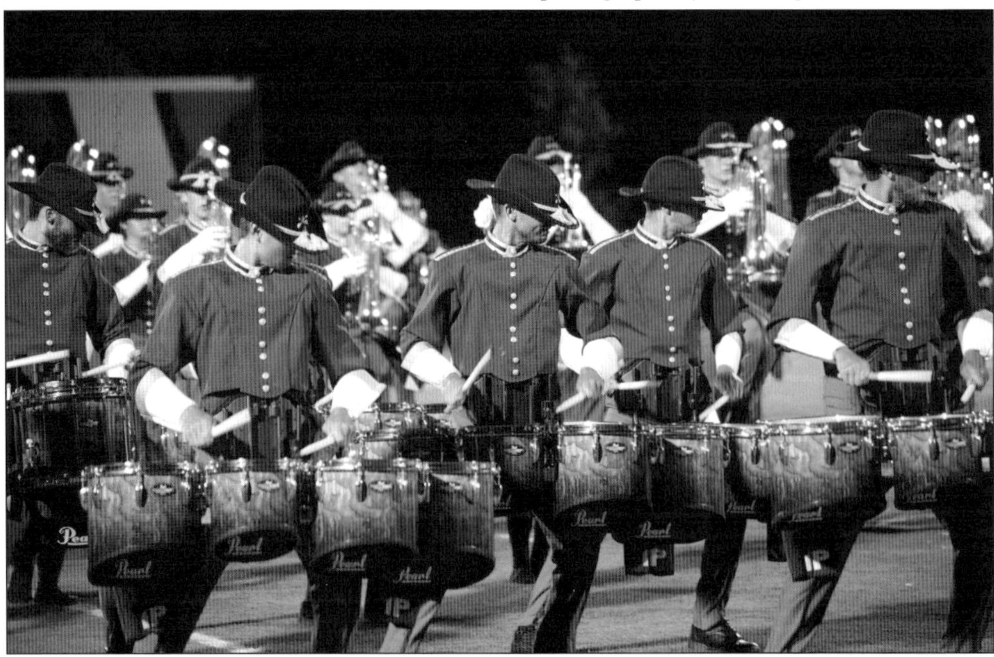

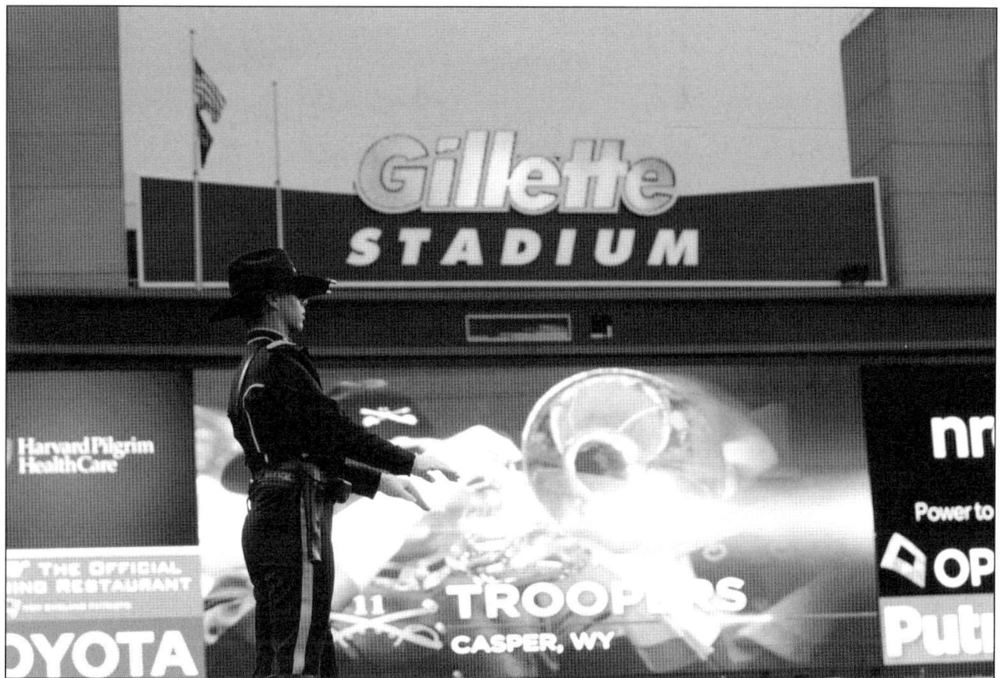

The Troopers perform at the East Coast Classic in Foxborough on July 2, 2015. Drum major Gabe Gallegos (above) conducts from the scaffolding at Gillette Stadium. He was drum major from 2015 to 2018. Below, the bass drummers march in a line. From left to right are David Gutierrez, Liam Shea, Christopher Cortez, Scott Taylor, and Alex Irvine. They finished in sixth place that day. The Troopers participated in 19 contests in 30 states in 2015. They spent most of their time in the eastern half of the United States at competitions from Georgia to Texas and Rhode Island to Minnesota. (Both photographs by Pat Chagnon.)

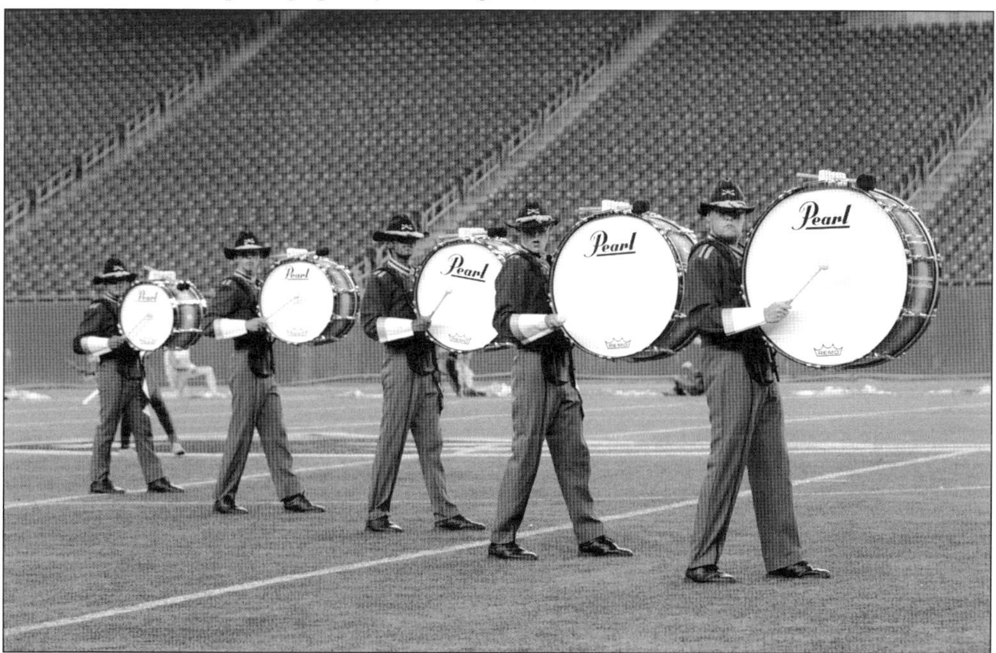

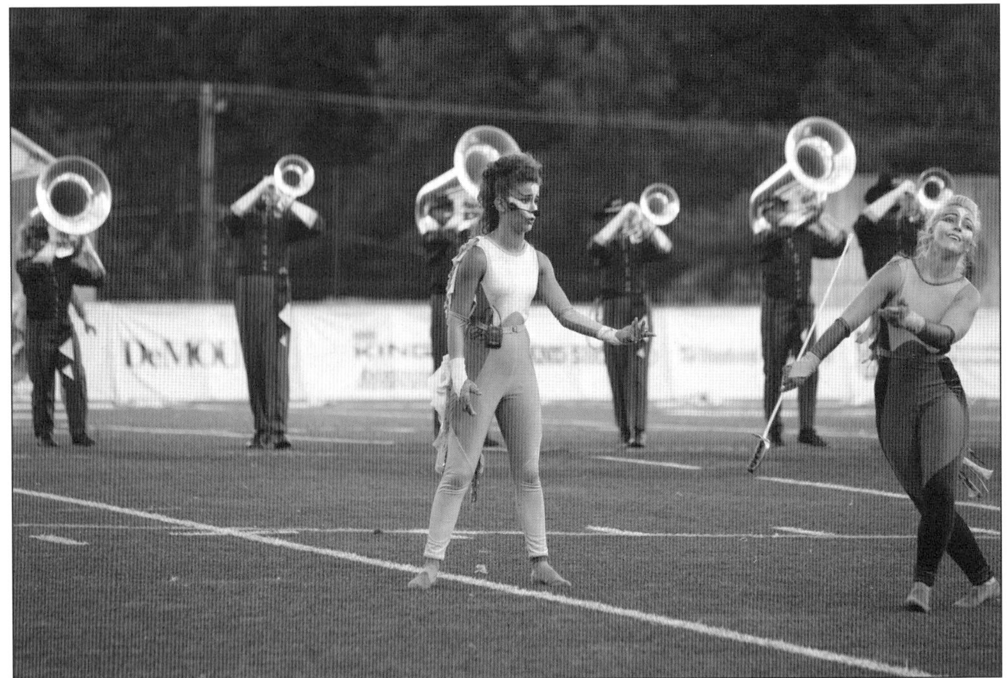

The Troopers perform at the DCI Eastern Classic in Allentown on August 1, 2015. Guard members Madison Smith (left) and Kat Latshaw are in front. Smith is singing "Wild Horses" by Natasha Bedingfield. From left to right in back are Alex Hubbell, Jason Weimer, Aaron Salazar, Kyle Gibbons, Jake Fortin, and Paul Davenport. This was the first time they had incorporated live singing into their performance. (Photograph by Pat Chagnon.)

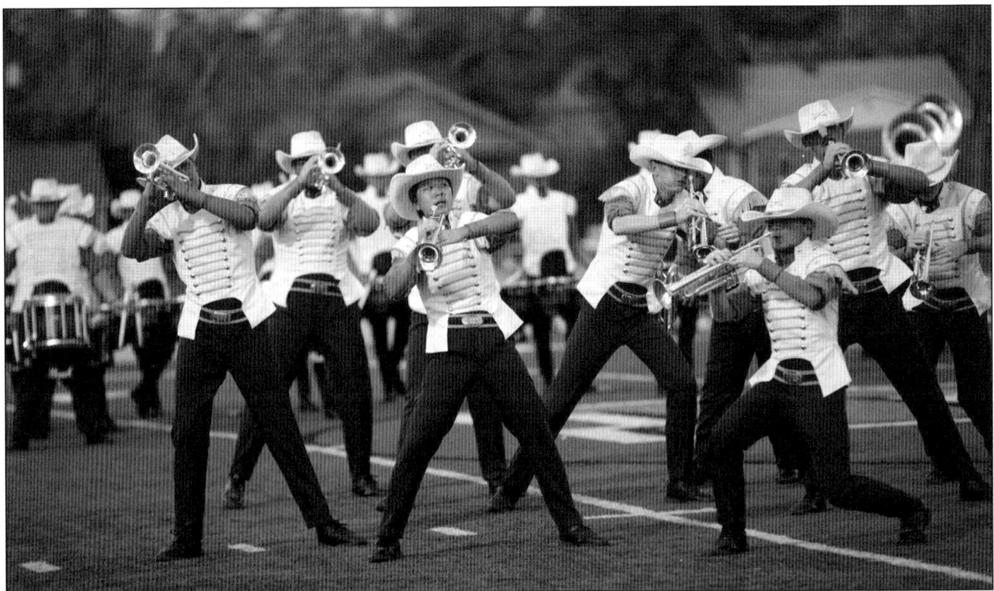

The Troopers sopranos perform at Drums Along the Rockies Casper Edition at Natrona County High School stadium in Casper on July 8, 2016. From left to right are Will Hoffman, Jacquelyn Fry, Tomoka Nakashita, Brook Peckham, Jaze Cayne, Branden Miller, and unidentified. (Photograph by Pat Chagnon.)

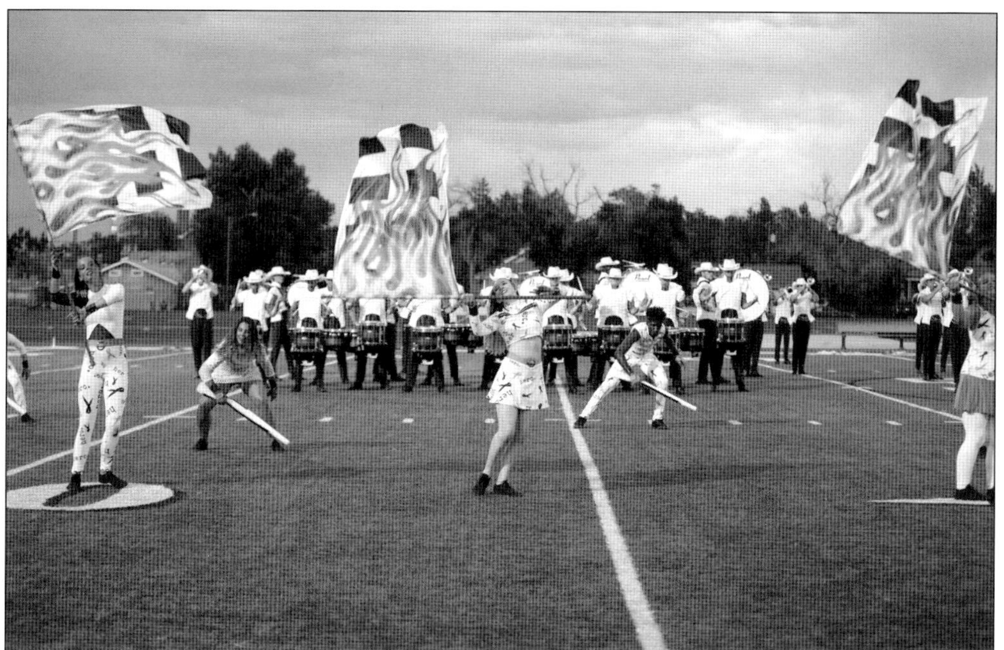

The Troopers guard twirl flags and rifles during their performance at Drums Along the Rockies Casper Edition at Natrona County High School stadium in Casper on July 8, 2016. From left to right are Hannah Robbins, Nicole Arbuckle, Raley Cherry, Stefon Lowery, and Lauren Weirich. (Photograph by Pat Chagnon.)

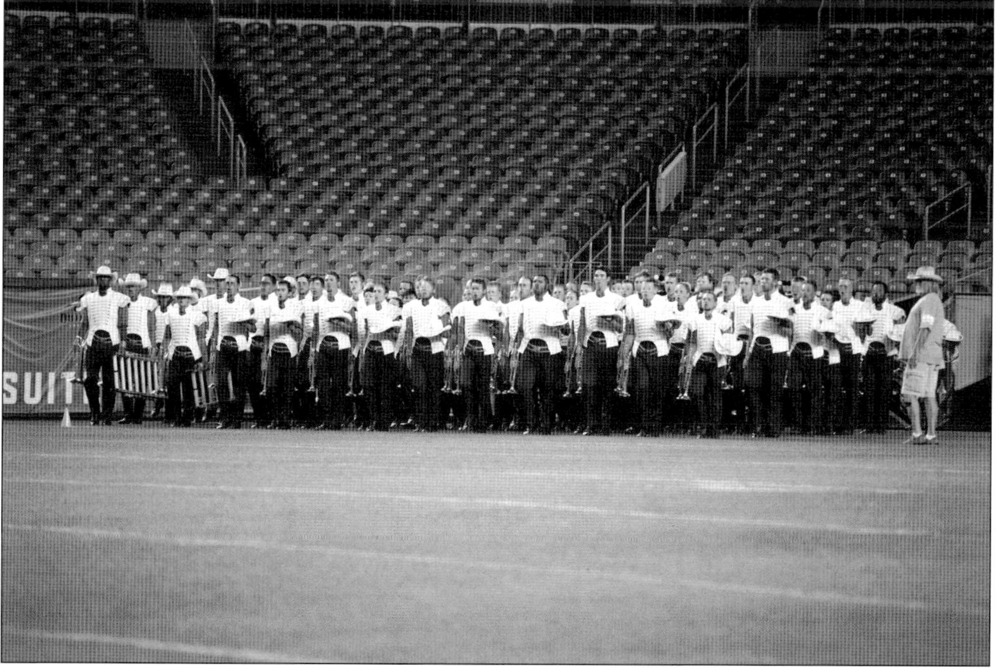

The Troopers take the field before their performance at Drums Along the Rockies at Sports Authority Field in Denver on July 9, 2016. Director Fred Morris stands to the right of group. They finished in second place that evening. (Photograph by Pat Chagnon.)

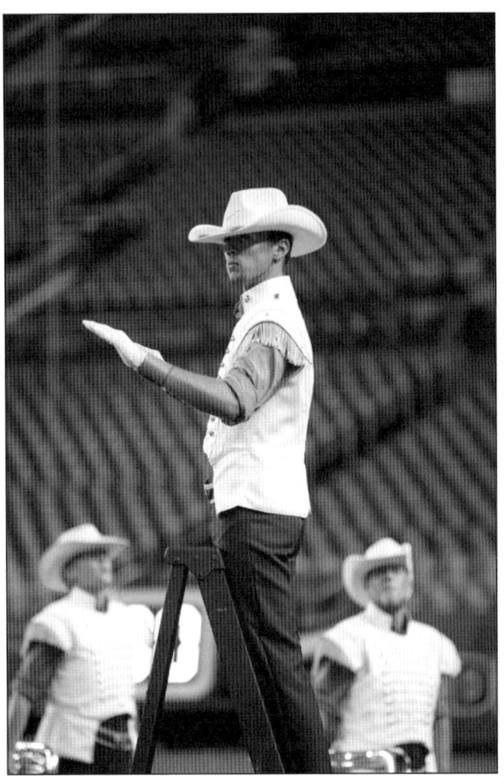

Troopers back field conductor Cameron Honnen is pictured during their performance at Drums Along the Rockies in Denver on July 9, 2016. Behind Honnen are Ian Calhoun (left) and Will Cole. The show theme that year was *Hero*, and the song selections were "Hero" by Robert W. Smith, "Walking with Heroes" by Paul Lovatt-Cooper, Symphony No. 1 by John Corigliano, and "Fix You" by Coldplay. (Photo by Pat Chagnon.)

The Fort Caspar Museum in Casper featured an exhibit about the Troopers in 2017 and 2018. Troopers: Celebrating 60 Years of the Troopers Drum & Bugle Corps was organized by the museum staff with assistance from the Troopers. The exhibit included photographs, posters, flags, uniforms, instruments, and souvenirs. Video footage of a number of past performances played to give visitors a sense of the corps' energy and skill. (Courtesy of Fort Caspar Museum.)

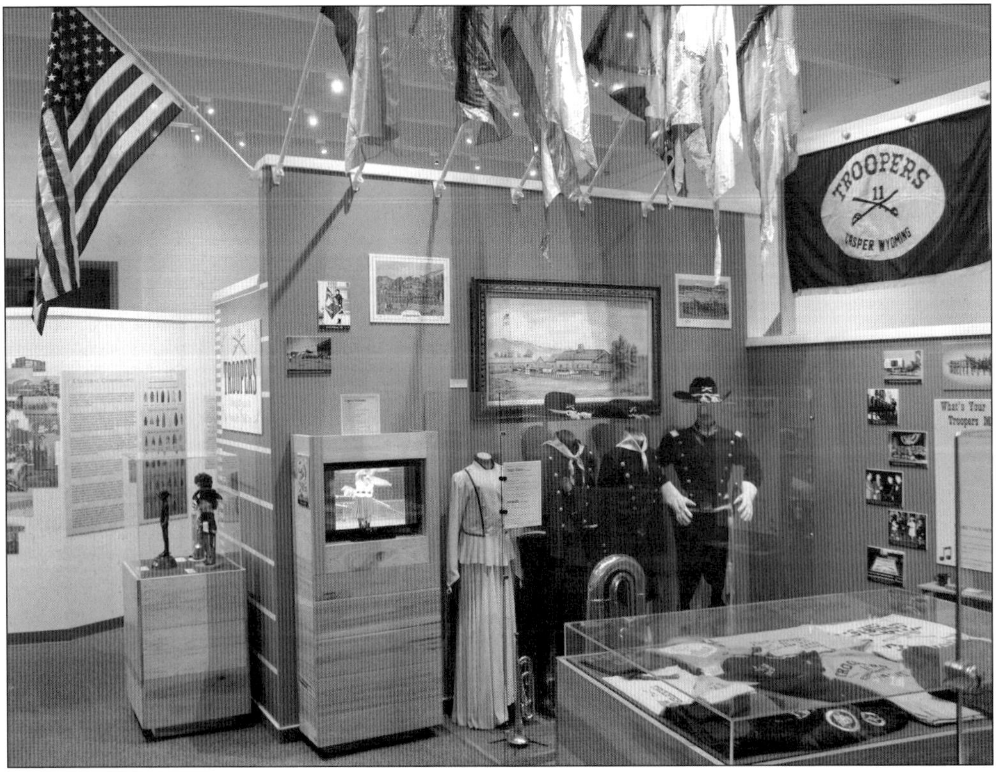

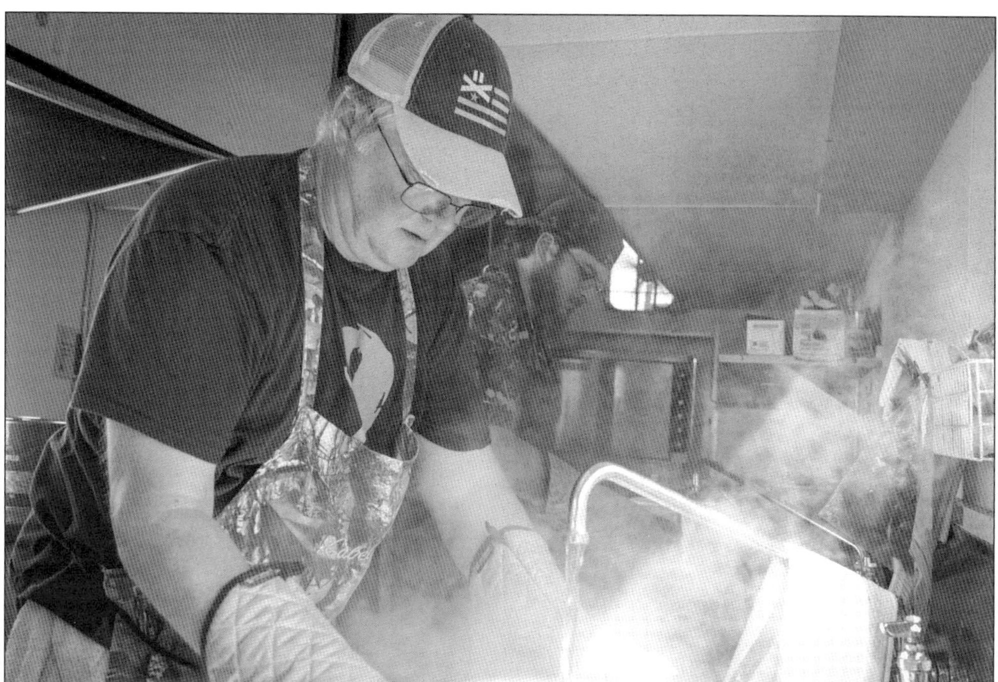

Working in the Troopers' food truck are food services manager Sterling Bock and his assistant Jeremy Cantu on May 29, 2017. The Troopers have their own semi-truck outfitted with a full kitchen that provides most of the meals during the summer. With 150 marching members and up to 50 support people, the mobile kitchen serves 200 people four meals a day. (Courtesy of the Troopers Drum & Bugle Corps.)

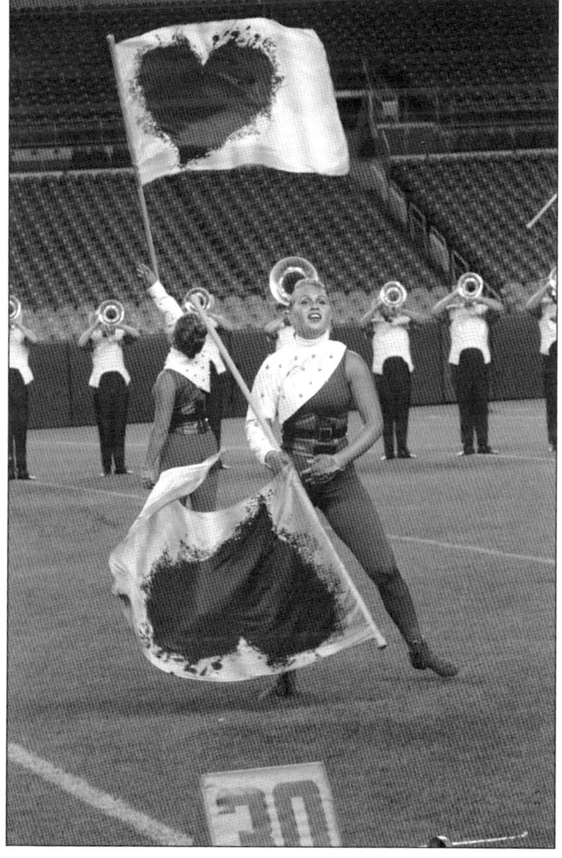

Troopers color guard Shelby Daughtery is shown during a performance at Drums Along the Rockies at Sports Authority Field in Denver on July 15, 2017. The 2017 program was anything but Western: *Duels and Duets* featured "Death of Tybalt Parts 1 and 2" from *Romeo and Juliet*, "Black Heart Tango," "Nessun Dorma Part 3" from *Turandot*, and "Foil." (Photograph by Pat Chagnon.)

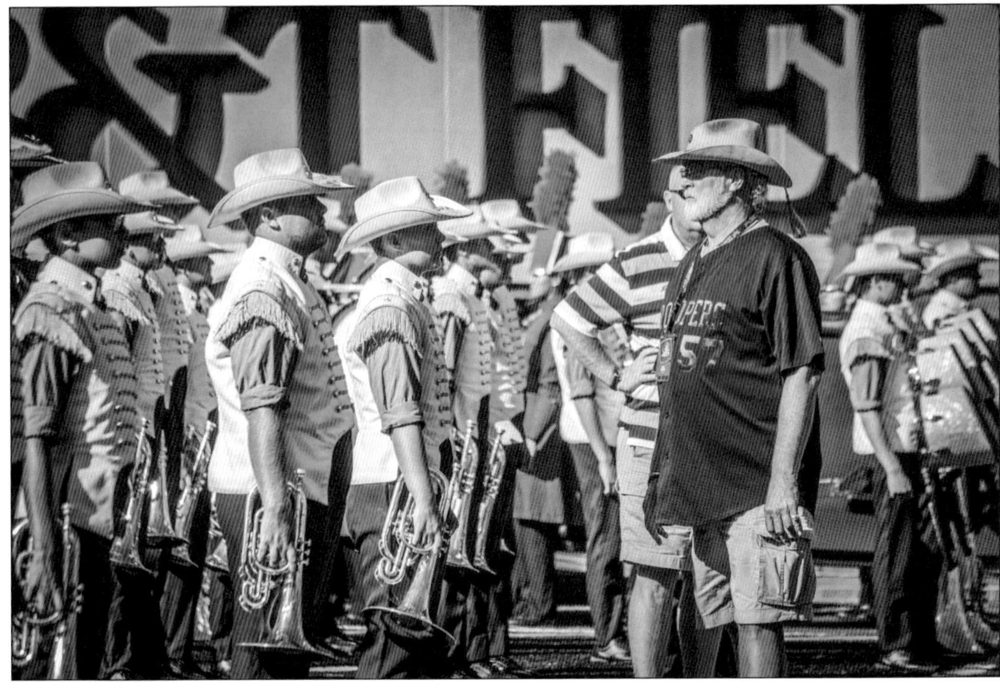

Troopers director Fred Morris stands on the field with the corps at the NightBEAT Tour of Champions in Winston-Salem, North Carolina, on July 30, 2017. Morris is setting the drum corps up on the starting line and waiting for the cue to enter the field. (Courtesy of the Troopers Drum & Bugle Corps.)

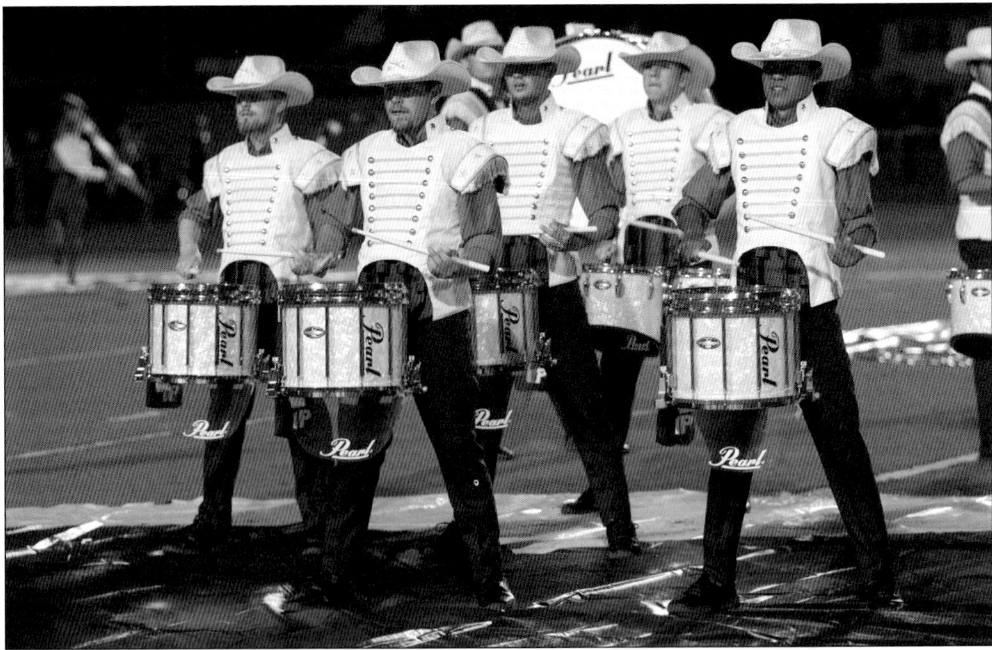

The Troopers drum line performs at Drums Along the Mohawk in Rome, New York, on August 6, 2017. From left to right are Adam Buckner, Niko Athanas, Ryan Willis, Ben Gostkowski, and Luis Sanchez. They finished fifth that day. (Photograph by Piper Nevins, courtesy of Pat Chagnon.)

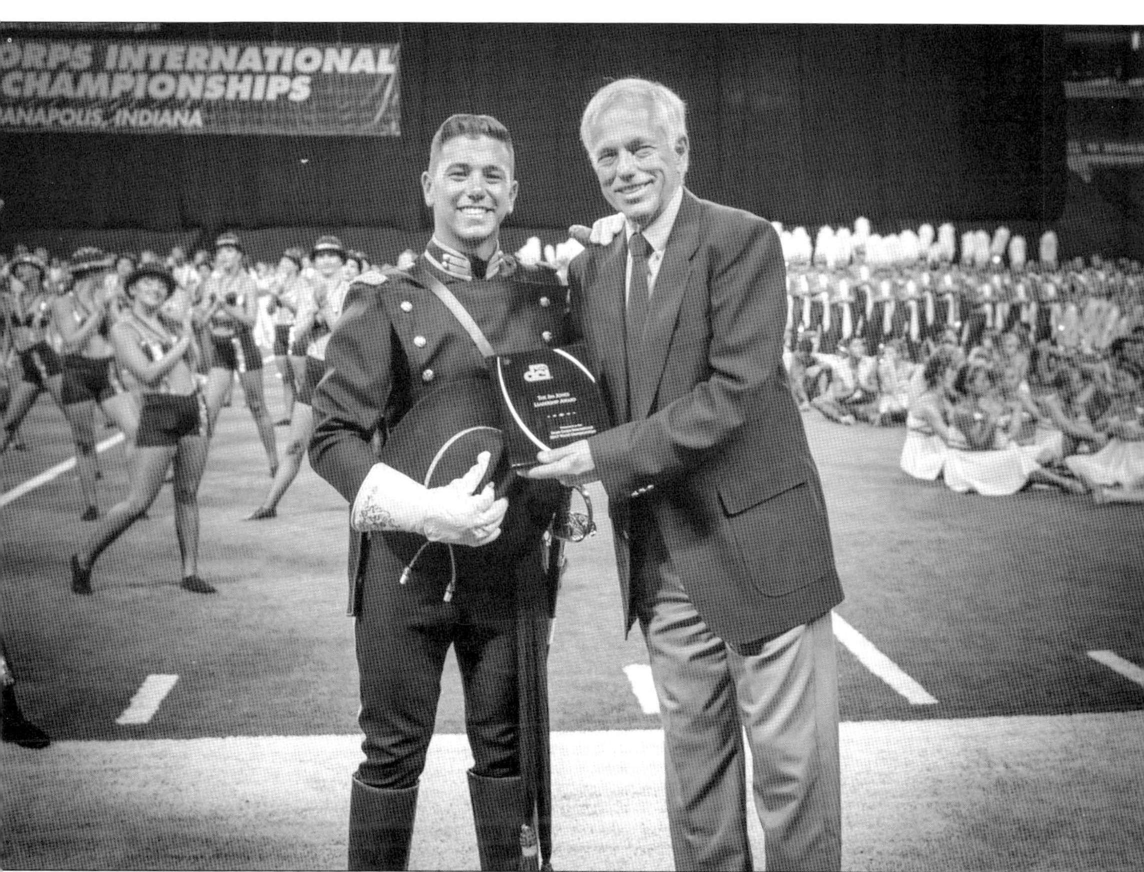

Troopers drum major Gabe Gallegos receives the Jim Jones Leadership Award from Gene Monterastelli at the DCI World Championship Finals award ceremony at Lucas Oil Stadium in Indianapolis on August 12, 2017. The Jim Jones Award is given each year to the drum major who demonstrates strong leadership skills, both on and off the field, and who also possesses exceptional conducting skill. This is the first time a Troopers drum major received the award. Gallegos exemplifies the Troopers trademarks of honor, loyalty, and dedication—learned and lived by everyone who has ever worn the uniform. (Courtesy of the Troopers Drum & Bugle Corps.)